FLORIDA STATE
UNIVERSITY LIBRARIES

FEB 25 1999

TALLAHASSEE, FLORIDA

Sustaining Amazonia

MANCHESTER
UNIVERSITY PRESS

Issues in Environmental Politics

Series editors Tim O'Riordan, Arild Underdal *and* Albert Weale

As the millennium approaches, the environment has come to stay as a central concern of global politics. This series takes key problems for environmental policy and examines the politics behind their cause and possible resolution. Accessible and eloquent, the books make available for a non-specialist readership some of the best research and most provocative thinking on humanity's relationship with the planet.

already published in the series

Animals, politics and morality Robert Garner

Sustaining Amazonia: grassroots action for productive conservation Anthony Hall

The protest business? Mobilizing campaign groups Grant Jordan and William Maloney

Environment and the nation state: the Netherlands, the European Union and acid rain Duncan Liefferink

Valuing the environment Raino Malnes

Life on a modern planet: a manifesto for progress Richard North

The politics of global atmospheric change Ian H. Rowlands

European environmental policy: the pioneers Mikael Skou Anderson and Duncan Liefferink (eds)

The new politics of pollution Albert Weale

Realism in green politics Helmut Wiesenthal

Sustaining Amazonia

Grassroots action for productive conservation

Anthony Hall

Manchester University Press
Manchester and New York
Distributed exclusively in the USA by St. Martin's Press

Copyright © Anthony Hall 1997

Published by Manchester University Press
Oxford Road, Manchester M13 9NR, UK
and Room 400, 175 Fifth Avenue, New York, NY 10010, USA

Distributed exclusively in the USA
by St. Martin's Press, Inc., 175 Fifth Avenue, New York, NY 10010, USA

Distributed exclusively in Canada
by UBC Press, University of British Columbia, 6344 Memorial Road,
Vancouver, BC, Canada V6T 1Z2

British Library Cataloguing-in-Publication Data
A catalogue record for this book is available from the British Library.

Library of Congress Cataloging-in-Publication Data
Hall, Anthony L., 1947–
   Sustaining Amazonia : grassroots action for productive conservation /
Anthony Hall.
      p.   cm.—(Issues in environmental politics)
   Includes bibliographical references and index.
   ISBN 0–7190–4698–X (cl)
   1. Sustainable development—Amazon River Region.   2. Natural
resources—Amazon River Region—Management.   3. Sustainable
development—Brazil.   4. Environmental policy—Brazil.   I. Title.
II. Series.
HC188.A5H35   1997
333.7'0982'1—dc21   97–5366

ISBN 0 7190 4698 X hardback

First published in 1997

01 00 99 98 97   10 9 8 7 6 5 4 3 2 1

Typeset in Sabon
by Northern Phototypesetting Co. Ltd, Bolton
Printed in Great Britain
by Biddles Ltd, Guildford and King's Lynn

*To the people of Amazonia
and their courage
in the face of adversity*

Contents

About the author	*page* viii
List of illustrations	ix
List of tables	x
Acknowledgements	xi
Abbreviations	xiii
Preface	xxiv

1	Resource governance: mobilisation and participation	1
2	Environment and development in Brazilian Amazonia: evolving paradigms	45
3	Extracting a livelihood: the rubber tappers' movement	91
4	Fishing for a future	134
5	Survival on the Transamazon highway	171
6	Amazonia: towards productive conservation	213
	References	244
	Index	265

About the author

Anthony Hall has for a number of years been closely involved with development issues in Brazil. He has undertaken extensive field research in Amazonia and the north-east and was Oxfam's country representative in Brazil from 1977–81. He is presently Senior Lecturer in Social Planning in Developing Countries at the London School of Economics and Political Science. His major academic publications include *Drought and Irrigation in North-East Brazil* (Cambridge University Press, 1978), *Community Participation, Social Development and the State* (with J. Midgley *et al.*, Methuen, 1986), *Development Policies: Sociological Perspectives* (with J. Midgley *et al.*, Manchester University Press, 1988), *The Future of Amazonia: Destruction or Sustainable Development?* (with D. Goodman, Macmillan, 1990) and *Developing Amazonia: Deforestation and Social Conflict in Brazil's Carajás Programme* (Manchester University Press, 1991; published in Brazil under the title, *Amazonia: Desenvolvimento para quem?* Zahar, 1991).

Illustrations

Figures

3.1	Federal extractive reserves in Brazilian Amazonia	103
4.1	Mamirauá project area	140
4.2	Cross-section of upper Amazon *várzea* ('flooded forest')	142
5.1	Areas covered by the CAT and PAET programmes along the Transamazon highway	177

Plates

Plates appear between pp. 70 and 71.

1. A cattle ranch in southern Pará
2. A family of settlers on the Transamazon highway
3. Timber extraction by small farmers
4. The grave of Chico Mendes
5. A rubber tapper and his family
6. Rubber tappers and their handicrafts
7. Floating guardposts protect Mamirauá from commercial invaders
8. Two locals fishing in a lake reserved for restocking
9. The fourth community assembly of sector representatives at Mamirauá
10. The RECA project in Acre state
11. The sustainable extraction of palm hearts
12. A small settler on the Transamazon highway plans to start agroforestry
13. A community tree nursery on the *Transamazônica*

Tables

1.1 Dimensions of community participation in productive conservation — 26
3.1 Extractive Resettlement Projects (PAEs) in Brazilian Amazonia — 101
3.2 Federal extractive reserves in Brazilian Amazonia — 104

Acknowledgements

During the researching and writing of this book I have received help from many. Rafael Rueda and Carlos Aragón of the National Centre for the Sustainable Development of Traditional Populations/Brazilian Institute of the Environment and Renewable Resources (CNPT/IBAMA) in Brasília provided me with extensive information on extractive reserves. In Acre, Júlio Barbosa and his colleagues within the National Rubber Tappers' Council (CNS) and the Agro-Extractivist Cooperative of Xapurí (CAEX) were the source of numerous insights into local-level issues and problems. Márcio Ayres, Deborah Lima and Marise Reis gave me valuable field support at Mamirauá. Jean Hébette was always ready to supply crucial documents and discuss key issues arising from his pioneering projects on the Transamazon Highway. At the Agro-Environmental Centre of the Tocantins (CAT) in Marabá, 'Mano' Wamberg, Aluizio Solyno, Nicolette Burford, Sr. Almir, Márcia Muchagata and Olivier Topall were extremely helpful. In Altamira, Christian Castellanet, Bernard David, Juliette Alves and their colleagues were also highly supportive. In Brasília, Gordon Armstrong, the Overseas Development Administration's (ODA) Brazil representative, gave constructive advice which assisted my research, while Don Sawyer and his staff at the Institute for Society, Population and Nature (ISPN) facilitated access to their rich archives on Amazonia, as did Mary Allegretti and colleagues at the Institute of Amazon and Environmental Studies (IEAA).

Those not mentioned individually will, I hope, forgive me, in the knowledge that their contributions were equally valued. To all of my field contacts, I would like to express my profound gratitude for their collaboration and forbearance inthe face of questions which must at times have seemed unduly intrusive. I hope they were able to forgive such inquisitiveness, which was driven solely by the need to understand these pioneering productive conservation initiatives and learn lessons for the future.

I would like to thank the Nuffield Foundation and the LSE for their financial assistance, without which my research would not have been possible. Lastly, but by no means least, a very special vote of thanks is owed to Bruno Pagnoccheschi of the ISPN, whose continual advice and support greatly facilitated my work.

Abbreviations

AEA	Associação dos Empresários da Amazônia (Association of Amazon Businessmen)
APA	Area de Proteção Ambiental (Area of Environmental Protection)
ASAREAJ	Associação dos Seringueiros e Agricultores da Reserva Extrativista do Alto do Rio Juruá (Association of Rubber Tappers and Farmers of the Alto do Juruá Extractive Reserve)
ASGM	Associação dos Seringueiros de Guajará Mirim (Guajará Mirim Rubber Tappers' Association)
ASPRUVE	Associação dos Produtores Rurais Vencedores (Association of Victorious Rural Producers)
BASA	Banco da Amazônia S.A. (Bank of Amazonia)
BHN	Basic Human Needs
BNDES	Banco Nacional de Desenvolvimento Econômico e Social (National Bank of Economic and Social Development)
CAEX	Cooperativa Agro-Extrativista de Xapurí (Agro-Extractivist Cooperative of Xapurí)
CAMTA	Cooperativa Agropecuária Mixta de Tomé Açu (Mixed Agro-Livestock Cooperative of Tomé Açu)
CAPEB	Central de Associações de Produtores de Brasiléia e Epitaciolândia (Consortium of Producer Associations for

	Brasiléia and Epitaciolândia)
CAPOIB	Conselho de Articulação dos Povos e Organizações Indígenas do Brasil (Coordinating Council for the Indigenous Peoples and Organisations of Brasil)
CAT	Centro Agroambiental do Tocantins (Agro-Environmental Centre of the Tocantins)
CCZEE	Comissão Coordenadora do Zoneamento Ecológico-Econômico do Territôrio Nacional (Coordinating Commission for the Ecological-Economic Zoning of National Territory)
CEB	Communidade Eclesial de Base (Community Religious Group)
CEDI	Centro Ecumênico de Documentação e Informação (Ecumenical Centre for Documentation and Information)
CEPASP	Centro de Educação, Pesquisa e Assessoria Sindical (Centre for Education, Research and Union Advice)
CEPLAC	Comissão Executiva do Plano de Lavoura Cacaueira (National Cacao Research and Extension Programme)
CIDA	Canadian International Development Agency
CIMI	Conselho Indigenista Missionário (Indian Missionary Council)
CIRAD	Centre Internacional en Recherche Agronomique pour le Développement (International Agricultural Research Centre for Development)
CNBB	Conferência Nacional dos Bispos do Brasil (National Conference of Brazilian Bishops)
CNPq	Conselho Nacional de Desenvolvimento Científico e Tecnológico (National Council for Scientific and Technological Development)

Abbreviations

CNPT	Centro Nacional para o Desenvolvimento Sustentado das Populaçães Tradicionais (National Centre for the Sustainable Development of Traditional Populations)
CNS	Conselho Nacional dos Seringueiros (National Rubber Tappers' Council)
COAPEX	Cooperativa Agrícola de Produtores Extrativistas (Agricultural Cooperative of Extractive Producers)
COCAT	Cooperativa Camponesa do Araguaia-Tocantins (Small Farmer Cooperative of the Araguaia-Tocantins)
COICA	Coordinadora de Organizaciones Indígenas de la Cuenca Amazónica (Coordinating Body for Indigenous People's Organisations of the Amazon Basin)
CONAIE	Confederación de Nacionalidades Indígenas Ecuatorianas (Confederation of Indigenous Nations of Equador)
CONAMA	Conselho Nacional do Meio Ambiente (National Environment Council)
CONAMAZ	Conselho Nacional da Amazônia Legal (National Council for Legal Amazonia)
CONFENAIE	Confederación de Nacionalidades de la Amazonia Ecuatoriana (Confederation of Indigenous Nations of the Equadorian Amazon)
CONTAG	Confederação Nacional dos Trabalhadores na Agricultura (National Federation of Agricultural workers)
CPATU	Centro de Pesquisa Agropecuária do Trópico Úmido (Agro-Livestock Research Centre for the Humid Tropics)
CPR	Common Property Rights/Regime/Resource
CPT	Comissão Pastoral da Terra (Church Land Commission)

CRV	Centro Regional de Vigilância (Regional Vigilance Centre)
CSN	Conselho de Segurança Nacional (National Security Council)
CTA	Centro dos Trabalhadores da Amazônia (Amazon Workers' Centre)
CUT	Central Única do Trabalho (Unified Labour Centre)
CVP	Cernambi Virgem Prensado (Pressed Virgin Rubber)
CVRD	Companhia Vale do Rio Doce (Vale do Rio Doce Company)
DAZ	Agriculturas Familiares Amazônicas e Desenvolvimento Agro-Ambiental (Amazonian Family Farming and Agro-Environmental Development)
EELM	Estação Ecológica do Lago Mamirauá (Lake Mamirauá Ecological Station)
EIA	Environmental Impact Assessment
EMATER	Empresa de Assistência Técnica e Extensão Rural (Technical Assistance and Rural Extension Company)
EMBRAPA	Empresa Brasileira de Pesquisa Agropecuária (Brazilian Agro-Livestock Research Agency)
ESG	Escola Superior de Guerra (Higher War College)
EU	European Union
FAO	Food and Agriculture Organisation
FASE	Federação de Órgãos de Assistência Social e Educacional (Federation of Organisations for Social and Educational Assistance)
FATA	Fundação Agrária do Tocantins-Araguaia (Agrarian Foundation of the Tocantins-Araguaia)
FCAP	Faculdade de Ciências Agrárias do Pará (Faculty of Agrarian Sciences of Pará)
FETAGRI	Federação dos Trabalhadores na Agricultura (Federation of Agricultural Workers)

Abbreviations

FINAM	Fundo de Investimento da Amazônia (Investment Fund for Amazonia)
FINEP	Financiadora de Estudos e Projetos (Funding Agency for Studies and Projects)
FLONA	Floresta Nacional (National Forest)
FNO	Fundo Constitucional de Financiamento do Norte (Constitutional Fund for the North)
FPR	Farming Participatory Research
FSR	Farming Systems Research
FUNCATE	Fundação de Ciência, Aplicações e Tecnologia (Foundation for Science and Space Technology)
FUNTAC	Fundação de Tecnologia do Estado do Acre (Technology Foundation of Acre State)
FUNAI	Fundação Nacional do Índio (National Indian Foundation)
GEBAM	Grupo Executivo do Baixo Amazonas (Executive Group for the Lower Amazon)
GEF	Global Environmental Facility
GETAT	Grupo Executivo das Terras do Araguaia-Tocantins (Executive Group for the Lands of the Araguaia-Tocantins)
GPD	Grupo de Preservação e Desenvolvimento (Preservation and Development Group)
GRET	Groupe de Recherche et d'Echanges Technologiques (Group for Research and Technological Exchange)
GTA	Grupo de Trabalho da Amazônia (Amazon Working Group)
IBAMA	Instituto Brasileiro do Meio Ambiente e dos Recursos Renováveis (Brazilian Institute of the Environment and Renewable Resources)
IBASE	Instituto Brasileiro de Análises Sociais (Brazilian Institute for Social Analysis)

IBDF	Instituto Brasileiro de Desenvolvimento Florestal (Brazilian Institute of Forestry Development)
IBGE	Fundação Instituto Brasileiro de Geografia e Estatística (Brazilian Institute of Geography and Statistics)
IBRD	International Bank for Reconstruction and Development (The World Bank)
ICDP	Integrated Conservation and Development Project
IDB	Inter-American Development Bank
IDESP	Instituto do Desenvolvimento Econômico-Social do Pará (Institute for the Economic and Social Development of Pará)
IEA	Instituto de Estudos Amazônicos (Institute of Amazon Studies)
IEAA	Instituto de Estudos Amazônicos e Ambientais (Institute of Amazon and Environmental Studies)
IEF	Instituto Estadual de Florestas (State Forestry Institute)
IIED	International Institute for the Environment and Development
ILO	International Labour Organisation
INCRA	Instituto Nacional de Colonização e Reforma Agrária (National Institute for Colonisation and Agrarian Reform)
INESC	Instituto de Estudos Sócio-Econômicos (Institute of Socio-Economic Studies)
INPA	Instituto Nacional de Pesquisas da Amazônia (National Institute for Amazonian Research)
INPE	Instituto Nacional de Pesquisas Espaciais (National Institute for Space Research)
IPAAM	Instituto de Proteção Ambiental do Estado de Amazonas (Environmental Protection Institute of

		Amazonas State)
IPEA		Instituto de Pesquisa Econômica Aplicada (Institute of Applied Economic Research)
ISPN		Instituto Sociedade, População e Natureza (Institute for Society, Population and Nature)
ITERON		Instituto de Terras de Rondônia (Rondônia Land Institute)
ITTO		International Tropical Timber Organisation
IUCN		International Union for the Conservation of Nature
LAET		Laboratório Agro-Econômico da Trans-amazônica (Agro-Economic Laboratory of the Transamazon Highway)
LASAT		Laboratório Sócio-Econômico do Tocantins (Socio-Economic Laboratory of the Tocantins)
MDB		Movimento Democrático Brasileiro (Brazilian Democratic Movement)
MEB		Movimento de Educação de Base (Movement for Basic Education)
MIRAD		Ministério da Reforma e do Desenvolvimento Agrário (Ministry of Reform and Agrarian Development)
MMA		Ministério do Meio Ambiente, dos Recursos Hídricos e da Amazônia Legal (Ministry of the Environment, Water Resources and Legal Amazonia)
MPST		Movimento pela Sobrevivência na Trans-amazônica (Movement for Survival on the Transamazon Highway)
MST		Movimento dos Trabalhadores Rurais Sem Terra (Landless Rural Workers' Movement)
NAEA		Núcleo de Áltos Estudos Amazônicos (Nucleus of Higher Amazonian Studies)
NGO		Non-Governmental Organisation
NTFP		Non-Timber Forest Product

ODA	Overseas Development Administration (now renamed the Department for International Development – DfID)
OECD	Organisation for Economic Cooperation and Development
ORSTOM	Office de la Recherche Scientifique Outre Mer (Office for Scientific Research Overseas)
OSR	Organização dos Seringueiros de Rondônia (Organisation of Rubber Tappers of Rondônia)
PAD	Projeto de Assentamento Dirigido (Directed Resettlement Project)
PAE	Projeto de Assentamento Extrativista (Extractive Resettlement Project)
PAET	Programa Agro-Ecológico da Transamazônica (Agro-Ecological Programme of the Transamazon Highway)
PAF	Projeto Agro-Florestal (Agroforestry Project)
PBD	Placa Bruta Defumada (Smoked Rubber Sheet)
PC do B	Partido Comunista do Brasil (Communist Party of Brazil)
PCN	Projeto Calha Norte (Calha Norte Project)
PESACRE	Grupo de Pesquisa e Extensão Agroflorestal do Acre (Acre Agroforestry Research and Extension Group)
PFD	Pesquisa, Formação, Desenvolvimento (Research, Training, Development)
PIFI	Plano Integrado de Florestamento Industrial (Integrated Industrial Forestry Plan)
PIN	Plano de Integração Nacional (Plan for National Integration)
PLA	Participatory Learning and Action
PLANAFLORO	Plano Agropecuário e Florestal de Rondônia (Rondônia Agricultural, Forestry and Livestock Plan)
PMACI	Programa de Proteção do Meio Ambiente e

	às Comunidades Indígenas (Programme for the Protection of the Environment and Indigenous Communities)
PNMA	Plano Nacional do Meio Ambiente (National Environment Programme)
PNRA	Programa Nacional de Reforma Agrária (National Agrarian Reform Programme)
POEMA	Pobreza e Meio Ambiente na Amazônia (Poverty and Environment in Amazonia)
POLAMAZONIA	Programa de Polos Agropecuários e Agrominerais da Amazônia (Programme of Agro-Livestock and Agro mineral Poles for Amazonia)
POLONOROESTE	Programa de Desenvolvimento Integrado do Noroeste do Brasil (Integrated Development Programme for the North-West Region of Brazil)
PORP	Participatory Organisation of the Rural Poor
PRA	Participatory Rural Appraisal
PROBOR	Programa de Incentivo à Produção da Borracha (Incentive Programme for Rubber Production)
PROCERA	Programa de Crédito Especial de Reforma Agrária (Special Credit Programme for Agrarian Reform)
PRODEX	Programa de Apoio ao Desenvolvimento do Extrativismo (Commission for the Assistance Programme for the Development of Extractivism)
PT	Partido dos Trabalhadores (Workers' Party)
REBRAF	Instituto Rede Brasileira Agroflorestal (Brazilian Agroforestry Network Institute)
RECA	Projeto de Reflorestamento Econômico, Consorciado e Adensado (Mixed, Economic and Concentrated Reforestation Project)
RESEX	Reserva Extrativista

	(Extractive Reserve)
RTF	Rainforest Trust Fund
SAE	Secretaria de Assuntos Estratégicos (Secretariat for Strategic Affairs)
SESAU	Secretaria de Saúde (Secretariat of Health)
SCM	Sociedade Civil Mamirauá (Mamirauá Civil Society)
SEMA	Secretaria Especial do Meio Ambiente (Special Secretariat for the Environment)
SIPAM	Sistema de Proteção da Amazônia (System for the Protection of Amazonia)
SISNAMA	Sistema Nacional do Meio Ambiente (National Environment System)
SIVAM	Serviço de Informação e Vigilância da Amazônia (Information and Surveillance Service for Amazonia)
SNUC	Sistema Nacional de Unidades de Conservação da Natureza (National System of Nature Conservation Units)
STR	Sindicato dos Trabalhadores Rurais (Rural Workers' Union)
SUDAM	Superintendência do Desenvolvimento da Amazônia (Superintendency for the Development of Amazonia)
SUDEPE	Superintendência do Desenvolvimento da Pesca (Superintendency for the Development of Fishing)
SUDHEVEA	Superintendência da Borracha (Superintendency for Rubber)
TORMB	Taxa de Organização e Regulamentação do Mercado da Borracha (Tax for the Organisation and Regulation of the Rubber Market)
UDR	União Democrática Ruralista (Farmers' Democratic Movement)

Abbreviations

UFPa	Universidade Federal do Pará (Federal University of Pará)
UNCED	United Nations Conference on the Environment and Development
UNDP	United Nations Development Programme
UNEP	United Nations Environment Programme
UNI	União das Nações Indígenas (Union of Indigenous Peoples)
UNRISD	United Nations Research Institute for Economic and Social Development
USAID	United States Agency for International Development
WCED	World Commission on Environment and Development
WCI	World Conservation International
WWF	World Wide Fund for Nature

Preface

The first critical accounts of official development strategies in Brazilian Amazonia which appeared in the 1970s were highly pessimistic in their evaluations of regional progress. It was thought that, in the drive to 'modernise' and integrate the Amazon into mainstream national development, traditional culture would be largely eradicated, while remaining rural producers would become wholly subservient to large-scale capital, marginalised and dominated by hostile government policy. The authors of Brazil's economic 'miracle' and their political allies viewed the region's natural assets as a resource base to be opportunistically exploited, either as a boost to export income and GNP or as a source of short-term, financial profit for the advantage of a powerful few, with some benefits 'trickling down' to the regional population. Social conflict and environmental degradation were seen as the inevitable price which had to be paid in this apparently unidirectional process of societal transformation, one which has been extensively documented in the relevant literature and on film.

Yet while the above scenario still accurately describes much of what happens in present-day Amazonia, the picture is far less black and white than it may have appeared during the 'decade of destruction'. The research upon which this book is based was inspired by the observation that a quiet revolution has been taking place which challenges the paradigm that has dominated so far. All over Amazonia, local initiatives are attempting to exert control over the productive process as it affects their livelihoods. 'Productive conservation', as I have called this process, is based on the economic use of Amazonia's forests and waterways by local populations alongside the preservation of natural resources for the benefit of present and future generations. Yet although traditional producer groups have taken the initiative in defending their livelihoods while conserving nature, domestic policy-makers and international aid donors have also begun to recognise the potential economic, social and environmental benefits of harnessing the skills and power of local resource-user groups.

Chapter one brings together three conceptual areas which underpin the idea of 'productive conservation'. Firstly, theories of new social movements suggest why hitherto socio-politically fragmented populations may band together in support of unifying causes such as ecosystem defence. Secondly, a discussion of common property regimes rejects the inevitability of a 'tragedy of the commons' and suggests that individual and collective interests can inspire collaboration amongst natural resource-users in common-pool situations, based both on traditional arrangements as well as upon more institutionalised structures. Thirdly, notions of community participation illustrate what forms such involvement may take at various stages of the inception, planning and implementation of productive conservation strategies.

Following a review in chapter two of how development and environmental policies for Amazonia have evolved over the past three decades, three major case-studies of productive conservation experiences are considered. Chapter three examines the pioneering rubber tappers' movement, which, measured in both spatial and political terms, has arguably had the most significant impact on policy-making for Amazonia through the formation of extractive reserves. Chapter four considers the often-forgotten inland, traditional fishing communities of Amazonia and how, rather like the rubber tappers, they have been obliged actively to defend their livelihoods against external threats from commercial fishermen, while going on to formulate a longer-term resource-management strategy. Mamirauá is the most important example of such action for aquatic-resource conservation and development in Brazilian Amazonia. Chapter five analyses the efforts of two small settler programmes around Marabá and Altamira to develop mixed agroforestry farming systems which could break the vicious circle of slash-and-burn farming, sedentarising the population, while preserving the remaining rainforest.

Finally, chapter six reviews some general lessons which may be learned from these diverse, pioneering experiences with rubber tappers, fisherpeople and colonist farmers. It attempts to show how grassroots groups may contribute in distinctive ways to the process of productive conservation, in collaboration with other institutions such as non-governmental organisations (NGOs), the state and international donors. The fundamental point made here and, indeed, throughout the volume is that without the active participation of the community, productive conservation would simply not be viable. The speculative, predatory and destructive methods of resource extraction which have fuelled Amazonia's development since the 1960s are not sustainable in the long run.

The forest and its peoples must be allowed to continue to exist under conditions which facilitate their gradual adaptation to more sustainable forms of resource-use. This is not to imply that Amazonia's *caboclos*, Amerindians and peasant farmers should be preserved in aspic as some kind of monument to an idyllic or mythological past. However, their right to a voice in the development of the region and to determine their own livelihoods should be recognised with all the potential economic, social and environmental benefits that this condition would generate. Productive conservation, although by no means a panacea for the problems which beset Amazonia, and still embryonic, with many problems to be overcome, offers one major avenue for helping to achieve this goal. If this challenge were eventually to be fully accepted by policy-makers perhaps the future of Amazonia, together with its rich natural and social fabric, could then be regarded with something approaching optimism.

Anthony Hall

1
Resource governance: mobilisation and participation

The productive use of natural resources is fundamental to sustaining rural peoples' livelihoods in developing countries. In the Brazilian Amazon, official development policies have encouraged terrestrial and aquatic-resource destruction both by prioritising speculative and large-scale commercial interests such as cattle-ranching and logging, while at the same time failing to assist small settlers to progress towards the adoption of better adapted farming and land-use methods. As livelihood resources have come under increasing pressure, users have been obliged to engage actively in defensive struggles to protect themselves. Such conflicts have become a prominent feature of daily life in many parts of the world. Indigenous peoples, traditional fishing communities and forest-dwellers as well as frontier settlers have been obliged actively to resist attempts by more powerful groups at encroachment upon their resource base. What was until the mid-1980s a silent war is now an increasingly loud battle.

It is no coincidence that grassroots resistance to resource degradation has been especially marked in fragile environments such as Amazonia's. To many in the Amazon and elsewhere, the protection of natural resources is a *sine qua non* for the maintenance of their livelihoods. For indigenous and peasant populations who depend almost entirely upon farming, fishing and various forms of extractivism for their sustenance, preservation of natural assets is not a luxury but a question of survival. The failure of government to protect the rights of local populations in disputes over access to both common property and private resources in Amazonia has frequently left local groups with little option but to be driven out or resist and organise their own defensive strategies.

Although such action is by no means a novel phenomenon, it has become more pronounced since the 1980s. What will here be denominated 'productive conservation' initiatives or movements represent an attempt by resource-user groups to reconcile the twin goals of supporting people's livelihoods while conserving the natural resources upon which these are based. It is argued in this volume that, although grassroots action is clearly no panacea for the problem of resource depletion in Amazonia or elsewhere, it is one of the most important prerequisites for any sustainable development strategy involving local populations in resource protection. In other words, resource-users must become actively involved in resisting encroachment as well as in designing and implementing long-term, planned productive conservation strategies. It is, therefore, absolutely crucial that planners and policy-makers accept this fundamental premise. They must understand not only how grassroots movements originate and are sustained; in particular, it is vital to comprehend their very distinctive contributions at all levels in the design and execution of productive conservation projects and programmes.

There is no single paradigm in the social sciences which provides a unified theoretical basis for explaining the origins and functions of grassroots socio-environmental movements. However, a number of relevant conceptual areas can be identified which, considered together, constitute a loose framework which facilitates analysis. The framework presented in this study draws upon three areas relevant to the present discussion: firstly, *new social movements* concern the emergence of group action around socio-environmental issues related to the administration of natural resources; secondly, *governance of common property* relates to the exercise of collective choice by local groups for the self-governance of natural resources; finally, *community participation* describes the particular ways in which such collectivities contribute with their skills and efforts towards the definition and execution of purposeful, productive conservation strategies. All three areas fall broadly within a 'post-modern' perspective, which eschews deterministic and reductionist meta-theories in favour of an action-centred approach based on the power of local agency to influence the course of events.

Before considering these three areas and their links with productive conservation endeavours, the concept of 'sustainable development', as adopted in this volume, needs to be clarified. Sustainable development is a vague and relative concept; it has given rise to a myriad of definitions which are often contradictory and flawed (Lélé, 1991). Like beauty, it seems to exist largely in the eye of the beholder rather than in any absolute sense. The Brundtland Report (WCED, 1987) set broad parameters based on the notion of development which meets the needs of both present and future generations. For present purposes in the context of Amazonia, however, 'sustainable development' can be best defined as: 'development which allows the productive use of natural resources for economic growth and livelihood strengthening, while simultaneously conserving the biodiversity and sociodiversity which form an integral and indispensable part of this process' (Hall, 1995: 4). Thus, the attainment of 'sustainability' will depend upon meeting a number of complementary and mutually interdependent goals in terms of biophysical preservation, economic feasibility, organisational competence and socio-political solidarity.

Productive conservation movements

Although local communities in Amazonia have always been involved in the systematic management of their natural resource base in what nowadays would be called a 'sustainable' manner, productive conservation movements are a fairly new phenomenon. The growing practice of communities under threat to actually band together to defend their livelihoods and set up sustainably managed systems is a relatively recent trend. Along with other forms of collective action which have emerged over the past twenty years, this has posed a challenge to conventional functionalist and neo-Marxist interpretations of social movements. As reductionist paradigms, both schools aim to identify universal laws on the basis of which specific events can be understood. Functionalist interpretations see social movements as irrational manifestations which are disruptive of an assumed social order, while Marxist analyses perceive such activity as a necessary reflection of class conflict within society. Not only do such views belie reality, they are of precious little use to policy-makers and planners given their inherently pessimistic interpretation of the potential for human agents to bring about progressive, piecemeal change. They are also extremely patronising and condescending in their view of poorer groups as essentially ineffectual victims of processes totally beyond their control.

Although grassroots environmental action as a phenomenon has been noted for its significance as a force for conservation,[1] there has been little reformulation of social science conceptualisations to help explain the origins and specific roles of such mobilisation. One area relevant to the present discussion concerns the theory of 'new social movements' as collective social actors. This set of ideas was developed from the 1960s to explain new, group-based responses to novel grievances which have emerged as a result of structural changes in modern society (Touraine, 1988; Melucci, 1989). Notions of inevitable class solidarity and linear, historical determinism have little place in this paradigm. Furthermore, there is little affinity between the demands of new social movements and the territorial or class interests of political parties. Under the banner of 'new' movements, socially and ecologically driven group initiatives, whether in the industrialised or the developing world, are characterised, above all, by their diversity of structure. No higher level, reductionist theory such as functionalism or Marxism can offer a full explanation for the rise of these movements. As Scott notes (1990: 7–10), they 'are not a unified sociological phenomenon which can be explained with reference to any single set of social-structural changes ... [and] ... cannot be viewed as a coherent sociological category'.

Notions of heterogeneous composition and flexible response to new livelihood challenges fits well with an action-based perspective on social change. An actor-oriented view frees analysis from the deterministic, universalist interpretations of functionalist and neo-Marxist paradigms. While allowing for the influence of structural factors in determining the emergence or otherwise of social action, this conceptualisation recognises the central importance of the social collectivity and its ability to exert influence. According to this viewpoint, groups of farmers, fisherpeople and extractivists are most usefully seen as proactive rather than as simply passive participants in the process of change, who are in fact '"knowledgeable" and "capable". They attempt to solve problems, learn how to intervene in the flow of events around them' (Long and Long, 1992: 23).

Such groups are credited with the power of agency as legitimate, collective social actors. The outcomes of change processes are, thus, not predetermined, but may be strongly affected by the action of groups and alliances formed in particular 'interface' or contact situations. Structural characteristics may lay down certain prerequisites for group action to be feasible, but they by no means guarantee that it will emerge. Context-specific factors, such as the strategies adopted by actors in organising their resources and in negotiating with other participants in the change process, will be far more important in determining the eventual outcome. The discussion below on categories of community participation attempts to disaggregate the forms which such involvement may take. In the final analysis, as Long (1988) and Mouzelis (1990) have pointed out, it is necessary to combine both actor-oriented and historical-structural analyses to obtain a complete picture of the evolving situation.

What is evident in the Amazonian context is that particular groups cope in very different ways with threats to the depletion of their natural resource base. Traditionally in Amazonia, as will be shown in chapter two, many have succumbed to the onslaught of public policy-driven development models, which have supported private commercial interests while neglecting those of small-scale producers. Since the 1970s, through land struggles and, from the mid-1980s, via resource-conservation and production-based projects, others have successfully resisted these outside interventions and set their own agendas for action. Far from being passive victims, therefore, small producers are increasingly proactive in their dealings with private business and government agencies, aiming to establish their own priorities in what is a 'socially constructed and negotiated process' shaped by the kinds of interactions which develop in given situations (Long and Long, 1992: 35). As will be seen from the three major case-studies in this volume, this applies to all levels of negotiation, from the local to the regional, national and even international spheres.

Environmental movements in the industrialised nations have been concerned with broad issues of global ecology and sustainable development, often linked to 'green' party politics. Similarly, the middle-class environmental lobbies of developing countries such as Brazil have been limited to raising public awareness in the large urban centres about deterioration of the environment generally, while action is largely restricted to 'ecologised discourse' (Viola, 1993: 20). These are very different from the livelihood battles of grassroots groups struggling daily to conserve their natural wealth and meet their basic needs in the face of growing destructive pressures. If there are parallels to be drawn between productive conservation initiatives and other kinds of action, it is with new social movements in the Third World rather than 'green' environmentalism that comparisons may best be made.

Despite their inherent diversity, however, such movements share certain basic features. They need not be class-based, but may unite a range of groups around a common theme or external threat. In the case of the present analysis, the theme of livelihood preservation based on resource conservation provides this underlying motivation, although this coincides in the three case-studies with a relatively uniform socio-economic status amongst group members (rubber tappers, fisherpeople and small farmers). The range of group or community adherence to conservation activity will be closely determined by the area of influence of the natural resources in question, such as the existence of a common property regime benefiting, say, rubber tappers or fisherpeople. In the Amazon context, therefore, membership will tend to be drawn from similar resource-user groups in a broadly shared situation.

What tends, with varying degrees of intensity, to unite participants of productive conservation movements is not a desire for radical political change as such, but for reform of the existing system in order to safeguard people's rights and livelihoods. Coupled with this is the perception that direct grassroots action is essential in order for people to be able effectively to defend their individual and collective interests, as they know that they can rarely rely on formal political or bureaucratic channels, at least in the initial stages. Such community-based action is thus a challenge to 'social closure', a search for avenues of participation in formulating policies and taking decisions, given the failure of political parties and state machinery to provide for this. The observation by Scott (1990: 6) with regard to new social movements can equally well be applied to productive conservation movements in Amazonia, especially in their more conflictive, formative stage: 'they have mass mobilisation, or the threat of mass mobilisation, as their prime source of social sanction, and hence of power.'

Be that as it may, however, there are conceptual and methodological problems inherent in trying to define what is a social or conservation 'movement'. Internally, such collective action is bound to be heterogeneous and diverse despite observers' sometimes spurious imputations of group solidarity. Yet this may be something of a red herring with regard to the current discussion. A more important question is whether *sufficient* group unity can be achieved at critical junctures to enable conservation and production objectives to be met; for example, in the key phases of initial resistance and policing of natural resource protection as well as, later, in the design and execution of a long-term management plan. As the examples considered in this volume demonstrate, different forms of collective action are required by the community at different stages in this process, each in its own way critical to the success of the exercise. Furthermore, the propensity of a group to act collectively in its own interests is not a fixed or permanent feature, but flexible and changing depending upon the demands of the situation, the challenges posed and the effectiveness of methods used for mobilising the group.

As already mentioned, it is necessary to link the concept of overall structure with that of local agency to show people as social actors engaging in strategic relationships with broader systems and institutions. In the action model of resource conservation being put forward here, the propensity for a productive conservation movement to emerge in a given situation will therefore depend on both structural and context-specific factors. In structural terms, the likelihood of cooperation amongst resource-users will be conditioned to a large extent by the nature of the economic base and dependent livelihood patterns, as well as by the degree of shared group identity. In terms of the local context, the nature and extent of community participation will closely determine how groups cooperate to defend and manage their natural resource base, how they define membership and what means are adopted to enhance commitment to the group's cause. Before examining the role of local participation, structural factors will be discussed in more detail.

Increasingly, social scientists are seeking explanations for the nature and pace of socio-economic change in a combination of macro-level or structural determinants together with situation-specific, social agents as rational choice-makers faced with alternative courses of action in their efforts to maximise advantage. In terms of the case-studies considered in this volume, it is possible to identify certain key features which can, broadly speaking, be said to constitute prerequisites for the emergence of productive conservation action. These are, as it were, a basic minimum requirement, although their presence by no means guarantees that such collective action will necessarily take place. For this to happen, other factors will also be operative, building upon and maximising the organisational potential resulting from these preconditions. In terms of their characteristics as collective social actors, at once defending and managing access to key natural resources, such movements require two major structural features; firstly, livelihoods which are underpinned by direct access to and productive use of natural resources, and secondly, some notion of group identity. These will be considered in turn.

Natural resource-based livelihoods
As an instrumental basis for individual and collective motivation, perhaps the overriding precondition for a productive conservation movement to emerge is that members' livelihoods be strongly underpinned by access to a clearly defined stock of natural resources. This may take the form either of a common property resource such as a lake or reserve, or privately owned assets, such as plots of land. Whatever the degree of common access or use, the most critical feature from the point of view of introducing productive conservation initiatives is that such resources actually play a key role in people's livelihood strategies. If this is not the case, it will be extremely difficult to introduce incentives for their conservation. While this may seem self-evident, it is likely to have important implications for conservation policy, as rural people diversify their sources of income, especially in urban areas, and thus become less economically dependent upon natural resources.

Yet if this precondition does exist, it should be possible to strengthen or generate an awareness that the longer-term management of these resources will maximise benefits both for individuals as well as for the user group as a whole. The motivation to maximise personal profit as opposed to pursuing the collective good arising from these activities, whether fishing, timber extraction or gathering of non-timber forest products, will depend very much on the nature of the resource and the historical-institutional context in which it is being harnessed.

As will be discussed in greater detail below, 'collective choice' or 'resource-mobilisation' theories can be broadly divided into those that stress instrumental motivation and those that emphasise shared identity as a basis for collective action (Cohen, 1985). In their discussions of new social movements, Latin American researchers have tended to stress identity-centred theories as the basis for autonomous action, while neglecting other more utilitarian aspects

(Escobar and Alvarez, 1992). Productive conservation initiatives or movements, by definition, are sustained in large measure by the sheer economic necessity felt by resource-users to conserve their productive assets rather than engage in short-term, destructive behaviour.

In the three cases studied here, access to various kinds of natural resources is critical for meeting the most basic livelihood needs of user groups. If people are unable to tap forest products, are unable to fish the rivers and lakes or are prevented from establishing sedentary forms of agroforestry, their existence as small cultivators in Amazonia becomes increasingly unviable. They are then obliged to engage in more diversified livelihood strategies, some of which may be environmentally damaging; the trek to a new agricultural frontier to begin another destructive cycle of slash-and-burn farming, for example, or prospecting for gold. The increasingly common combination of rural production with urban informal sector activities, while necessary, may prove to be unreliable and financially unrewarding. In short, economic and basic needs considerations figure very prominently in motivating natural resource-users in Amazonia to collaborate in devising more immediately defensive as well as longer-term conservation strategies to protect these assets from destruction.

Group identity
Although economic-utilitarian factors are clearly of central importance in motivating users to protect their natural resources, collective action for conservation requires additional sources of group solidarity to make it viable on a long-term basis. As Cohen (1985: 691) points out, 'the logic of collective interaction entails something other than strategic or instrumental rationality'. This is especially so when the resource-management strategy or plan requires the direct and active participation of user-group members at successive stages of project design and execution. Such an approach will require that users be prepared to forgo short-term, individual benefit maximisation in the interests of preserving assets for their sustainable use on a longer-run basis by the group as a whole. This is particularly important if the so-called 'freerider' problem in common property situations is to be successfully dealt with. Thus, in order to strengthen the likelihood of continued local involvement for both planning and operational purposes, as well as to reconcile individ-

ual with collective interests, there must be some sense of shared identity and a certain community of purpose, irrespective of the gains accruing to individual group members.

Popular movements in defence of access to land or to conserve natural resources in Amazonia are usually based upon backgrounds of struggle against hostile forces. In fact, such clashes with aggressors seem to be almost a precondition for productive conservation to be undertaken. Small-scale initiatives such as stand-alone community projects which address economic and conservation issues are quite feasible and indeed not uncommon in Amazonia, even in the absence of direct outside threats. Yet attempts at forming more broadly based programmes, such as the rubber tappers' movement or concerted action by small famers on the Transamazon highway, are often enhanced by the unity of purpose resulting from conflicts with external interests.

As chapter two will show in more detail, public policy has offered little support for small-scale producers in Amazonia, while at the same time it has channelled vast subsidies to large corporate and individual landowners in their pursuit of ecologically damaging activities such as cattle-ranching and logging. All over the region, communities of farmers, extractivists, fisherpeople and indigenous groups have been obliged to unite and collectively fight off attempts by powerful commercial interests to appropriate common and personal assets, whether in the form of land, trees or fish. All of the movements studied in this volume, in Acre, Rondônia, Pará and Amazonas, have cut their teeth, so to speak, on the conflicts of the past, giving people some sense of collective purpose. In addition, the struggles of rural trade unions and 'popular education' movements supported by the radical Catholic church and NGOs especially during the military regime, have also supported and strengthened grassroots action.

Theories of new social movements have addressed the issue of *why* people mobilise around certain issues, but have largely ignored the more operationally important question of *how* they mobilise to defend their interests (Foweraker, 1995). This is clearly a fundamental problem which has to be faced, and care must be taken not to romanticise the inherent virtues and stability of community cooperation. It is important as a means of binding conservation movements together and, for this very reason, should not be taken for granted. As the history of the rubber tappers shows, conservation movements are as prone as any other group to internecine conflicts. It is, indeed, almost axiomatic that latent conflicts tend to reveal themselves once the initial solidarity induced by fighting a common enemy has passed.

Institutional mechanisms and strategies are therefore needed, which capitalise upon and augment incentive systems conducive towards sustaining productive conservation strategies. Where external conflicts do not exist or have been surpassed, such initiatives should include techniques for binding together social groups faced with the challenge of devising and implementing a resource-management plan. This is a key issue, which is, however, often neglected. Cohesiveness is automatically assumed to exist by virtue of previous demonstrations, however transitory, of collective action. Structures of resource governance, educational programmes and economic incentives may all be used to enhance collective solidarity. These matters will be further explored in the following sections on the regulation of natural resources and on the role of community participation.

The governance of common property resources

'Common property' may be defined in three major ways: firstly, as an all-embracing category of good with no single claimant and which cannot be privatised or legally appropriated, such as the atmosphere or the international seas, usually referred to as the 'global commons'; secondly, resources which are freely accessible to a number of user groups but which may eventually come under some form of state or private ownership; and thirdly, resources governed by a structured, common property rights (CPR) regime, such as community forests and lakes, to which access is controlled (*de facto*, if not necessarily *de jure*) to varying degrees by the principal users, managers or owners.

Many rural communities in the developing world are wholly or partially dependent for their livelihoods on access to common-pool natural resources, which are either open access or, more commonly, under some form of local control. This is the case with the rubber tappers and fishing communities, discussed in chapters three and four of this volume. Yet even where land is privately owned or secured, as along the Transamazon highway settlements analysed in chapter five and to some degree in the extractive reserves, regional commons issues are important; for example, in terms of controlling deforestation on individual plots in order to retain environmental services provided by the rainforest, such as climate regulation and biodiversity preservation.

Traditional conceptual models of common-pool resource-use are, however, extremely pessimistic with regard to the potential for conservation. They assume that, eventually, such natural assets are bound to be degraded and depleted through excessive use. It is thought that there is an inherent contradiction between the interests of individual users, out to maximise short-term gains without taking into account the full costs of their actions, and the interests of the user group as a whole, whose collective good would be best served by a longer-term conservation strategy based on more measured and gradual use of natural resources. Such apparent incompatibility has become known as the 'freerider' problem. Resource-users are thought to be incapable of cooperating in a manner which reconciles their own individual interests with the collective interests of the community.

This argument has been most forcibly expressed by Garrett Hardin (1968) in his discussion of the 'tragedy of the commons', which suggests that degradation of the environment is inevitable wherever natural resources are openly accessible.[2] This was formalised as the 'prisoner's dilemma game' by Dawes (1973), while Olson (1965) had elaborated a similar view in the 'logic of collective action'.[3] These theories all suggest very strongly that it is difficult, except under the most exceptional circumstances, to persuade individuals to pursue long-term, joint welfare goals rather than more immediate individual benefits. Traditional common property institutions, with their supposed inherent tendency towards 'freeriding', have often been blamed for the misuse of resources and subsequent environmental degradation.

The implication of such theories is that, as resource-users cannot be expected to adopt more conservationist behaviour of their own accord (since this would be 'irrational' when viewed in terms of individual versus group interests and the inherent tendency to freeride), they must be coerced by external forces. Policy-makers have tended to assume that resource-users are incapable of collectively running their affairs in a responsible manner and that central government must therefore impose controls. This must be achieved either through coercive state administration or privatisation.

In the first instance, a central authority would take direct charge of a resource system, effectively turning it into state property. Centralised control and regulation of natural resources has formed the basis of environmental policy in developing countries, including Brazil, despite its demonstrably limited effectiveness. Alternatively, the government may privatise resources by parcelling out property rights and allowing individuals to follow their own interests within this system. These kinds of policy recommendations have been based on Western assumptions that individual private property rights will provide sufficient incentive for the adequate management of natural resources. This is in spite of strong evidence that such arrangements have failed to prevent and have, indeed, frequently exacerbated resource degradation.

The inbuilt pessimism of the theories cited above concerning the abilities of groups collectively and sustainably to manage common-pool resources is based on some fundamental misconceptions about the nature of common property, about the rationale underlying its collective use and about decision-making processes within user groups. A clear distinction must be made between large-scale, open-access regimes (*res nullius*), which permit an uncontrolled free-for-all along the lines suggested by Hardin and others, and smaller-scale, authentic common property regimes (*res communes*). In fact, very few resources are truly open to everyone.[4] In genuinely open-access situations, where either no system of cooperation has been developed, where a previously existing system has broken down completely, or where state jurisdiction is weak, there may well be a tendency towards resource degradation. In contrast, controlled access CPRs constitute a form of collective private property in which individuals have both rights and obligations and where management authority is vested in the group and/or its recognised leaders.

For centuries in Europe, resource management was governed by common property institutions specifying rules for joint use, until the enclosure movements forced land into private ownership. In the modern developing world also, such arrangements prevail in situations which, to outside observers, may appear as open access. Many groups have evolved systems with 'structured ownership arrangements within which management rules are developed, group size is known and enforced, incentives exist for co-owners to follow the accepted institutional arrangements, and sanctions work to ensure compliance' (Bromley and Cernea, 1989: iii). There is ample evidence from around the world of traditional management systems which successfully balance individual and communal interests in the use of scarce or renewable natural resources.[5]

This principle is usually applied to situations where the population is almost entirely dependent upon CPRs for their livelihoods; that is, in the collective administration of renewable and living resources such as forests and fish, as in the cases of extractive reserves and the Mamirauá Ecological Station considered in chapters three and four respectively of this volume. In addition, however, the same principle is applicable in part to those more commonplace circumstances in Amazonia where a degree of collective management responsibility is essential to maintain a conservationist and productive enterprise based on private ownership, such as the small farmer organisations Agro-Environmental Centre of the Tocantins (CAT) and Agro-Economic Laboratory of the Tocantins (LAET) on the Transamazon highway, analysed in chapter five. These examples from contrasting ecological sub-systems of Amazonia are analysed with a view to showing how ideas taken from traditional resource-management regimes can be adapted to address contemporary pressures and problems.

Evidence from many sources shows that there is no inevitable tendency for people sharing a common-pool resource to be automatically caught up in a vicious circle of environmental destruction. As Ostrom (1990: 21) notes, 'some individuals have broken out of the trap inherent in the commons dilemma, whereas others continue remorsefully trapped into destroying their own resources'. The case-studies in this volume from Amazonia attempt to show how, in three very different sets of circumstances, institutional arrangements are being worked out which, if successful over the long term, will permit the sustainable management of terrestrial and aquatic natural resources in the interests of the user groups involved. In some instances, these efforts are building upon longer-standing systems of resource management (Mamirauá), while in others (extractive reserves and *Transamazônica* settlers) new arrangements are necessary to encourage user cooperation. The underlying premise is that those who depend on natural resources for their livelihoods will eventually perceive a vested interest in their non-destructive use and that, consequently, it is possible to harness such commitment in order to design solutions which fit local circumstances.

These will entail contrasting sets of agreements, rules and sanctions, as well as a variety of collective and individual ownership arrangements. As Runge (1986: 633) notes, there are no universal prescriptions for natural resource management, and, 'private exclusive property is not always comparatively advantageous in the villages of less developed economies ... The search for appropriate institutional responses must respect both the traditions and the constraints of local needs in specific choice environments.' Common property systems evolve not just through pure chance or as a cultural idiosyncrasy, but because they play a number of distinctive roles (Berkes, 1989). These revolve around protecting livelihoods through the application of shared rules, as the basis of non-destructive production systems, guaranteeing equity of access, while mediating conflicts over asset use, conserving resources which would otherwise be degraded and offering the hope of longer-term sustainability.

Moves towards formalised, productive conservation arrangements in Amazonia, where the preservation of people's livelihoods is inextricably tied to the conservation of the natural resource base, are best viewed within a rational choice paradigm. In this sub-context, involving relatively small and clearly defined rural producer groups in CPR-type situations, a modified 'collective choice' or 'resource-mobilisation' framework seems appropriate. As we have said, this approach combines two essential elements. Firstly, it argues that organised groups such as those discussed in this volume are principally rational-utilitarian in their objectives, basing their strategies on the likely benefits and costs accruing to both the individual and to wider groups. Following Ostrom (1990: 33), resource appropriators may be viewed as 'broadly rational individuals who find themselves in complex and uncertain situations'.

This notion is useful for helping to understand collective action in relatively small-scale resource-conservation situations where socio-political action is closely tied to economic goals, although, as discussed further below, non-materialistic objectives may be equally rational and utilitarian in their own way. Resource-users do have strong material incentives to conserve their productive base. They depend strongly for their survival on natural resources, which are coming under increasing demographic, technological, political, commercial and environmental pressure. The high financial costs, and the practical and legal difficulties of establishing private property rights, are legion. These problems, together with sheer poverty and the resulting uncertainty of life, signify that many producers have little or no cushion against imminent catastrophe, whether naturally or human-induced. They 'can make a necessity out of joint use rights that elsewhere might seem more virtuous ... [and] an incentive structure that can make common property a comparatively rational solution to certain problems of resource management' (Runge, 1986: 624–5).

The second basic feature of this approach is recognition of the fact that the behaviour of individuals and groups will vary depending on local conditions, and that appropriate institutional rules can be established to influence people's actions. Rational individuals, it is assumed, will 'participate' in the conservation exercise by contributing goods and services or in a number of other ways, as long as others do the same. It rejects the assumption contained in the 'free rider' notion that decisions are entirely individualistic and that there is no place for cooperation unless this is imposed from outside. In our alternative paradigm, decisions within a group are seen as interdependent and determined by other people's choices as well as the individual's initial perceptions. Thus, with appropriate information-sharing, consultative and organisational mechanisms and incentive structures in place, it should be possible to raise expectations to a level at which the principle of reciprocity operates in a situation of collective choice. Participants can thus develop confidence that a sufficiently large proportion will cooperate in the conservation exercise to make it worth everyone's while to collaborate.

This has also been labelled an 'institutional rational choice' approach, in which structures and regulations may be set up to allow 'local individuals to play critical roles in designing the institutional rules, in monitoring compliance, and in enforcing sanctions', and to permit the exclusion of those who do not comply (Sabatier, 1993: xx). The organisational mix in any given situation is bound to vary considerably and, as discussed in the case-studies, may involve a combination of local, regional, national and international bodies in order to establish and maintain an appropriate institutional structure.

Some theorists of the 'rational-utilitarian' school such as Olson (1965) have been condemned for what are perceived by critics as their overly simplistic neo-classical, economistic assumptions and their neglect of other determinants of both individual and group behaviour. However, the economic dimension is clearly central in the case of Amazonia's productive conservation experiments. In the cases examined in this volume, people's livelihoods depend very heavily upon preserving natural resources, since they derive a large proportion of their sustenance from these assets, whether collectively or individually managed. Destroy the rubber trees or overfish the lakes, and economic catastrophe will surely follow for the resource-users involved.

As we have said, the motivations and actions of resource- users depend heavily upon informal calculations, at both individual and group levels, of economic benefits and costs arising from particular conservation strategies. In addition, however, as noted above, collective interests also form part of the equation. As highlighted by Bates (1988) in his version of rational choice theory, it is also necessary to consider other, non-economic features such as shared perceptions arising from common experiences and community solidarity in the face of external threats.

These less tangible factors are also important for explaining the formation of new institutions to protect a natural resource base, whether wholly or partially shared. Localised settings, where communities of individuals have lived in relatively close proximity and have developed interrelationships may well 'possess social capital with which they can build institutional arrangements for resolving CPR dilemmas' (Ostrom, 1990: 184). Like new social movements, discussed above, action groups for productive conservation can also be understood as 'a collective actor constituted by individuals who understand themselves to have common interests and, for at least some significant part of their social existence, a common identity' (Scott 1990: 6). Such characteristics do not guarantee that solutions will be encountered, but they do constitute certain basic minimum prerequisites, without which the commons dilemma would be more difficult to resolve through local management.

Research into group dynamics has shed some light on those factors which are conducive towards the successful resolution of potential 'freerider' situations, or 'social dilemmas ... [where] ... [t]he challenge is to induce individuals to contribute to common causes when selfish actions would be more immediately and personally beneficial' (Glance and Huberman, 1994: 58). Very much in the tradition of the more instrumentalist version of resource-mobilisation theory, it is observed that 'an individual caught in a social dilemma forms a strategy for conditional cooperation from a calculation of the expected pay-off'. Yet this observation begs the more fundamental question of how such a 'pay-off' is expressed.

Conventionally, such rewards are thought of in terms of purely material benefits accruing to the individual, either in cash or in kind. Yet a 'pay-off' may equally well be perceived as a contribution towards some form of collective, less tangible advantage accruing to the group which enhances its strategic position in the struggle over resource management; for example, a strengthening of administrative skill or productive capacity. As Popkin (1979) points out in his study of the Vietnamese peasantry, rationality is not necessarily equated solely with self-interest defined in terms of personal welfare. Other considerations related to the situation and well-being of broader groups such as family and community also determine action and decision-making. In the final analysis, individual and collective as well as material and non-material benefits and costs may well be inextricably bound up with each other in situations such as those discussed in this study.

From their research into group dynamics in a range of social situations, Glance and Huberman (1994) conclude that, in the absence of a central authority, the successful sharing of a common good depends upon individuals' expectations as conditioned by two major related variables: group size and length of members' time horizons. Cooperation was found to be far more likely in small groups whose members were in prolonged contact with each other and who expected the endeavour to continue on a long-term basis. It was also discovered, conversely, that cooperation was unsustainable in groups beyond a certain size, since individual defectors were unlikely to be called to account for their actions and there was no disincentive effect, especially if the group activity in question was expected by members to be short-lived.

Another related variable concerns group homogeneity. Sugden (1984), for example, argues that cooperation is increasingly difficult as the group becomes more heterogeneous. Rules become more difficult to enforce as they fail to respond to the needs of diverse sub-sectors within the conservation unit. On the other hand, breaking down the collective management task into small, locally administered but coordinated sub-units is liable to facilitate resource management over geographically extensive areas in which the population is widely scattered. This approach is being tried, for example, at Mamirauá and on the extractive reserves. The extent to which increased group size and growing heterogeneity acts as a serious constraint upon cooperation, and the policy implications for promoting more effective community-based, productive conservation, will be discussed in the following chapters.

Glance and Huberman (1994) also note that the likelihood of cooperation is conditioned by the quality, volume and timing of information received by group members. Based on this observation, it seems likely that the efficient communication of relevant news and data on conservation issues as they affect the interests of a given group, if transmitting appropriate messages in a comprehensible fashion, may well increase incentives to cooperate. Particularly in the case of the large Amazonian producer groups with which this present study is concerned, which tend to be scattered over large areas, such information-sharing will play a critical role in various aspects of resource planning and management. Above all, it can serve to bring about a transition in expectations from a short to a long time horizon, encouraging collaboration in the pursuit of joint goals. In the large geographical areas involved, decentralised decision-making and management of CPRs through a network of localised groups can provide a sense of security and responsibility. Poor communications, on the other hand, may frustrate the whole exercise, leading to uncertainly, mistrust of the collective programme and 'selfish' behaviour.

Thus, a 'collective' or 'institutional' rational choice approach offers a useful conceptual basis for the formulation and implementation of policies designed to encourage productive conservation strategies. In the first place, it recognises the underlying, self-interested rationality of collective action amongst natural resource-user groups. Not only does this allow, in purely technical terms, for the justified introduction of a system of incentives and sanctions to encourage resource conservation. Even more importantly, in a political sense, this concept legitimises for the first time the development needs, or even the development 'rights', of large sections of the productive population which have hitherto been 'invisible' to the eyes of policy-makers, and whose vital contribution to environmental sustainability has gone largely unrecognised in official circles. In the second place, the adoption of a multi-institutional approach permits a great deal of creativity and flexibility in the design and execution of appropriate packages for dealing with contrasting conservation challenges in Amazonia and elsewhere.

There are, nevertheless, several major limitations to the rational choice model. These range from its inherently utilitarian bias, its use of the deductive method and definitions of individual versus group interests, to the efficacy of information distribution amongst resource-users and the notion of freedom of choice. Notwithstanding these criticisms, however, rational choice is 'the one political science paradigm which focuses centrally on the factors explaining variations in the extent to which different actors are likely to mobilize politically' (Moore, 1990: 242). For the purposes of the present analysis, the notion of rational, collective choice within the context of a social movement to protect natural resources is a useful analytical and prescriptive tool. Our third conceptual area, that of community participation, allows further disaggregation of the ways in which group members may become operationally involved in productive conservation strategies.

Community participation

Much has been written since the 1970s on the role of grassroots or community 'participation' in development. As one of the most used (and abused) pieces of development rhetoric, the term 'participation' should be treated with extreme caution. However, the idea of participation, if carefully defined and employed, is useful both for analysing the dynamics of local community movements as well as for helping to define and operationalise a normative basis for prescriptive change. It is particularly relevant in the context of productive conservation exercises in Amazonia, whose existence has been determined by the fact that resource-user groups have been able to organise themselves and make demands as collective entities in particular ways. Locale-specific modalities of resource-user involvement have had a major impact upon the nature and evolution of conservation movements in different parts of Brazilian Amazonia. The success of this incipient process of natural resource governance will depend heavily on the precise manner in which users are engaged, and what kinds of support are subsequently given to management procedures by other institutions taking part.

Origins of participation
Current ideas about promoting development through community participation owe their origins to various intellectual traditions. In

the West, for example, building up neighbourhood democracy involved the creation of small, local political institutions, while, in the Third World, populist leaders in newly independent nations espoused the virtues of cooperative and community-based forms of social and economic organisation, frequently as panaceas for the problems of underdevelopment (Midgley *et al.*, 1986). The notion of grassroots mobilisation for the purposes of promoting popular protest and local development as being more appropriate to local needs can be traced back many years to the influence of Gandhi and Mao. During the 1950s and 1960s, the widespread policy in Africa, Asia and Latin America of encouraging 'community development' was seen as a tactic for achieving mobilisation of the rural population for development purposes. However, this was a heavily state-directed and generally manipulative form of community involvement, which allowed people little influence on decision-making, whether under capitalist or socialist regimes (Hall, 1986).

During the 1970s, the participation ideal was adopted by the United Nations as a critical ingredient of anti-poverty initiatives. It was hoped that, if the rewards of material progress had not automatically 'trickled down' to the poorer sectors of society, as had been (rather conveniently) assumed by modernisation theorists, people's direct involvement in the development process would ensure a fairer distribution of benefits. The Basic Human Needs (BHN) approach was based firmly on participatory principles, and the International Labour Organisation (ILO), shortly after launching its BHN policy in 1977, introduced the Participatory Organisations of the Rural Poor (PORP) programme (Streeten *et al.*, 1981). The concept of primary health care was also grounded in the idea of community participation, as were other policies which emerged during that period, such as that of self-help housing (Turner, 1967; World Bank, 1975). The United Nations Research Institute for Social Development (UNRISD) initiated a major series of case-studies of popular participation in its various guises (Pearse and Stiefel, 1979). Several other analyses have attempted systematically to break down the concept of 'participation' in a development context, as a guide to project analysis and policy formulation.[6]

A number of studies have gone so far as to speak of participatory development as constituting a new paradigm in which people have become active subjects rather than merely passive objects, playing a major role in determining the direction of socio-economic change;

such ideas have been well expressed in all-encompassing works such as *Development by People* (Gran, 1983) and *People's Self-Development* (Rahman, 1993). Other publications (Burkey, 1993) have offered more pragmatic advice in terms of drawing up practical guidelines on how to apply some of these participatory principles to solving development problems in specific situations. Debate over the need for techniques such as Participatory Action Research (PAR), Participatory Learning and Action (PLA), Participatory Rural Appraisal (PRA) and Farmer Participatory Research (FPR) also testifies to the continuing importance of more democratic, 'bottom-up' methods as a means of helping to ensure more effective planning and implementation (Chambers *et al.*, 1990; Chambers, 1992; Okali *et al.*, 1994). Not only are they held to be technically more efficient research tools for gathering information, but, it is thought, they assist in the gradual process of reconditioning professional attitudes and values so that they are more consonant with the need to direct development efforts towards the underprivileged and resource-poor sectors of developing countries. These ideas have been most clearly and forcibly expressed by Chambers (1983, 1993, 1995) in his calls for a new development professionalism based on 'reversals' in learning and management.

The 1990s have seen a resurgence of official interest in the potential of local participation to promote development of the poorer sectors of society. 'Inadequate participation' is highlighted by the World Bank as a major cause of project failure, while donors and recipients are chastised for not having been 'sufficiently aware of the important role that the poor themselves can play in initiatives designed to assist them' (World Bank, 1990: 133). In a similar vein, the United Nations Development Programme (UNDP, 1993: 1) states in the opening sentence of its *Human Development Report*: 'People's participation is becoming the central issue of our time.' Even in the USA, where the political and economic ethos is founded on self-interested individualism, the 'communitarian movement' has attempted to resurrect and reaffirm the notion of personal obligations towards collective goals (Etzioni, 1993).

This renewed emphasis on popular or community participation in the developing world may be attributed to a number of factors. These include neo-liberal arguments in favour of state withdrawal, the promotion of 'good governance' and greater local self-reliance, underpinned by international bodies such as the World Bank. At the same time, however, there has been a more pragmatic concern in the light of heavy international criticism over the poor record of official development aid.[7] As discussed in greater detail below, research demonstrates that the closer involvement of project beneficiaries invariably leads to greater efficiency in the spending of aid funds.

In Brazil, participatory development concepts were heavily influenced by the ideas of Paulo Freire and his notion of conscientização or 'awareness-raising', as expressed through literacy training programmes during the early 1960s in north-east Brazil (Freire, 1975). In passing, it is worth noting that the profound influence of Freirian pedagogy on the development of social and environmental action both in Brazil and further afield is only now being fully appreciated (McLaren and Lankshear, 1994). Throughout the period of military rule in Brazil, but especially in the 1970s when political opposition was effectively banned, the radical Catholic church became a major channel for the promotion of grassroots development.

Closely tied to Freirian precepts, the influence of 'Liberation Theology' grew significantly after the Second Conference of Latin American Bishops (Vatican II) held in Medellín, Colombia, in 1968, and the papal enclyclical *Populorium Progressio*. A large network of community religious groups (CEBs), numbering some eighty thousand, with over two million members by the early 1980s, was formed by church and lay activists (LAB, 1982). At a time of intense political repression, the church addressed issues of social justice and human rights such as land conflicts in Amazonia and elsewhere, culminating in its landmark 1977 declaration, 'Christian Demands for a New Order'.

During this period, many small-scale, community-based development projects were set up based on local CEBs, whose influence is still strongly felt. In fact, many of today's NGO-sponsored local schemes (such as Mamirauá, the subject of chapter four) have their roots in church-supported initiatives. However, the policy of the church hierarchy in Brazil, under pressure from the Vatican, has been to withdraw from more 'politicised' activities and let civic organisations such as NGOs and rural unions take over. Yet despite these more recent changes, in the space of only a few years a marked transition took place in the kinds of local development undertaken in Brazil (Hall, 1993a).

Church and NGO influence resulted in the progression from a

paternalistic, welfarist orientation, characterised almost entirely by charitable and relief operations during the 1960s, to a more politicised and participatory style from the 1970s, which was intended to encourage self-determination by traditionally powerless groups of peasants, urban-dwellers and Amerindians. Many of the participatory goals and ideals expressed by the large, official international organisations during the 1970s and 1980s originally found their expression in the grassroots philosophy of NGOs. As will be discussed below, the more recent brokerage and lobbying roles performed by NGOs since the mid-1980s have been crucial in creating the circumstances for productive conservation programmes to become viable propositions.

Concepts and dimensions of participation
The underlying premise of the present study is that active local mobilisation must underpin productive conservation efforts in Amazonia and that, without such grassroots involvement, attempts to reconcile the preservation of natural resources with their active use for livelihood support are highly likely to fail. A case has been argued for resource-mobilisation theory as a valid initial framework within which the motivation to conserve natural resources could be rationalised. Within this paradigm, both economic-instrumentalist and shared identity factors were considered important prerequisites for explaining individual and group motivation behind such activities. Principles derived from the literature on new social movements offered theoretical insights for explaining the broader context within which productive conservation groups have formed in response to specific socio-ecological threats.

The aim of the first two sections of this chapter, on governnance of common property resources and on collective action respectively, was to demonstrate that there is a conceptual logic, both internal and external, behind the rise of social movements for productive conservation. In terms of drawing out lessons for present and future development efforts in this field, however, it is also important to be able to demonstrate how such movements mobilise and how they actively contribute to the effective implementation of productive conservation processes. Although these experiences are highly context-specific, whose outcomes cannot be deduced from higher order laws, it is possible to look for key propensities based on how conservation movements evolve and the roles they play. For this purpose, the literature on community participation offers some useful conceptualisations and operational definitions.

The notion of 'participation' in development is multi-faceted and often vague. It frequently lacks conceptual clarity and can mean all things to all people, a feature which is useful for some development practitioners, who 'limit themselves when convenient to general proclamations and advocacy of participation without having to spell out the practical implications, the political aspects, and thus the power consequences of participation' (Stiefel and Wolfe, 1994: 223). While it has all too often been used as a rhetorical catch-phrase, some attempts have, nevertheless, been made to establish more precisely *what* participation entails and what is its potential value as a development tool, *who* is involved in this process and *how* it can be more effectively promoted.

At the most general level, the UN defined participation in 1981 as 'The creation of opportunities to enable all members of a community and the larger society to actively contribute to and influence the development process and to share equitably in the fruits of development' (cited by Midgley *et al.*, 1986: 24). Three main elements thus identified by the UN consist of: people contributing directly to the development effort; a degree of equity in the sharing of the resulting benefits; and involvement in decision-making with respect to project-planning and policy-making. In the latest terminology, these features are collectively referred to as 'stakeholder participation', which is defined as 'the process whereby all those with an interest [stakeholders] play an active role in decision-making and in the consequent activities which affect them (ODA, 1995: 94).[8]

In the present analysis, it is important to define more precisely the ways in which participation is important for development purposes and, more particularly, for local resource management. Whether in the context of extractivism, forest management, fishing or agroforestry, their common feature is that, in all cases, small and geographically dispersed groups have organised themselves into larger associations for the purpose of defending their livelihoods and their natural resource base. These communities may be diversified in socio-economic terms, but their commonality of interests is sufficiently great to unite them at strategic junctures in the pursuit of productive conservation. Table 1.1 presents a guide to the broad dimensions of participation adopted here. The categories used are adapted from existing studies,[9] and distinguish between four major dimensions of community participation according to its objectives, scope, strength and timing. Use of the term 'community' is justified by the fact that all of the experiences studied here involve communal action by groups with broadly shared production conservation goals, regardless of their spatial distribution, which does not usually adhere to the standard western model of a nuclear rural settlement.

Table 1.1 *Dimensions of community participation in productive conservation*

Objectives	Scope	Strength	Timing
Cost-sharing	Coverage (APR/DPR)*	Passive participation	Late involvement
Product efficiency			
Project effectiveness	Strategic alliances	Proactive participation	Early involvement
Capacity-building			
Empowerment			

* APR   Aggregate Participation Ratio
  DPR   Differential Participation Ratio

Objectives of community participation   Five major objectives of community participation may be identified (Paul, 1987). Although these can be conceptually disaggregated, in practice they usually overlap and merge, with several aims often being pursued simultaneously within a single project or development initiative. Sometimes this produces complementarity, a social multiplier effect which strengthens the community's role. On other occasions, however, conflicts and contradictions become apparent which may undermine collective unity and action.

(a) *Cost-sharing*   This refers to contributions by participants of labour and cash which help support conservation activities, either in setting up initiatives or for longer-term operation and maintenance of infrastructure. This kind of participation is frequently treated in the literature as the most cursory and manipulative form of people's involvement, the argument being that state authorities frequently shirk their responsibilities in this way. It is sometimes referred to by critics as 'development on the cheap'.

However, as the case-studies will show, cost-sharing can be a powerful tool for obtaining commitment from those who might otherwise become dependent on paternalistic handouts. In the world of clientelistic Latin American politics and social formations, this is an important consideration. Depending on the context and the way in which it is carried out, therefore, community resource mobilisation may help to break negative dependency ties rather than reinforce them.

(b) *Project efficiency* By ensuring the timely provision of beneficiary contributions and securing agreement to cooperate, it is argued that costs can be reduced, services provided efficiently and wastage minimised. Once again, it is sometimes suggested that project participants may be unduly controlled or manipulated in the interests of sponsors. However, in the fragile ecosystems under discussion here, such efficiency is critical for the introduction of conservation measures which, as we shall see, depend so heavily on comprehensive community participation in order to ensure sustainability. This is true both at the design as well as at the implementation and monitoring stages.

(c) *Project effectiveness* This refers to the extent that project objectives are achieved, leading to a 'better match of project services with beneficiary needs and constraints' (Paul, 1987: 3). In this case, the overarching goal is the reconciliation of livelihood and resource-conservation aims. Increasing efficiency also refers to what Cernea (1991a) has called better 'project fit': recognition that, for a project to be designed in a manner which is appropriate to the socio-cultural requirements of beneficiaries, participation must go hand in hand with a multidisciplinary planning process which incorporates social science inputs.[10]

This consideration is particularly critical in the conservation experiences under examination here, due to the strong dependence for success on proper organisation of conservation strategies at community level, involving large numbers of people. It is, therefore, especially important that a 'farmer first' or a 'putting people first' approach be adopted, which designs strategies 'around the social actor rather than starting with technical factors ...[and which] ... concerns, primarily the shaping of development *policy* and secondarily the shaping of *project* design' (Cernea, 1991a: 21). It is also critical that such an approach be mindful of the essentially political nature of the knowledge-generation process and that participatory

mechanisms are put in place which allow traditional or local wisdom to be effectively harnessed (Scoones and Thompson, 1994).
(d) *Capacity-building.* Closely related to increasing project efficiency and effectiveness is the goal of enhancing the management capacity of intended beneficiaries. Once more, this objective is particularly relevant to the examples being considered in the present study because the concept of productive conservation is heavily dependent on the direct involvement of resource-users throughout the various stages of the project, from identification and design through to execution, monitoring and evaluation. Strengthened local management capacity is especially crucial in situations where common property resources figure prominently, and in which individual and collective interests must be harmonised. Both the rubber tappers' extractive reserves and Lake Mamirauá fall into this category, although the principle is also relevant to other experiences.
(e) *Empowerment.* This refers to the greater sharing of decision-making powers with beneficiaries, 'so that they are able to initiate actions on their own and thus influence the processes and outcomes of development' (Paul, 1987: 3). Expressed somewhat more forcefully and reflecting more accurately its conflict theory origins, empowerment consists of acquiring 'access to, and control of, the resources necessary to protect livelihood' (Oakley and Marsden, 1984: 25). Empowerment is often considered the ultimate goal of 'authentic' participation, a no-strings-attached 'end' in itself which gives beneficiaries greater, perhaps total control over planning and implementation of development activities. A parallel may be drawn here with Freire's discussion of people's liberation through awareness-raising education, which, he claims, should lead to their active 'involvement' rather than 'pseudo-participation' (1975: 61).

Empowerment is often contrasted with the other, above-mentioned objectives of participation: namely, cost-sharing, efficiency, effectiveness and beneficiary capacity. These are frequently viewed more as instrumental 'means' for achieving aims predetermined by outsiders and, hence, less 'pure' forms of involvement. A related distinction has been made between 'participatory development', which refers to people's involvement in activities prescribed by outsiders, and the notion of 'people's self-development', which 'leads to self-reliant development and confers on the group or organisation the necessary clout to negotiate on new terms with powerholders, parties and the state' (Stiefel and Wolfe, 1994: 203; Rahman, 1993).

The 'ends' versus 'means' debate is, in fact, a largely sterile one and something of a red herring. All the objectives of participation are vehicles for achieving some further goal, whether explicitly or implicitly. Be that as it may, however, there is bound to be much variation in the degree to which outcomes are predetermined by outsiders, as well as the extent to which project or policy design can be modified during the process of implementation by direct participants. Furthermore, early instrumental-type activities such as cost-sharing and enhancing capacity may well lead to beneficiaries becoming more 'empowered' as the people involved acquire more skills and self-confidence to manage their affairs autonomously.

The case-studies analysed in this volume certainly bear witness to the beginnings of an evolution towards more authentic and effective participation. A useful working definition for the present study is that provided by UNRISD in terms of 'the organised efforts to increase control over resources and regulative institutions in given social situations, on the part of groups and movements of those hitherto excluded from such control' (Stiefel and Wolfe, 1994: 5). Empowerment in this sense is directly relevant to the quest by communities for sustainability, as part of an enhanced capacity 'to reflect on the factors that shape their environment and to take steps to effect changes to improve their situation' (Singh and Titi, 1995: 13).

Use of the term 'empowerment' has, rather like 'participation' itself, become too free and imprecise in the development literature, and it is necessary to establish clearer definitions of what is meant. Friedmann (1992: 33) distinguishes between three kinds of power in people's livelihood struggles: social, political and psychological. Social power refers to the bases of household productive wealth such as 'information, knowledge and skills, participation in social organizations, and financial resources'. Political power concerns people's access to decision-making both through formal political channels or via collective action such as a socio-environmental movement or trade union. Finally, psychological power at once derives from and reinforces the sense of potency acquired from successful action in the social and political spheres.

In the case-studies examined here, social, political and psychological strength are all crucial aspects of empowerment, given the importance of access to natural resources for livelihood sustainability, the key role of conservation movements and individual or communities' self-confident behaviour when viewed against a history of powerlessness in the face of adversity. It has been shown (Berkes, 1995) that institution-building based on traditional practices for more sustainable common-pool resource management can be a major tool of local empowerment, an argument which is supported by the cases from Amazonia examined in the following chapters.

Scope of community participation   This refers both to the degree of coverage enjoyed by a movement at local or regional level, as well as to the network of strategic alliances established with outside groups. It may be broken down as follows.
(a) *Coverage.*   This can be assessed in either aggregate or differential rates of participation. What is here called the aggregate participation ratio (APR) is a measure of the overall level of involvement within the geographical area covered by a movement. This will give a broad idea of the general level of people's participation in conservation activities. However, on its own the APR may convey a false picture, since it takes no account of the fact that neither communities nor socio-environmental movements are homogeneous entities. It is thus necessary to disaggregate this indicator into its constituent components in the light of their internal dynamics.

The differential participation ratio (DPR), as denominated here, will provide a better indication of how particular sub-groups are involved during different phases of conservation projects. Distinctions therefore need to be made on the basis of class, ethnic, religious, gender, age and spatial dimensions. In view of the similarity of socio-economic backgrounds amongst natural resource-users in given sub-ecosystem movements, class differentiation is not usually a major factor which affects levels of participation. However, there is likely to be a divergence of interests, for example, between wealthier group members with commercial interests such as middlemen and merchants, and the mass membership. This may give rise to internal friction over the aims and procedures to be adopted in managing natural resources, especially where common property rights are concerned. Given Brazil's history, it is, on the other hand, likely that group unity may be undermined by ethnic clashes between, for example, indigenous peoples and settlers from other regions pushing forward the agricultural frontier, as in southern Pará. Religious differences have also exerted an influence in this respect, as evangelical sects have spread rapidly.

Differential participation may also be assessed in terms of gender.

Resource governance

Women's participation in conservation activities may be discussed in terms of their 'triple' productive, reproductive and community managing/community politics role (Moser, 1993). The gender issue is important in Amazonia, where the demands of both productive activities as well as struggles over access to land have resulted in important modifications to women's roles as well as men's. This has been due in large measure to the fact that men have frequently been obliged to diversify family income sources by migrating to seek work as temporary labourers in towns or on larger estates. It has been estimated, for example, that in Brazilian Amazonia, small-scale, informal sector gold-prospecting (*garimpagem*) employs upwards of 800,000 people altogether, both directly and in ancillary activities (Wilson and Alicbusan-Schwab, 1991).

Women have also been drawn more heavily into community-management activities around issues of collective consumption. Research in southern Pará and in Acre shows unequivocally, for example, that females have played a major role alongside their menfolk in land-access struggles at the frontier-occupation stage (Hébette and Colares, 1990; Bakx, 1990). One consequence of this behaviour is that old taboos have gradually been broken and more women are now active members of rural trade unions. Women's involvement in conservation project elaboration and management has become pronounced and, as the case-studies below will show, has had a major influence in ensuring project effectiveness and enhancing the capacity of local communities to manage their own affairs.

Age factors tend to be neglected in discussions about community participation, yet different age groups are involved in contrasting ways. Children have often been included in passive resistance tactics adopted by communities against land invasions, as in the case of the *empates* by rubber tappers. Their inclusion has an important symbolic and strategic significance, as a reflection of the struggle for livelihood. Older members of the community with a lifetime of experience in traditional systems of resource management usually possess historical and technical knowledge which is undocumented and thus invaluable to contemporary researchers and community planners in their efforts to devise appropriate conservation techniques. It is therefore crucial that their participation is guaranteed so that the benefits of such knowledge can be shared.

Geographical considerations also exert their own influence on participation rates. Productive conservation units in Amazonia tend to house widely dispersed populations, which encounter serious transport and communications problems. The likelihood of effective participation taking place is greater, all other things being equal, in those areas closer to the hub of project operations. Contacts with more distant groups will usually tend to be less frequent, and it is sometimes more difficult to engage these communities in the collective effort. The case study of Mamirauá below provides examples of this kind of operational constraint.

According to the implications of resource-mobilisation theory, the greater difficulty of communications with more distant groups may hinder the emergence of a shared identity or community spirit. Members of outlying communities may participate less frequently in strategy meetings, for example. The adverse consequences of physical separation will be exacerbated if, in addition, a divergence of economic interests exists between core and periphery communities. Thus, the latter may perhaps feel less constrained about the unsustainable extraction of common property resources such as fish or timber. It is, therefore, extremely important that, in order to engage resource-user groups successfully in a group management strategy, an efficient system of communications and decentralised decision-making be established which embraces the whole conservation unit.

(b) *Strategic alliances*   As discussed above, the scope of community involvement within individual projects can be gauged according to aggregate and differential participation rates by factors such as class, ethnicity, age, gender and spatial distribution. However, an additional indicator of how successfully a conservation movement can mobilise support lies in the nature and range of alliances established with outside organisations. On their own, localised movements have limited power; they are a necessary but not a sufficient prerequisite for a successful productive conservation exercise. Increasingly, the potency of such movements is being substantially enhanced via the involvement of external agencies, both official and non-governmental. This notion of joint action is consistent with the 'institutional perspective' on social development, which 'seeks to mobilize diverse social institutions including the market, community and state to promote people's welfare' (Midgley, 1995: 139).

The assistance of major domestic and international institutions with an interest in promoting productive conservation efforts in

Amazonia has produced what could be called a socio-political multiplier effect. In the past, such external support would, more likely than not, have come exclusively from NGOs in Brazil and overseas. Nowadays, however, a much larger range of entities is involved, including bilateral and multilateral aid agencies, federal and state government bodies, universities and even private companies. Not only is this diversified pattern of support conducive to greater financial stability, but it also strengthens the overall legitimacy of community-based conservation as a viable development strategy for Amazonia.

For many years, NGOs have provided key financial and logistical support for micro-level projects, given their advantages over official bodies in terms of being able to gauge expressed needs at grassroots level as well as to respond more quickly and appropriately. The number of socio-environmental NGOs in Brazil has expanded rapidly in since the 1980s.[11] In all three case-studies examined in this book NGOs have provided key monetary, moral, technical and political support to assist the conservation movements in their embryonic stages. Without this backing, many projects which are today active and well established might never have got off the ground. It has to be remembered that during the formative period for these community movements under military rule in the 1970s and 1980s, NGOs (including the Catholic church) were the only source of support for community projects which have since grown.

Since the mid-1980s, especially in Latin America and Asia, NGOs have expanded their activities from purely operational support to advocacy in the national and international arenas (Korten, 1987). While this has often involved lobbying on global issues of trade, commerce, debt and adjustment, for example, NGOs have increasingly sought to exert pressure on policy-makers over individual projects and sectoral issues as a means of 'scaling-up' their activities (Clark, 1991; Edwards and Hulme, 1992). Such confrontational tactics have been successfully employed on several occasions by the powerful North American NGO environmental lobby, together with campaigns by Brazilian organisations, in relation to multilateral agency funding for controversial projects in Brazil.[12]

Yet although networks of overseas and Brazilian NGOs have achieved notable successes based on exerting leverage and the use of oppositional tactics, procedures in the more democratic 1990s have begun to change significantly. While this more confrontational approach has by no means been entirely eschewed, there has, nevertheless, been an approximation of state and civic society in the pursuit of development objectives. The potentially critical role of NGOs as actors in local development has also been officially recognised by major organisations such as the World Bank (Cernea, 1988; World Bank, 1992). From another, perhaps more ambitious perspective, NGOs, social movements and grassroots community initiatives have enough in common to constitute a new 'Third Sector' in Latin America (Fernandes, 1994).

Although attempts have been made at operational involvement and policy dialogue, NGO participation in the design phase of Bank-funded projects is still very limited (Edwards and Hulme, 1992). Furthermore, despite growing collaboration between NGOs and the state, they remain, as one recent study of NGO involvement in sustainable agricultural development in the Third World concluded, 'reluctant partners', with ambivalent feelings towards each other (Farrington and Bebbington, 1993: 177). In order to avoid the danger of cooptation, the need has been recognised for NGOs to be more concerned with developing performance monitoring and accountability criteria as part of their strategic planning (Edwards and Hulme, 1995).

In Brazil, this ambivalence is certainly present, but relationships between NGOs and the state are now based far more on consultation and negotiation than in the past. Both sides recognise that, for much of the time at least, this is in their mutual interest. NGOs acquire financial support and a voice in policy-making, while state bodies are keen to utilise the accumulated expertise and local knowledge of NGOs for the more efficient design and speedy execution of development projects. In the developing world generally, 'interest is clearly growing in the extent to which there are practical complementarities between NGO and government, and to which NGO approaches might be incorporated into governmental programmes' (Farrington and Bebbington, 1993: 180). In the Amazonian projects studied here, however, it is government which has tended to complement NGO-supported grassroots conservation initiatives, rather than vice versa. This fact serves to underline the leading supportive and catalytic role played by NGOs in the productive conservation field within Amazonia, both at the operational and policy levels.

In spite of NGOs' pioneering stance, however, the viability of conservation endeavours and the scope of community participation is also increasingly dependent upon complementary support from state agencies and other quasi-official bodies such as universities. Funding for basic research and training activities has come from the National Council for Scientific and Technological Research (CNPq), while technical support has been provided by the Brazilian Agro-Livestock Research Agency (EMBRAPA). Support from the Ministry of the Environment (MMA) and its monitoring arm, IBAMA, in enforcing controls is likely to become more important, especially in the case of Lake Mamirauá and the extractive reserves, where attempts at encroachment by commercial interests have been commonplace. University researchers have been working collaboratively with grassroots organisations in designing, executing and monitoring the conservation projects studied here.

International cooperation is proving to be a vital ingredient in productive conservation initiatives for Amazonia. Aid-funded technical assistance from the UK and France has, for example, been critical in the agricultural research and agroforestry fields. Research inputs are especially important in conservation initiatives given the existing lack of systematically documented knowledge on the relationships between natural resources and their appropriators and its importance for devising sustainable management strategies. Country-to-country aid from major industrial powers such as the UK, Germany, Japan, the USA and France, has been used to set up basic infrastructure and to pay for running costs, either directly under bilateral programmes or through the Group of Seven (G7) Pilot Programme, discussed in chapter two. Further details of these supportive activities will be provided in the case-studies, but the basic point to bear in mind is that these more conventional sources are no less important than NGOs in sustaining productive conservation projects in Amazonia in the longer run, even if their role is less pronounced in the preliminary stages.

A major indicator of the scope of participation and the degree of resource-user empowerment relates to the level of influence enjoyed by the movement in question, whether this is limited to influencing local project design, or whether it can go beyond this to affect policy formulation and execution at the regional or sectoral level. Although Brazilian Amazonia is characterised by a high degree of diversity, particular ecosystems such as those of the rubber tappers, riverine (*várzea*) fisherpeople or terra firma peasant farmers encompass large geographical areas with substantial human populations. Thus, participatory innovations on individual projects relating to productive conservation almost certainly have a wider relevance. The potential therefore exists for lessons learned locally to be incorporated into new policy initiatives. As will be discussed below in chapter three, the extractive reserves are the best example so far in evidence of a local struggle leading to the introduction of new policies with region-wide and even national repercussions.

Strength While analysis of 'objectives' and 'scope' tell us about the extent of community participation, these categories shed little light on the strength or intensity of the process. Such an understanding is crucial to the present discussion, since it is important to establish what degree of control local movements exercise over interventions which affect their natural resource base, and in what ways populations may become more closely involved in devising and managing conservation strategies. In terms of assessing the strength of community involvement, two major categories are distinguished which represent the opposite ends of a continuum: 'passive participation' and 'proactive participation'.

(a) *Passive participation.* This follows the 'blueprint' approach in which development aims are pre-established by outsiders, largely according to their own interests. Involvement of participants is likely to be of the more instrumental kind and limited to cost-sharing, with contributions of labour and other local resources being elicited in the name of participation. Critics would label this variety as 'manipulative' and 'pseudo' in nature. Community groups may be provided with limited information about the proposed intervention, or they may even be consulted about key aspects of the project with a view to improving project efficiency or effectiveness, within the terms of the original design. In this approach, local groups are not involved in basic decision-making and have little or no control over the form or execution of the scheme in question. As Rondinelli (1983) and others have pointed out, in the field of development planning, passive community participation – where community involvement exists at all – is the norm rather than the exception.

(b) *Proactive participation.* In a growing number of instances, local groups have managed to press successfully for a greater say in decision-making about project design and implementation. Far from succumbing to the dictates of government planners, local groups have been able to negotiate the process of guided change and to initiate action, so that community interests are placed higher on the agenda than they would otherwise have been.

This proactive quality may be observed in different ways and at various levels, as the case-studies will demonstrate. At the crudest level it may entail policing duties such as those carried out by rubber tappers and fisherpeople. From this purely confrontational level, proactive involvement may develop into extensive consultation with the authorities and other project partners over the detailed planning and execution of conservation strategies. This may even evolve into more sophisticated lobbying at national and international levels in order to bring about wider policy change, as occurred in the case of the rubber tappers (*seringueiros*) in the setting up of numerous extractive reserves in Amazonia and other parts of Brazil.

In order for local groups to have any significant influence over natural resource-conservation strategies in Amazonia and elsewhere, it is essential that the participatory process becomes proactive. More passive forms of local involvement will probably co-exist with this to form part and parcel of a participatory planning strategy. However, the major thrust must be towards proactive involvement, in the sense that community organisations should always retain the ability to initiate action, at whatever level, in support of their own livelihood interests.

As the case-studies will demonstrate, this is necessary to ensure that outsiders, whether government bureaucrats, aid agencies or commercial enterprises, do not ride roughshod over the wishes of the local population. Positive action by enlightened planners and policy-makers at federal and regional levels is clearly important for the legitimisation of innovatory conservation strategies and their introduction onto the statute books. However, productive conservation movements lend vital strategic and political support to this process, acting as a major countervailing power, perhaps the single most critical force against hostile commercial interests anxious to encroach upon Amazonia's fragile ecosystems. In such large and isolated areas, where the state is either unwilling to act or has limited powers to do so, local groups must take the initiative if they are to survive.

Timing Traditionally in the process of development planning, when local populations have been consulted at all, it has tended to be at the monitoring and evaluation stages of a project or programme. This has often consisted of belated attempts by embarrassed officials to discover why a particular intervention has failed to achieve its objectives. Since the 1980s, there has been a greater effort to involve beneficiaries in the design or project preparation phase when, although basic aims and parameters have already been determined in a 'blueprint' fashion by outsiders, there is nevertheless a perfunctory attempt to tailor some project features to meet certain expressed community needs. Such procedures are, however, invariably manipulative and pay only lip-service to the notion of community participation.

In order to maximise the extent to which community interests are taken into account, grassroots organisations and their project partners have to ensure that they engage themselves as early as possible in the planning process, well before even the design stage has been reached. Ideally, they should become involved at the time of identification and appraisal, when a particular conservation strategy is being conceived, and when no major decisions have been taken nor basic parameters set. Only in this way can local movements fashion the process of guided change to serve livelihood interests as the priority objective, pre-empting efforts by commercial and other outside groups, which wish to appropriate the natural resource base in question for their own purposes. In the case-studies under examination in this volume, the respective grassroots organisations have in large measure been able to do this and, it will be argued, this has been a major factor contributing towards their relative success so far in setting up productive conservation programmes in extremely diverse contexts.

It is during the pre-design phase that there is considerable potential for communities to have their needs placed high on the agenda for action. A vital component of this process is the use of socially and environmentally sensitive planning techniques, which are necessary in order to ensure better project fit from a socio-cultural standpoint by 'putting people first' (Cernea, 1991b).[13] However, while the incorporation of socially sensitive planning skills is essential, especially in experiments with productive conservation, social planners and environmentalists need support from the grassroots in order effectively to design and implement such a strategy. This complementarity has already proved to be a powerful instrument for project modification and even policy reform in Brazil, notably in the field of involuntary resettlement due to hydropower development.[14] As the case-studies will show, such joint activities may involve a variety of forms of local participation, ranging from policing to information-gathering and lobbying. When they do take place, such partnerships can be highly positive; yet when they fail to materialise, for whatever reason, the implementation of productive conservation strategies can be seriously compromised.

The nature of community involvement in this process can, of course, change significantly over time, sometimes with dramatic consequences. Initially strong, confrontational forms of grassroots action may, for a number of reasons, not evolve into more systematic and organised dialogue by the people with planners and policy-makers. Conversely, movements which start by taking a modest, almost passive stance in relation to outside threats, can acquire self-confidence and mature forms of organisational competence. Thus, grassroots participation in conservation initiatives is by no means a fixed and stable phenomenon, but is variable and constantly evolving, sometimes for the better and at other times for the worse.

Any discussion of grassroots action in this context would, of course, be incomplete without mention being made of the numerous obstacles which exist to the realisation of such participatory ideals. How such constraints are identified and addressed depends very much on the ways in which participation is conceived. Planners and policy-makers who see community action as an instrument for achieving goals defined largely in the interests of outsiders, and with precious little regard for the aspirations of the communities taking part, will identify operational barriers to participation. These will tend to focus on managerial and technical problems relating, for example, to over-centralised management, inappropriate technologies, poor project design and local coordination, amongst other factors.

At the other end of the spectrum, those who view participation as a means of 'empowering' local groups and enabling them to acquire a degree of influence over the planning process place far less emphasis on operational problems. They see the major barriers to change in more fundamental societal structures, which are antithetical to the Western notion of power-sharing embodied in the idea of 'participation'. These relate to the very bases of society, such as cultures, ideologies and belief systems, as well as to the distribution of wealth and political power. It is not surprising that more conventional and officially accepted forms of participation such as cost-sharing and improving project efficiency, notwithstanding the undoubted operational problems which have to be surmounted, have been far easier to realise than those which challenge the status quo in their attempts to 'empower' beneficiaries.

There is a widespread assumption that the structural obstacles to people's participation are so entrenched that 'empowerment', as defined here, is almost impossible to achieve. The Food and Agriculture Organisation (FAO) concluded in the late 1970s that 'authentic popular participation seldom occurs'.[15] Yet it is also being realised that such a black and white scenario is simplistic and unhelpful. Clearly, empowerment implies some redistribution of power in favour of the disadvantaged. However, the process of acquiring power is not linear, purist or absolute, as implied by earlier critiques. As recent studies, including this one, have taken pains to stress, participation is a multi-dimensional concept with no clear progression from less genuine to more 'authentic' forms. Different kinds of community involvement take place at various junctures, often simultaneously, in the development of local movements, following no fixed pattern. Although confrontational tactics may be more typical of the early stages of community resistance to resource destruction, this will mature over time to include other forms of action. Increasingly, this involves the mediation of structures and institutions previously considered completely opposed to such change.

Thus, in the context of Brazilian Amazonia grassroots movements have established alliances with government agencies from local to national level as well as foreign aid donors, in addition to trade unions, research institutions and other bodies involved in the complex process of planning, funding and implementing strategies. The highly diverse range of social actors engaged in the pursuit of conservation goals in any given context is illustrative of the many interests being served and of the contrasting rationalities behind their involvement. These range from a commitment to advancement of the community, the need to spend aid funds quickly, the quest for institutional self-preservation and the desire to secure short-term political gains via a 'successful' project.

In the past, such diversity tended to be seen by participation 'purists' as a weakness and a potential source of conflict which would undermine the aims of the exercise. This danger might indeed be present but, viewed in more pragmatic terms it can also be perceived as a source of strength in which a number of contrasting aims and institutional efforts effectively complement each other in the combined effort to devise an innovative conservation strategy. The end product is the same, even if the underlying motivations are invariably different. It is these diversities and complementarities, as well as the constraints and obstacles, which will be explored in the following case studies of productive conservation movements in the Amazon region of Brazil.

Concluding comments

Three major strands of social theory within a broad rational choice framework have been identified, which, considered together, are highly pertinent to the challenge of simultaneously preserving natural resources and livelihoods. Firstly, the 'productive conservation' initiative was identified as a distinctive type of collective action practised by a variety of groups which make use of vulnerable natural resources. This constitutes a relatively recent phenomenon in response to external threats to those stocks of natural assets, based wholly or partly on common property resources, upon which communities depend for their livelihoods. The community-based social response has become an increasingly important vehicle through which the desire for natural resource preservation may be expressed and conservation strategies operationalised.

Secondly, conceptualisations were considered of how self-interested groups may be motivated by utilitarian or shared identity goals, and institutions thus established to conserve common- pool and, indeed, private resources, thus challenging the notion of an inevitable 'tragedy of the commons' scenario of resource destruction. In principle, therefore, a conceptual rationale exists for reinforcement of traditional resource-management strategies which reconcile the immediate interests of individuals with the longer-term interests of the group as a whole.

The manner in which such collective protection and governance can be operationalised is suggested by the third set of concepts, relating to grassroots or community participation. Disaggregating the notion of community involvement in terms of major dimensions provides a useful analytical tool for identifying ways in which communities may become directly involved with, and exert a decisive influence upon, the design and management of resource-conservation initiatives.

After considering the history of Amazon settlement and the evolution of environmental policy for the region in chapter two, the subsequent three chapters discuss major examples of such productive conservation activities within contrasting ecosystems in Brazilian Amazonia: rubber tappers' extractive reserves, the Mamirauá fishing conservation project and small farmer settlement on the Transamazon highway. These diverse experiences are all directed at reconciling the preservation of a natural resource base together with its productive use by local populations to sustain livelihoods without resorting to destructive practices which might undermine the longer-term sustainability of these activities. Although the physical, social, economic and political circumstances of each case vary considerably, they have one common feature. All three are based on the direct involvement of local populations of resource-users as an integral part of the development-conservation planning process.

Notes

1 On the topic of grassroots environmental action see, for example; Redclift (1987), Ghai and Vivian (1992), Friedmann and Rangan (1993), Barraclough and Ghimire (1995), Collinson (1996).
2 Although by no means the first to observe the tendency to environmental degradation whenever many individuals use a scarce resource in common, Garret Hardin's seminal article in *Science* (1968), which employed the grazing commons as a metaphor for overpopulation, highlighted the problem. The possibility of a 'tragedy of the commons' has since been raised with reference to many resource-dependent situations, from famine and fisheries to firewood crises.
3 The 'Prisoner's Dilemma' game (Dawes, 1973) is seen as a non-cooperative exercise, in which individuals choose a profit-maximisation strategy independently of each other in the use of a common resource. This creates a paradox that 'individually rational strategies lead to collectively irrational outcomes ... [and] ... seems to challenge a fundamental faith that rational human beings can achieve rational results' (Ostrom, 1990: 5). This suggests that it is impossible for rational people to cooperate with each other, an imputation which, in an increasing number of situations, is simply not borne out by the facts.

In his theory of the 'Logic of Collective Action', Olson (1965) also raises serious doubts about whether self-interested individuals have the

Resource governance

capacity to unite to serve group interests, thus challenging the optimism of group theory which maintained that 'individuals with group interests would voluntarily act so as to try to further those interests ... [and]... that the possibility of a benefit for a group would be sufficient to generate collective action' (Olson, 1965: 5–6).

4 Even the oceans have come under a greater degree of control through the International Law of the Sea (1982), either by individual governments or under international jurisdiction.

5 For further details of such cases, see, for example, Berkes (1989), McCay and Acheson (1987), Bromley and Cernea (1989), *The Ecologist* (1992, 1995).

6 See, for example, Oakley and Marsden (1984), Paul (1987), Bamberger (1988), Marsden and Oakley (1990), Bhatnagar and Williams (1992).

7 This has ranged from the sweepingly condemnatory to the technically incisive. Examples of the former, fairly blanket critiques include Hancock (1991), Adams (1991), Adams and Solomon (1985) and *The Economist* (1994). A more comprehensive, but no less critical survey of the ineffectiveness of Organisation for Economic Cooperation and Development (OECD) bilateral aid in reaching the poorest can be found in ACTIONAID *et al.* (1993).

Some agencies have also been highly self-critical in this regard, notably the World Bank. An internal evaluation of lending procedures conducted by Willi Wappenhans blamed a project success rate of less than two-thirds on, amongst other factors, a failure to consult beneficiary groups and an excessive preoccupation with lending turnover at the expense of project implementation and supervision (Wappenhans, 1992). This has led to some restructuring of World Bank procedures, including the setting up of an Inspection Panel to deal with complaints about project impacts.

8 Other definitions of participation have drawn upon social science theories about state-society relationships to categorise 'modes' of participation: 'anti-participatory' and 'manipulative' modes based on Marxist and elite conceptualisations, contrasted with 'incremental' and 'authentic' participation founded on liberal-democratic and pluralist theories (Midgley *et al.*, 1986: 38–44). While useful for broad analysis, such general paradigms do not, however, permit disaggregation of participatory mechanisms at the project or programme level.

9 Among the most useful of these are Paul (1987), Oakley and Marsden (1984), Stiefel and Wolfe (1994) and Friedmann (1992).

10 Kottak's (1991) study of over seventy World Bank and USAID-supported projects in a variety of sectors demonstrated that socio-culturally sensitive planning based on participatory principles leads to a high rate of cost-effectiveness and efficiency. Projects which lacked such inputs

and were insensitive to people's needs were found to be far more likely to fail.
11 See chapter two for further details.
12 The temporary suspension in 1985 of World Bank loans for the POLONOROESTE programme in Rondônia, the recent freezing of Inter-American Development Bank funding for the paving of the BR364 highway in Acre state, and the 1988–9 campaign against construction of the Xingú hydropower complex in Amazonia, are examples of this growing NGO influence. The campaign for the creation of extractive reserves, following the murder of rubber tappers' leader Francisco 'Chico' Mendes in 1988, also falls into this category. See Goodman and Hall (1991), Rich (1994), Hall (1993b, 1996) and chapter two for further details.
13 These include, for example, social and environmental impact assessments, involving new methodologies such as Participatory Rural Appraisal (PRA), Participatory Farmer Research (PFR) and Participatory Learning and Action (PLA). For a detailed discussion of these methodologies, see Chambers (1992) and Okali et al. (1994).
14 At Itaparica in the São Francisco valley of north-east Brazil, a combination of grassroots pressure from the *Polosindical*, a federation of local rural trade unions and citizens, together with innovative policy reforms spearheaded by World Bank social scientists (along with advocacy by NGOs), was a major factor in the redesign of resettlement plans for that project. Similar reformulations have been brought about in other dam projects such as Itá in southern Brazil (Hall, 1992, 1994).

This combination of influences – internal pressure from Bank policy-makers and external pressure from the grassroots supported by NGOs – has led to the introduction of sectoral and not just project-related resettlement guidelines for hydroelectric expansion in Brazil, leading to the postponement of several socially damaging schemes (Serra, 1993; World Bank, 1994). See chapter two for further discussion of these issues.
15 FAO, *Participation of the Poor in Rural Organisations*, Rural Organisations Action Programme (ROAP), Rome, 1979. Cited by Oakley and Marsden (1984: 29).

2
Environment and development in Brazilian Amazonia: evolving paradigms

Three decades of destruction

Deforesting for development

The history of Amazonian occupation since the 1960s has been one of resource depredation for short-term gain.[1] The clearest single indicator of this increasing threat to Amazonia's natural resource base is deforestation. It is from the rainforest and its waterways that over two million inhabitants of the Amazon region (about half of the total regional rural population) derive a range of extractive products, from brazil nuts and latex to palm hearts and tropical fruits. Substantial destruction of natural forest cover signifies the permanent loss of biodiversity and productive capital for these populations. The wealth of species contained in Amazonia's rainforests, perhaps 50 per cent of the world's total, has been well documented elsewhere and need not be repeated.[2] Of more direct concern here is the social impact of deforestation, which is placing under ever greater pressure those fundamental natural resources upon which a large proportion of the rural population depends for its economic and cultural survival.

Calculation of virgin forest loss for Amazonia has become a highly contentious and politically charged issue. In 1970, when construction of the Transamazon highway commenced, only 2.4 per cent of Amazonia had been deforested. Even by 1978, this figure had risen to a mere 3.8 per cent, but rates of forest loss accelerated rapidly during the 1980s. A study of LANDSAT data by Fearnside (1993) put the figure for 1991 at 10.5 per cent, while the data published by the National Institute for Space Research (INPE) in July 1996 for the period 1992–4 suggests that 12 per cent of Amazonia's original forest-cover had been lost.

Deforestation was at its highest during 1978–88, averaging some 22,000 square kilometres annually. Peaking in 1987, rates subsequently declined to around half of this figure, a trend which has been attributed to a combination of economic recession and reduced government subsidies.[3] However, according to INPE, deforestation accelerated once more during 1992–4 to almost 15,000 square kilometres a year, representing a 35 per cent increase over the 1990–1 period. Record levels of forest burnings during 1995 once again raised the spectre of deforestation running out of control.[4] Official projections by the Institute of Applied Economic Research (IPEA) put Amazonia's forest loss for the year 2030 at 33 per cent, rising to 67 per cent by 2090.[5]

For the present, however, the total level of deforestation in Brazilian Amazonia, at around 12 per cent, remains relatively low compared with most other tropical countries. Yet the spatial distribution of deforestation in the region is highly uneven. Whereas Amazonas state has forfeited only 1.6 per cent of its forest, for example, the figure increases dramatically to 66 per cent in Maranhão, forty per cent in Tocantins, 16 per cent in Rondônia, 13 per cent in Pará and 7 per cent in Acre (Fearnside, 1993). Clearing is concentrated along the southern, eastern and north-western borders of the forested zone, and along highways such as the infamous BR364, which connects Porto Velho and Rio Branco with central and southern Brazil. Several areas of most intensive forest loss are home to large communities of natural resource-users; for example, the small farming population of the 'Brazilnut Polygon' in southern Pará, the rubber tappers of Rondônia and Acre, and the babaçú nut-gatherers of Maranhão. The middle stretch of the Amazon floodplain has been almost totally logged out, except for protected areas such as the Mamirauá Ecological Station, discussed in chapter four of this volume (Goulding *et al.*, 1996). The latest settlement frontiers for small farmers and loggers are being opened up in Amazonas state, along the western portion of the Transamazon highway and around Itacoatiara, near Manaus, respectively, the latter attracted from Paragominas (Pará) by governor Amazonino Mendes.

Integration, modernisation and conservation, 1964–85
Forest loss in Amazonia is the direct result of intensified occupation since the 1960s. New forms of land use have been encouraged

which contrast strongly with more traditional, less intensive and less destructive forms of resource extraction. The 'integration' of Amazonia was a high priority of the military regime, as it appeared to offer simultaneous solutions to a number of pressing internal and external problems. Not only could it alleviate growing social tensions within Brazil, but it could also promote regional as well as national economic growth and modernisation, while enhancing the country's strategic position in South America (Becker, 1982; Becker and Egler, 1992). Despite the military's strong geopolitical agenda for Amazonia, social and economic goals were, unsurprisingly, given the highest public profile. Whatever strategic motivations existed, settlement was publicly justified in terms of promoting economic development and alleviating human suffering.

During 1970–4, under Brazil's Plan for National Integration (PIN), official policy placed great emphasis on encouraging small farmers to settle the recently constructed Transamazon and Cuiabá–Santarém highways. In humanitarian terms, the *Transamazônica* would, it was hoped, absorb migrants forced to flee the periodic north-eastern droughts. Agriculturally, colonisation projects would produce essential staple food crops for the region, while agribusiness enterprises would supply export markets. At the same time, resettlement of 'excess' rural populations from potentially explosive situations such as those in the north-east, with its history of rural activism prior to the 1964 coup, was considered a productive social investment. By uniting 'men without land to land without men', this strategy would, it was hoped, perform a useful 'safety-valve' function, easing demographic or land conflict-induced tensions elsewhere and alleviating growing pressures for land reform.

In the south and north-east, land concentration due to state-subsided pasture formation and the spread of mechanised soybean and wheat production has forced small farmers off the land in growing numbers. In the north-east, subsidies for cattle-ranching, together with drought vulnerability amongst sharecroppers and smallholders in particular, has had a comparable effect (Hall, 1978). A similarly skewed structure has been reproduced in the Amazon region, where, in 1985, 6.5 per cent of farmowners possessed 80 per cent of the land (INCRA, 1986). A small number of especially powerful landowners (*latifundiários*) possess properties the size of small countries.[6]

Little did planners then realise that the violent land conflicts characteristic of the north-east and south of Brazil would not be eradicated in Amazonia, but merely reproduced there.

Economic integration through centralised regional and growth pole strategies was another driving force behind the occupation of Amazonia. In particular, Perroux's 'development pole' theory was enthusiastically adopted on the assumption that concentrations of investment would generate capital, profits and employment (Becker and Egler, 1992). The POLAMAZONIA programme of 1974, based on the channelling of federal and private funds into fifteen major growth poles, epitomised this strategy. Out of this grew the Carajás Iron-Ore Project and Programme (Hall, 1991). Centrally controlled development of the region was designed both to tap Amazonia's great natural wealth to serve national growth, while at the same time neutralising potentially obstructive regional political elites through federal intervention. Yet, as predominant as these were, broader geopolitical aims provided an additional and perhaps overriding logic.

Concerns had been expressed in Brazil even before the military coup over the dangers of 'international greed' (*cobiça international*) directed at Amazonia's natural resources and the implications for national sovereignty.[7] This geopolitical theme was taken up after 1964, as the military sought to populate Amazonia and secure definitively Brazil's territorial space against possible outside incursions: 'to integrate in order not to forfeit' ('*integrar para não entregar*'), in the catchphrase of the day. Strongly influenced by the Sorbonne group of the Higher War College (ESG), this thinking had three basic strands (Gross, 1990). Firstly, that the state was technocratically competent and powerful enough to direct regional development, excluding public participation as being inefficient and potentially subversive. Secondly, the dualistic notion that 'modern', Western production technologies had to replace Amazonia's presumed 'primitive' and 'backward' systems. Thirdly, and most conveniently, that Amazonia was a vast empty space just waiting to be occupied and 'integrated' into the mainstream of Brazilian industrial life. As expressed by General Golbery do Couto e Silva, arguably the military regime's principal strategist, the aim was to 'inundate the Amazon forest with civilisation'.[8]

Politically, as already mentioned, these initiatives represented an attempt to contain the influence of regional politicians, extending

Environment and development

the power and authority of the federal government. A series of unilateral decrees reorganised the bureaucratic structure, wresting control over access to major resources such as land, and transferred it to federal authorities.[9] From a counterinsurgency perspective also, settlement of the region and a military presence were seen as crucial in controlling an incipient Maoist guerrilla movement in eastern Amazonia led by the Communist Party of Brazil (PC do B).

The early disasters of directed resettlement along the *Transamazônica* have been well documented (Smith, 1982; Moran, 1983). Although a variety of reasons has been cited for this débâcle, from a lack of initial planning to the failings of the National Institute for Colonisation and Agrarian Reform (INCRA) and absence of infrastructural support or funding for settlers, the episode gave rise to a tradition of 'blaming the victims', whose influence can still be felt (Wood and Schmink, 1978). Agribusiness and construction company interests, anxious to secure access to the official subsidies which had hitherto been devoted to 'social colonisation', lobbied government for a change in development priorities in favour of large-scale, capital-intensive projects. Small colonisers, it was suggested, were destructive agents, unsuited for life on the Amazon frontier. The then Minister of Planning, João Paulo dos Reis Veloso, criticised the 'predatory occupation' of the region by small farmers, while the regional development Bank of Amazonia (BASA), the Superintendency for the Development of Amazonia (SUDAM) and the private São Paulo-based Association of Amazon Businessmen (AEA) all supported a policy change (Pompermeyer, 1984; Branford and Glock, 1985).

Yet while there is clearly some truth in the notion that small cultivators from outside Amazonia are indeed poorly equipped for pursuing non-destructive production techniques, evidence on deforestation supports the long-held view that, in Brazil at least, smallholders are relatively minor culprits. According to Fearnside (1993), data for 1991 indicate that only 30 per cent of forest loss in Amazonia can be attributed to small farmers, concentrated on properties of less than 100 hectares. Some 70 per cent of forest loss is caused directly by the activities of medium-sized and large ranching concerns on larger properties, especially on farms of over 1,000 hectares. Most of the cleared land is located in states dominated by large ranches, such as Mato Grosso, responsible for 26 per cent of the 11,100 hectares deforested in Amazonia during 1990–1.

Since Operation Amazonia was launched in 1966, ranchers have benefited from generous investment tax breaks and highly subsidised credit, amounting to no less than $US5.15 billion from 1971 to 1987, aimed at large ranches in particular (Schneider, 1992: 32). These subsidies have been significantly reduced in the wake of domestic and international criticism of their role in stimulating deforestation, most recently in 1996.[10] However, loopholes remain and subsidised rural credit continues to be available, while lax income and corporate tax laws as well as a range of other benefits continue to encourage deforestation by large landowners (Binswanger, 1991).[11] This situation is likely to continue thanks to the extremely powerful agrarian lobby (*bancada ruralista*) within Congress. Yet government subsidies have not been the only factor behind the growth of Amazonian cattle herds. These have expanded due to burgeoning urban demand in the region and the expansion of the crop and livestock frontier (Schneider, 1992). Furthermore, land purchase and pasture formation continue to be popular as a hedge against high rates of domestic inflation, as reflected in rapidly increasing land values (Hecht, 1985, 1989; Fearnside, 1993).[12]

The primarily speculative rather than productive role of subsidised Amazonian livestock 'enterprises' was clearly demonstrated by an official Brazilian government evaluation which found that, of 631 livestock projects approved and subsidised by SUDAM, only 92 had been completed, average production was just 16 per cent of planned levels and, furthermore, many so-called ranching 'projects' had no cattle on them whatsoever (Gasques and Yokomizo, 1986). It is well known that there is a market in 'borrowed' cattle herds within Amazonia, which are used as fronts by estate-owners for the acquisition of subsidised finance. Contrary to popular myth, Brazilian Amazonia is not part of the 'hamburger connection' (as is Central America) and remains a net importer of beef. The negative ecological impact of livestock production has also been widely documented: namely, rapid pasture degradation, weed invasion, soil compacting, erosion and nutrient loss (Hecht, 1985; Eden *et al.*, 1990).

Other causes of Amazonian deforestation include logging, mining and hydropower development, the latter accounting for about 1 per cent of forest loss, mainly through flooding. Timber extraction is largely a by-product of land clearance for smallholder cultivation and pasture formation and, in so far as it is possible to disaggregate this factor from related issues, is thought to be responsible for some 5 per cent of current deforestation.¹³ Most Amazonian timber currently produced is for the domestic market, but, as south-east Asian stocks become exhausted, direct extraction for export of valuable strands from areas of virgin forest will become more common, facilitated by the spread of the highway network. Commercial timber extraction is usually based on selective logging, which can be highly destructive of adjacent forest. There are about 350 commercially valuable species in Amazonia, but production is concentrated on a few of the most valuable such as mahogany (*Swietenia macrophylla*), which is reputedly in danger of extinction within the next fifteen years.¹⁴ Areas such as the Zona Bragantina of northern Pará have been especially affected by the concentration of about 3,000 extremely profitable sawmills, although 100 of these have transferred operations to Itacoatiara in Amazonas, encouraged by the state government.¹⁵

The consequences of logging are also increasingly intensive in other regions such as the Carajás railway corridor, where charcoal-fired pig-iron smelters associated with the Rio Doce Valley Company (CVRD) iron-ore project have significantly speeded up the rate of deforestation (Hall, 1991; Redwood, 1993). Given the lack of effective controls on current methods of extractive lumbering and the inherent cost advantages of mining the forest as opposed to engaging in sustainable management, there is little likelihood that this scenario will change in the foreseeable future. Pressure on Brazilian Amazonia's rainforest has also increased substantially as Asian timber companies have moved into the region from neighbouring Guyana and Surinam, taking advantage of lower labour costs.¹⁶

Although a major rationale for Amazonian settlement has been the 'safety valve' function, supposedly alleviating social and demographic pressures in more densely occupied and potentially conflict-ridden areas in the centre-south and north-east of Brazil, the region's ability to perform this role effectively is becoming seriously constrained. The heavy latifundium bias of settlement policy for Brazilian Amazonia has resulted in a pattern of land tenure which is heavily concentrated. In Amazonia as a whole, some 60 per cent of lands settled between 1970 and 1980 were occupied by farms of over 1,000 hectares. In 1985, three-quarters of land within agricultural establishments was occupied by properties of over 500 hectares (Hall, 1991; May and Reis, 1993). There has been a tendency towards aggregation of smaller units due to colonist failure and land speculation, while there is some evidence of division of larger properties.[17] Large establishments have the smallest proportion devoted to forest reserves and the largest percentage of idle productive land. Since land clearing and pasture formation, as evidence of 'productive' use, continue to provide a legal basis on which to claim property rights in Brazil, small farmers are encouraged to deforest beyond what is required for immediate livelihood purposes.

The human occupation of Brazilian Amazonia throughout the 1960s, 1970s and 1980s has thus been driven by a 'frontier economics' perspective, which views nature as offering an infinite supply of physical resources for economic development and as a sink for pollution and environmental degradation (Colby, 1990). Resources are perceived as non-scarce and need not, by definition, be used efficiently; there is, therefore, no reason to include them in economic calculations of the benefits and costs of growth. Little or no thought is given to the human groups and local economies which depend on these natural assets, and official policies are not directed at serving their needs. Indeed, the presence of indigenous or traditional populations such as Amerindians and *caboclos* is frequently considered an obstruction to mainstream development strategy, and their very physical presence, not to mention their economic importance, is often severely underplayed or even denied outright. Official strategies for Amazonia based on encouraging ranching, small farmer occupation, commercial logging and large-scale mining, underpinned by geopolitical considerations, fall squarely into this paradigm.

The period 1930–64 in Brazil saw the rapid rise of government-sponsored industrialisation, which placed a strong priority on the exploration of natural resources such as iron-ore, oil and fish, through state monopolies.[18] At the same time, several legal codes were enacted in the areas of water, mining and forestry (all in 1934), fishing (1938) and hunting (1943), while an inter-municipal pollution control agency was set up in São Paulo.[19] The Brazilian Institute of Forestry Development (IBDF), now part of the Ministry of the Environment, was set up in 1967. A commercially, politically and socially inspired 'assault on the Amazon' (Bourne, 1978), unfettered by obstructive environmental controls, commenced in the mid-1960s and has continued largely uninterrupted to the present day.

Such a crude 'frontier economics' ideology has been tempered by recognition of the need for some form of environmental protection. This involves legalising the environment as an economic externality and devising policies for damage limitation. In this approach, command-and-control regulatory mechanisms, such as environmental legislation and protection agencies, as well as impact assessments, become institutionalised. Small areas of common property are set aside for perpetuation in their original pristine condition as national parks, wilderness reserves or conservation areas, increasingly nowadays linked to eco-tourism. At the global level, the World Conservation Strategy has, since the early 1980s, advocated a wide-ranging approach based on neo-Malthusian assumptions about the need to curtail demand for scarce resources through measures such as population control and identifying the carrying capacity of ecosystems. Closely echoing a wildlife management approach, ecology is seen as setting strict limits on human intervention for development in a 'conservation-or-disaster' scenario (Adams, 1990: 47).

In Brazil, as elsewhere, conservationism has been the major approach adopted by policy-makers for environmental care. Brazilian conservationist policies were heavily influenced by US experience. The First Brazilian Conference on the Protection of Nature took place in Rio de Janeiro in 1934, a year in which Brazil's Forest Code (*Código Florestal Brasileiro*) also entered the statute books and introduced the concept of the reserved area. Between 1937 and 1961, some twenty national parks and biological reserves were created, covering over one million hectares (Guimarães, 1991).

During the immediate post-colonial period, conservationism tended to be rejected by newly independent nations due to its imperial associations. Biological conservation had acquired a new global legitimacy with the founding of the International Union for the Conservation of Nature (IUCN) in 1948. This was reinforced during the 1970s by strong support from the UN, such as for the system of Biosphere Reserves established by UNESCO.[20]

Already practised in Brazil, as noted above, conservation was reaffirmed during the period of military rule from 1964, for both scientific and political reasons. On scientific grounds, the setting up of priority conservation areas in Amazonia was justified by Pleistocene Refuge Theory and Island Biogeography Theory, developed during the 1970s (Foresta, 1991).[21] Strategically, the notion of centrally controlled conservation units appealed to the military, as it fitted in well with the move towards developing a strong federal focus from which to direct the nation's modernisation process and place political control at the centre. In practice, Brazil's 1979 plan for a national system of conservation units was informed as least as much by military and political considerations as by the above scientific criteria.[22]

In 1973, the Special Secretariat for the Environment (SEMA) was set up following the Stockholm Conference on the Human Environment, held the previous year. Although the conference had recommended the creation of such specialised agencies and the time was ripe, SEMA was in fact set up as an emergency response to deal with a particular incident of contamination by a wood-pulp plant in Rio Grande do Sul.[23] In the second plan for Amazonia (PDA II) for 1975–9 and in the linked POLAMAZONIA strategy, consideration was given to protecting the resource base. Reserves of various kinds were to be strategically located between development poles to protect the environment from the harsher excesses of national progress, in an attempt to reconcile conservation and development. The 1978 Treaty of Amazon Cooperation also placed a strong emphasis on biological conservation.

Attached to the Ministry of the Interior, it is widely acknowledged that SEMA had little executive power and could not itself be involved in the formulation or implementation of environmental policy. Staffed by technicians with predominantly natural science backgrounds, to whom were allocated tasks of pollution control and resource conservation, the creation of SEMA was seen as an attempt by the Brazilian government to neutralise potentially conflictual environmental issues. Despite these drawbacks, however, SEMA did represent a significant step forward in several respects. It was responsible for the National Environment Act of 1981, and also laid the basis for the setting up in 1985 of CONAMA, Brazil's first National Environment Council, which included representatives from central and state government as well as from groups in civic society, such as NGOs.

In 1986, under the new civilian government of President Sarney, CONAMA made environmental-impact assessments mandatory for new, large-scale public and private projects. SEMA also set up the first federal ecological stations, which by 1992 numbered twenty-six and covered 3.2 million hectares (Nogueira-Neto, 1992). The agency's broader role in encouraging debate about environmental

Environment and development

issues and in stimulating cooperation between government and the scientific community was important, although SEMA's role always remained constrained by the limited support it received from the Sarney government (Viola, 1993).

Throughout the 1970s and early 1980s, during the period of military rule, environmental control was reduced largely to natural resource management, 'understood as meaning the preservation of examples of Brazilian ecosystems' (Guimarães, 1991: 162). For Brazil's bureaucratic-military alliance, national economic progress as measured in aggregate growth rates took precedence over nascent considerations of resource conservation or the more rational use of natural assets. The twin spectre of Brazil's sovereignty and national security was periodically raised to harness nationalist opinion against any outside suggestion that these policies should be reconsidered. Environmental management became tightly compartmentalised in an attempt to contain and depoliticise it.

Regulation, protection and innovation: 1989 and beyond
In spite of settlement policies for Amazonia which suggest little in the way of government sensitivity to ecological or indeed social issues, environmental legislation in Brazil has made significant strides since the early 1990s. There has been at least a partial evolution in the way that Amazonia's ecological problems are perceived and in the assessment of which solutions are deemed to be most appropriate. In terms of the broad categories as defined by Colby (1990), the first signs can be observed of a shift in official thinking away from the crude 'frontier economics' paradigm which has predominated so far, and towards 'environmental protectionism' and 'resource-management' ideas in the 1980s and 1990s. Environmental considerations that, twenty years ago, were officially dismissed in Brazil as an irrelevant obstacle on the path to national prosperity, imposed by hostile foreign powers, are now widely (if not completely) accepted by the state and civic society as legitimate issues which need to be addressed. Although there is still a long way to go, it may be said that a policy context is forming in Brazil which is beginning to offer some support to productive conservation initiatives.

Although it did not appear significant at the time, a major step forward came with President Sarney's nationalistic *Nossa Natureza* ('Our Nature') programme, announced on 1 April 1989 in response to mounting international criticism on a number of highly publicised fronts over Brazil's apparent lack of environmentally sound development policies for Amazonia. Focuses of global attention included the death of rubber tappers' leader Francisco 'Chico' Mendes in December 1988 and the Altamira meeting against the proposed dam complex on the River Xingú early the following year.[24] Yet although heavily criticised at the time as a token gesture meant to appease critics, *Nossa Natureza* was, nevertheless, the first attempt by a Brazilian government to design a national environment policy. A number of measures were announced aimed at curtailing Amazonian deforestation: the suspension of SUDAM fiscal incentives, limits on round log exports, the creation of national parks in Acre, Amapá, Amazonas and Mato Grosso as well as a programme of environmental protection and research.

The main practical result of the programme was the creation in 1989 of IBAMA, Brazil's federal environmental protection agency, which currently forms the monitoring arm of the Ministry of the Environment (MMA).[25] Absorbing four major environmental agencies,[26] IBAMA's new remit was much broader and adversarial, assessing ecological damage and enforcing environmental laws in conjunction with state and federal police forces. In Amazonia, IBAMA was allocated the high-profile but unrealistic task of controlling illegal forest burnings. Although the agency subsequently claimed significant successes, it was in reality severely under-staffed and under-resourced at field level (despite a burgeoning Brasília-based central administration) for such a huge and, many would say, impossible task.[27]

For all its apparent environmental sensitivity, *Nossa Natureza* was, arguably, driven mainly by a less apparent military agenda. According to Viola (1993), it was the first geopolitical project for Amazonia to incorporate the idea of environmental protection. Echoing long-standing fears about the 'internationalisation' of Amazonia, both in terms of US military presence in neighbouring countries such as Guyana, as well as the penetration of private capital and acquisition of large landholdings, in 1989 General Leônidas Pires Gonçalves openly voiced such fears at an international meeting in The Hague. This rejected a proposal for the creation of an international body with supranational powers to address ecological problems in the region (*Latin America Regional Report* (Brazil), May 1994).

Concrete Brazilian proposals to increase substantially its military presence in the Amazon may be traced back to the Calha Norte Project (PCN), announced to Congress in 1987, over two years after the scheme had been secretly formulated.[28] The PCN was prepared by General Rubens Bayma Denys, head of the President's military household and general secretary of the National Security Council (CSN). The project, which is still operational, aims to increase Brazil's human occupation of 6,500 kilometres of frontier zone bordering Colombia, Venezuela, Guyana, Surinam and French Guiana. This includes the setting up of military posts, purchase of military equipment and improvement of transport facilities, taking up almost 80 per cent of the budget, as well as some colonist settlement and social infrastructure. In addition to its wider geopolitical objectives and border-strengthening activities, the PCN has been seen as a tool for limiting the territorial control of indigenous groups over areas deemed to have military and economic importance in terms of access to natural and mineral resources (Oliveira Filho, 1990). Now under the direction of the Secretariat for Strategic Affairs (SAE), the PCN has, since the mid-1990s, placed a stronger emphasis than previously on investment into social infrastructure along the border.[29]

Such geopolitical concerns notwithstanding, the introduction of environmental legislation has proceeded steadily. In response to vigorous pressure from the increasingly influential NGO lobby allied to progressive parliamentarians in the run-up to Brazil's hosting of the United Nations Conference on the Environment and Development (UNCED) in 1992, Brazil's new constitution of 1988 stressed the need to reconcile development with environmental preservation.[30] The National Environment Programme (PNMA) of 1990 laid down policies of agro-ecological zoning, demarcation of conservation units (such as national parks, Indian and extractive reserves) and a state-level network of environmental agencies to license and monitor activities such as logging and pasture formation.

Rondônia had in fact already taken the lead in this field, by carrying out a zoning exercise in the late 1980s under the auspices of the World Bank-funded Rondônia Agricultural, Forestry and Livestock Plan (PLANAFLORO), successor to the much-criticised Integrated Development Programme for the North-West Region of Brazil (POLONOROESTE).[31] The aim of PLANAFLORO is to tailor agricultural and forestry activities to natural resource capacity at the local level. Land has been divided into six zones, ranging from areas of intensive agricultural use to those designated for protection, such as Indian and extractive reserves. Providing a taste of things to come, however, strong political opposition to zoning in Rondônia has been encountered from many quarters (Nitsch, 1994; Millikan, 1994). Large landowners have objected to having limits set on lucrative activities such as logging and cattle-ranching, while small producers have complained about the apparent inability of the state government to implement the plan.

In 1995–6, local NGOs made strong representations to the World Bank's Inspection Panel to have PLANAFLORO subjected to independent audit, but this request was rejected in favour of an internal Bank review. Yet although, as Keck (1997) has convincingly argued, Rondônia NGOs were hamstrung by their inability to exert political leverage at the crucial local level, the situation created was sufficiently embarrassing and budget-threatening for all parties to prompt a major meeting in June 1996 to iron out these problems and reach agreement over the future of PLANAFLORO.[32]

Environmental protection is a necessary but not a sufficient strategy for protecting the environment and, on its own, has serious limitations as a tool for sustaining stocks of natural resources. Firstly, parks and reserves can never account for more than a small proportion of national territory, leaving the remainder, by definition, 'unprotected'.[33] Brazil has just 3.7 per cent of its area within conservation units, compared with a global figure of 5 per cent and 6.7 per cent for South America. Secondly, as we have seen with IBAMA, the management and policing capabilities of environmental agencies are seriously constrained, to the point of being farcically inadequate in an area as vast as Amazonia. Thirdly, the ecosystem is still seen as external to the economy and not an integral part of development policy-making. Neither environmental costs arising from destructive settlement strategies, nor environmental benefits accruing from traditional, sustainable resource-use systems, are properly recognised or accounted for. Yet while the creation of protected areas of various kinds and the halting of some sensitive projects were major steps forward, environmental policy still did not even begin to tackle the underlying economic and political forces driving deforestation and destructive settlement patterns.

Newly elected President Fernando Collor de Mello appeared to offer some hope for a more progressive stance on environmental policy when he took office in April 1990. Having laid strong emphasis on the environment in his campaign, one of his first measures was to set up SEMA, linked directly to the presidency. To international acclaim, Collor appointed as its head José Lutzenberger, one of Brazil's most distinguished and outspoken environmentalists. Commitments were immediately made on two key issues which had been the subject of much international criticism; removal of gold prospectors (*garimpeiros*) from Yanomami lands in Roraima and the restriction of deforestation to supply charcoal-fired iron-ore smelters along the Carajás railway corridor.[34] The ending of income-tax breaks for enterprises in areas of primary forest was also reaffirmed.[35]

A detailed plan of action was published which made a number of radical proposals, including: immediate action on illegal forest-burning, the incorporation of non-governmental and grassroots organisations into the formulation of public policy, favourable consideration of debt-for-nature swaps and, most importantly, the setting up of a new institutional framework for environmental policy. Changes were made to the national system of environmental administration with the setting up of a National Environment System (SISNAMA), while, in September 1990, a National Zoning Commission was set up under the new SAE to prepare for the ecological zoning of Amazonia, an exercise currently supported by the G7 Pilot Programme to Conserve the Brazilian Rainforest.[36] IBAMA was retained as the executive arm for policy formulated by SEMA, while CONAMA was created to perform an advisory role, with representatives from every ministry and the NGO sector as well.

Funding for the PNMA from 1991 to 1993, had been negotiated under the Sarney administration. Costed at $US166 million, the money came primarily from foreign loans.[37] However, due to a series of financial, bureaucratic and political problems, which included IBAMA's organisational and managerial inability to implement the PNMA, by 1993 only 9.4 per cent of available funds had been spent, the programme had to be restructured and a financial penalty was incurred (Ros Filho, 1994).[38]

In spite of the emphasis placed on conservation within Brazil's emerging environmental policy of the late 1980s and early 1990s, it was found that only one-third of the country's 350 conservation units were effectively operational, and only 20 per cent have adequate transport facilities for IBAMA officials.[39] Furthermore, the protected status of many conservation areas created since 1989 has been threatened by undue delays in legalisation. It is claimed that conservation units were set up hastily in order to impress international opinion in the run-up to the 1992 UNCED. Consequently, IBAMA claims, to legalise all Brazil's conservation units would now cost no less than $US1.2 billion.[40]

However, although these were extremely encouraging initial developments, which represented a significant shift in thinking compared with previous administrations, the honeymoon was short-lived, undermined by political and inter-institutional conflicts. Only six weeks after taking office, Lutzenberger fired the head of IBAMA, Werner Zalauf, over his decision to support a massive reforestation project in Amazonia without consulting SEMA.[41] Reflecting the contrasting perspectives on how Amazonia should be developed, the Secretary of the Environment also clashed with other ministers, such as those for Regional Development and Science and Technology, with their more technocratic and mainstream 'modernising' views, backed by powerful regional economic and political interests. Lutzenberger and Goldemberg, Minister of Science and Technology, had diametrically opposed views on energy policy. Goldemberg, for example, favoured large hydropower schemes in Amazonia, while Lutzenberger rejected this model, arguing for small dams serving local areas which, it was argued, would have less dramatic social and environmental impacts.

Gubernatorial elections in 1990 revealed the degree of state-level opposition to federal environmental policy, which was condemned in election campaigns as an unwarranted constraint on regional economic development. Gilberto Mestrinho, governor of Amazonas, rejected any form of environmentalism and promised in his campaign to be 'governor of the men and women of Amazonas, not of the animals and trees of Amazonas'.[42] In Roraima, Ottomar Pinto was elected largely on support from gold prospectors who were promised access to Yanomami lands. As if this were not enough, Lutzenberger was heavily criticised in government circles for being isolationist and for his apparent unwillingness to negotiate with other ministries. Most of these conflicts were set aside temporarily as Brazil hosted the 1992 UNCED.

Barely two years after taking office, José Lutzenberger was fired in March 1992, amidst rumours that President Collor had been under strong pressure from the timber industry, angry over his moves to curtail the alleged connivance of IBAMA in facilitating illegal logging.⁴³ José Goldemberg, by then Minister of Education, was appointed as interim Secretary of the Environment, followed briefly by Flavio Perri, a diplomat, and shortly afterwards by Fernando Coutinho Jorge, a senator from the state of Pará. After the impeachment of President Collor and his replacement by Itamar Franco, an institutional restructuring took place. In early 1993, SEMA was abolished and replaced by the MMA. Brazil's ambassador to Washington, the widely respected Rubens Ricúpero, was appointed Minister of the Environment in September 1993, replacing Coutinho Jorge.

Following the still recent turmoil of Lutzenberger's reign, and in the wake of the UNCED, Ricúpero adopted a non-confrontational approach. He sought in his pronouncements to reconcile competing interests in Amazonia and emphasise the potential contributions of all groups to the process of sustainable development in Amazonia. At the same time, however, Ricúpero stressed the need to 'add to the economic dimension of material progress those of social and environmental considerations',⁴⁴ portraying Amazonia not as a region of conflict but as an 'area of opportunity', where 'foreign interest could be valuable for funding, credit, investments and even tourism'.⁴⁵ A National Council for Legal Amazonia (CONAMAZ) was set up in December 1993, which later drew up a new set of development policy guidelines for Amazonia (Brazil, 1995a). Ricúpero held office for only a few months before being appointed, in mid-1994, as the new Minister of Finance, to be temporarily replaced as Minister of the Environment by Henrique Brandão Cavalcanti. On 1 January 1995, the new government of Fernando Henrique Cardoso took office and Gustavo Krause, ex-governor of Pernambuco, was appointed Minister of the Environment. A special secretariat was established within the ministry to deal with Amazon development policy, perhaps in recognition of the need to take innovative strides in addressing the urgent needs of the region.⁴⁶

It has been argued that federal environmental policy in Brazil 'exists only at the level of discourse, as a form of rhetoric', and that effective action, such as it is, takes place at state and municipal levels (Cleary, 1993a: 58). Although there is a large element of truth in this observation, the case is overstated. Since the early 1990s, there has been a significant evolution in the way in which environmental policy for Amazonia is being framed, as well as the beginnings of intervention which goes beyond a modernisationist 'frontier economics' or a limited conservationist approach to dealing with natural resource control. At one level, this has been reflected in the changing legislative and institutional framework for addressing Amazonia's environmental problems: the setting up of IBAMA and the MMA, some (albeit limited) punitive sanctions against illegal deforestation, the reduction of tax breaks for cattle-ranching and land speculation, and the gradual introduction of laws aimed at encouraging the sustainable use of forests. In terms of direct federal action also, the 1990s has seen several important initiatives; the commencement of agro-ecological zoning exercises in Amazonia, government support for a number of innovative grassroots productive conservation experiments such as those analysed in this volume, a substantial programme of aid under the $US250 million G7 Pilot Programme to Conserve the Brazilian Rainforest, and new policy guidelines for Amazonia, initiatives which are considered in further detail below.

Yet despite these advances, limited attention has been paid in Brazil to the kind of 'resource-management' approach advocated by the Brundtland Commission (WCED, 1987). This rejects the neoclassical notion of the environment as a costless sink, and that technology will automatically overcome any constraints to growth imposed by natural resource depletion. It endorses the calculation and incorporation of environmental costs and benefits into national accounts: 'ecology is being economized' (Colby, 1990: 23). The interdependence of ecosystems is recognised, along with the need to maintain both ecological processes and natural capital stocks as the basis for sustainable growth.

Policies advocated include energy efficiency, general resource conservation, ecosystem monitoring and 'the polluter pays' principle in order to internalise the social costs of degradation. Price incentives are seen as a major tool for encouraging sustainable environmental practices. As the case-studies below illustrate, providing the right market signals will be one important consideration in attempts to design livelihood strategies which rely on the sale of timber and non-timber forest products. However, extreme caution must be exercised by policy-makers in the assumptions made about the ability of small-scale producers to integrate successfully into economic markets.

Although the adoption of an economised, environmental management perspective has gained steady if slow acceptance in Europe and North America, it has had little practical impact in Brazil so far. As May (1993: 19) expressed it, 'welfare economics, benefit-cost analysis and its extensions in the economic analysis of environmental externalities are fields having limited penetration in Brazil'. Lack of trained professionals, insufficient data and the persistence of neo-classical ideas on the role of environment in the development process have all contributed to this lacuna. The apparent abundance and low financial cost of natural resources such as rainforest timber continues to encourage the mining of the environment and a corresponding lack of concern, either by government or private enterprise, to bother about calculating economic values.

Changes are, however, beginning to take place; Brazilian economists have become more involved in the field of environmental economics following the stimulus provided by UNCED, while major foreign funding institutions such as the World Bank and Inter-American Development Bank now expect the partial valuation of environmental resources to be built into impact-assessment procedures. Following regulations introduced by CONAMA in 1985, the Brazilian power sector has also embraced environmental impact assessment in its planning cycle.[47] Enforcing environmental protection while moving towards the adoption of more diverse natural resource-management strategies has, then, been a feature of Brazilian public policy since the mid-1980s in guiding development planning.

Yet, as we have seen, overriding military-geopolitical concerns, irrespective of regional and economic development objectives, have long had a major determining influence on the nature and scale of state intervention in Amazonia. This has found expression in a whole series of interventions. Chronologically, these may be listed as: the decision to build the *Transamazônica* at the end of the 1960s; the army's counter-insurgency campaigns against Maoist guerrillas in the Araguaia region of southern Pará during the early 1970s; the land regularisation agencies for the Carajás and Amazon estuary areas set up in 1980 – Executive Group for the Lower Amazon (GEBAM) and Executive Group for the Araguaia-Tocatins (GETAT); the *Calha Norte* programme formulated in 1985; President Sarney's nationalistic *Nossa Natureza* campaign inaugurated in October 1988; and the Programme for the Development of Western Amazonia's Borders (PROFAO).[48] The coordination of zoning activities by the SAE, successor to the CSN, is also indicative of continuing control over regional development issues by the armed forces. Persistent military concern with the 'internationalisation' of Amazonia has, according to some observers, led directly to a notable increase in the presence of the armed forces in the region since the early 1990s.[49] The theme of foreign 'threats' to national sovereignty, especially to Brazil's control over its Amazonian territory and natural resource base, is still regularly echoed in public forums.[50]

The ongoing strength of geopolitical preoccupations and military concern with Amazonia was further reflected in the government's announcement in early 1994 of a sophisticated radar and satellite surveillance system covering the entire Amazon Basin, known as SIVAM. The *Serviço de Informação e Vigilância da Amazônia*, or Information and Şurveillance Service for Amazonia, is coordinated by the SAE, attached directly to the Presidency of the Republic. SIVAM forms part of the wider System for the Protection of Amazonia SIPAM, under the aegis of the SAE.[51] Costing an estimated $US1.77 billion to implement, SIVAM's roles will include the defence of national sovereignty against possible military aggression, the prevention of drug-trafficking and smuggling, as well as environmental protection.[52]

Strongly backed by the Brazilian air force, SIVAM will involve 17 fixed and 6 mobile radars, 8 planes, 200 radio stations and 300 remote-sensing platforms for the collection of meteorological, mineral and environmental data. Information will also be obtained from a number of existing satellites: LANDSAT, SPOT, ERS-1, NOAA, GOES and CBERS. These will be fed to a network of Regional Vigilance Centres (CRVs) located in Belém, Manaus and Porto Velho, and then to the headquarters in Brasilia (Brazil, n.d., b). Despite intense controversy surrounding the awarding of the $US1.4 billion contract to the American company Raytheon, amidst widespread accusations of irregularities, delaying final approval and implementation, the measure was approved by Brazil's Congress in May 1996.[53]

Increasingly, a 'greening' of military policy in Brazilian Amazonia is taking place, in which the defense of national sovereignty is tied to, and justified by, protection of the environment and its natural resource base. SIVAM is described as 'supporting programmes related to the sustainable development of the region ... monitoring of the environment, the sustainable use of biodiversity, ecological and economic zoning, occupation and use of the soil, the fight against illicit activities, protection of indigenous reserves ...' (Brazil, n.d., b).

At the same time, there is a disturbing continuity in the emphasis placed by the SAE on small producers as the major force working against sustainability, which seems to underpin this latest surveillance strategy. Harking back to the 'blaming the victims' syndrome of the mid-1970s, it is stated that '... the major challenge facing the Brazilian government consists in promoting the Amazon's development without destruction and in opposition to the immediacy given rise to by the easy race for profits in which the thousands of migrants settled in the region take part' (Brazil, n.d., a).

Notwithstanding those more strategic or geopolitical concerns prioritised by the military establishment, it remains to be seen how strongly a genuine preoccupation with promoting rational resource-use will figure in the execution of SIVAM. To the extent that it relies on a command-and-control approach, its environmental impact is liable to be extremely limited. If it can, through the provision of scientific data, inform a more sensitive planning process, which attempts to reorient development priorities towards meeting the needs and supporting the productive conservation strategies of local resource-user groups, it may prove to be of some benefit for environmental management purposes.

While progress towards the more comprehensive adoption of a 'resource-management' approach has been slow, elements of the 'eco-development' paradigm have entered the policy arena. This approach is based on 'reorganizing human activities so as to be synergic with ecosystem processes and services', so that socio-economic and environmental goals are better matched. Development is based on reconciling activities which are ecologically sustainable with the livelihood needs of the population. Goals include using technologies which preserve the natural resource base, meeting basic human needs, adopting participatory planning from the grassroots, using indigenous knowledge, and the sound management of common property regimes (Colby, 1990; Adams, 1990). While justifiably dismissed as unduly populist and romantic in many of its more farfetched propositions, elements of an 'eco-development' approach can be observed as having gained ground in the context of both debates and action towards more sustainable (non-predatory) development in Amazonia. In particular, the notion of joint or collaborative resource-management programmes, involving local communities, NGOs, state agencies and overseas aid organisations, has gained considerable acceptance.

Following the inclusion of environmental concerns in Brazil's new 1988 Constitution, a new set of policy guidelines for Amazonia was drawn up. Couched in the post-UNCED language of sustainable development, the 'National Integrated Policy for Legal Amazonia' eschews total reliance on conventional 'preservationist' principles in favour of a development and environmental management model, which for the first time recognises the legitimacy of various interest groups '... from extractivism to the electronics industry' (Brazil, 1995a: 19). Development efforts should therefore, it is now argued, be directed not just at the modern manufacturing and mining sector, but also at strengthening the activities of more traditional economies with a view to improving the quality of life for the majority of Amazonia's population.

While the evident contradictions between these laudable objectives and the contextual realities of policy-making for Amazonia cannot be ignored, neither can it be denied that the 1990s have seen important changes, not just in development discourse but also in terms of action on the ground. One of the most significant initiatives is the G7 Pilot Programme to Conserve the Brazilian Rain Forest, a $US280 million aid package launched at the request of the Group of Seven industrialised countries at their 1990 Houston Summit.[54] In addition to its support for scientific research, environmental monitoring and control, zoning and other more conventional activities, the G7 Pilot Programme has provided support to a number of innovative productive conservation schemes. These include the extractive reserves (discussed in chapter three) as well as a series of income-generating projects in the field of agroforestry administered by community and farmer organisations.[55]

The case-studies examined below are promising examples of a new, albeit embryonic, productive conservation paradigm which is beginning to take hold in the region. In these projects, local socio-environmental movements have joined forces with a range of other national and international organisations to devise locale-specific solutions to the challenge of conserving natural resources while sustaining livelihoods. Essentially, this is an action-led phenomenon, in which national policy-makers have followed the lead set by coalitions of environmental activists in their support for distinctive projects in particular sub-ecosystems of Amazonia. Until the mid-1990s, environmental planning for Brazilian Amazonia, with its heavily conservationist bias, has largely ignored the human dimension. Little attempt has been made within mainstream official thinking to understand the relationships which have evolved between those diverse groups making productive use of Amazonia's natural resources and the region's varied and delicate sub-ecosystems, that is, to 'make people matter' (Hall, 1993b). While settlers have been repeatedly used by government as a vehicle for achieving predetermined economic, social or geopolitical goals, the basic needs of migrants and traditional populations have not been prioritised.

In the late 1990s, environmental issues in Amazonia acquired an importance which would have been unthinkable a decade earlier. The crude and simplistic, if politically convenient and (for some) profitable, 'frontier economics' paradigm, of which Brazilian Amazonia is such a fine example, has been somewhat ameliorated since the 1980s in the direction of a more environmentally rational concern for economic and human dimensions. It is, perhaps, not unduly optimistic to regard these small but significant changes as representing the beginnings of a partial paradigm shift in Amazonia: away from the essentially destructive, 'profits-and-settlement-at-any-cost' philosophy of the 1970s, towards a more careful and balanced strategy which attempts to reconcile economic growth and livelihood support with the sustainable use of natural resources.

Yet while notable successes may have been chalked up locally, there remain formidable obstacles to the achievement of such a goal at regional level. As far as policy is concerned, many lacunae still exist which directly contradict efforts being made in the direction of socially and ecologically sensitive planning. Pasture-led deforestation, for example, continues to expand despite cuts in fiscal incentives. Commercial logging in Amazonia is on the rise as Asian and African stocks dwindle, and is likely to continue in this direction given the almost total absence of sustainable timber management in the region. In 1975, Amazonia provided just 14 per cent of Brazil's wood production, but by 1987 this figure had leapt to 54 per cent, representing in absolute terms more than a five-fold increase.[56]

There has, in particular, been a marked increase in the illegal extraction of vulnerable species such as mahogany from indian reserves and other conservation areas, where the largest concentrations are now to be found, a process fuelled by growing demand from the USA and UK (Bonner, 1994; Monbiot, 1992; Veríssimo *et al.*, 1995). Although some groups such as the Kayapó have managed to profit, benefits tend to be monopolised by male leaders. In general, most indigenous groups are either excluded or duped into selling cheaply.[57] Research evidence shows that even selective logging of valuable species contributes significantly to regional deforestation by speeding up conversion to cattle pasture.[58]

IBAMA's ability to implement its programme of environmental action, even taking into account the political obstacles, is further constrained by inadequate and poorly supported field operations staff. Consistency in this regard is not helped by the high turnover of environment Ministers and top advisors. Although much emphasis is currently being placed on agro-ecological zoning, there are few laws to back up recommendations, except in the case of conservation areas such as parks and reserves. In the case of zoning, as with environmental monitoring and control, implementation remains a politically sensitive question, frequently undermined by powerful ranching and logging interests, as well as an ineffectual, omissive or corrupt judiciary and police force.

Despite the flurry of activity in Amazonia during the 1990s, concrete action on executing progressive environment policy has been most marked in the centre-south of Brazil and even the north-east. State governments in Ceará, Minas Gerais, São Paulo, Paraná, Santa Catarina and Rio Grande do Sul have given priority to basic sanitation and river clean-up projects. At municipal level, environmental policy has led to impressive achievements in cities such as Santos, Victoria, Belo Horizonte, Natal and especially Curitiba, where mayor Jaime Lerner has even been spoken of as a future presidential candidate on the strength of his accomplishments in this field.

Joint action, livelihoods and resource management

In spite of continuing drawbacks, policy-making has advanced significantly from the legitimised destruction of the 1970s, underpinned by a 'frontier economics' growth paradigm, to the increasing, if fragmented, concern for promoting more sustainable forms of resource management in the 1990s. Underpinning this change has been a rapidly growing body of research which demonstrates that the majority of small producers in Amazonia are not destructive of the environment, but, on the contrary, are its main defenders. While migrant settlers are frequently trapped by economic and institutional factors into an ecologically destructive system of slash-and-burn agriculture, this is far from being a total picture.[59] Small farmers and extractivists in a range of sub-ecosystems, from the fertile floodplains to degraded uplands, have developed a range of adapted, non-destructive agricultural and resource-management systems without major outside assistance, a fact which is often overlooked.[60]

Resource-users have demonstrated both individual as well as shared, collective interests in protecting those natural assets – land, forests, rivers and lakes – which form the very basis of their livelihoods. Within the paradigm of Amazonian integration prevalent since the 1960s, such groups have tended to be actively dismissed as quaint and 'backward' vestiges of pre-modern times, which should be encouraged to disappear. Yet a fast-growing body of research is demonstrating the diverse ways in which many rural groups in Amazonia have evolved agricultural and tree-based production systems which conserve natural resources. These populations have not only managed to secure their livelihoods, but also provide valuable environmental services for society which are almost totally unacknowledged in development policy formulation.

Most of the Amazon's rural population depends to a large degree upon continued access to natural resources for its survival. Without the ability to make use of the rainforest for its timber and other products, or fish the rivers and lakes, prospects for the region's Amerindian, *caboclo* and many recently arrived settlers would be bleak indeed. Unable to earn their livelihoods in any stable rural situation, they would be forced either into the familiar pattern of repetitive and destructive frontier settlement, or be obliged to inflate rapidly growing towns and cities in the region.

Some 55 per cent of Amazonia's population is now concentrated into urban nuclei, which are seen as the major centres for economic activity and organisation of regional labour markets in the process of frontier expansion. Countering popular images of a 'green hell', Amazonia has been described as an 'urbanised jungle' (Becker, 1987, 1992). Yet in terms of the demographic dynamics which fuel regional development, it is impossible to separate town and countryside. Close links exist between rural and urban informal sectors to create diversity and flexibility in livelihood and employment strategies.

Arguably, the failure of development policy to support rural populations or encourage sustainable natural resource-use has accelerated urban growth to unprecedented levels. The urban population of Brazilian Amazonia now outnumbers rural inhabitants and has been growing twice as fast since the 1980s.[61] According to census (1990) figures, the northern region has a population of over nine million, four million of whom live in rural areas. About half of these, at least two million people, are so-called 'traditional peoples' rather than recent migrants (indigenous groups, rubber tappers and other extractivists on terra firma forests, as well as floodplain populations of small farmers and fisherpeople), who earn their living at least in part from extractive activities.[62] Inclusion of other groups within the larger 'legal' Amazonia, such as the babaçu nut-gatherers of Maranhão and Tocantins, would substantially increase the figure.[63] This fact belies the image usually perpetuated by corporate landed interests and rabid modernisers of the small producer in Amazonia as an ignorant, itinerant destroyer of the rainforest.

Apart from the adaptive capacities of rural producers themselves, one of the most important factors behind whatever successes have so far been achieved in the field of productive conservation has been growing cooperation between grassroots movements and NGOs. Together, they have come to constitute an increasingly powerful force which has pushed forward the frontiers of environmental policy and action in Brazilian Amazonia. Strategic alliances between community-based movements and NGOs, both Brazilian and international, have been instrumental in the design of new and adapted forms of environmental management. Furthermore, in terms of translating such innovation into broader policy changes and practical strategies, this partnership has played a key political role in lobbying the government for legislative change and material support, frequently in the face of severe opposition from entrenched vested interests.

According to the latest figures, Brazil boasts about 5,000 NGOs. The number concerned with environmental matters has risen drastically from around 400 in 1985, to 700 by 1989 and 1,300 in 1992. By 1995, some 2,000 NGOs spent $US18.5 million in projects, although this capacity has come under severe financial pressure since economic stabilisation.[64] Nationally, it is estimated that about 40 per cent of these organisations are devoted to environmental protection. Of this total, perhaps 90 per cent are located in

1 This cattle ranch in southern Pará is typical of the land-use pattern prioritised by official development policies for Amazonia since the 1960s. Fiscal incentives and subsidised credit have encouraged land conflicts and the rapid depletion of natural forest cover in many areas, most notably in Pará, Maranhão, Rondônia, Tocantins and Mato Grosso.

2 A typical family of 'spontaneous' settlers on the Transamazon highway which has engaged in the conventional slash-and-burn cycle of subsistence crop production shown below in Plate 3.

3 Extraction of timber has in recent years become an increasingly important cause of Amazonian deforestation. Small farmers usually sell valuable lumber such as mahogany to sawmills for a small fraction of their real market value.

4 The grave of rubber tappers' leader Francisco 'Chico' Mendes, in the municipal cemetery of Xapuri, Acre. He was murdered on 22 December 1988 on the orders of hostile landowners opposed to the seringueiros' cause.

5 A rubber tapper and his family at home. Their pensive expressions perhaps capture some anxieties over the future of extractive reserves.

6 Rubber tappers in Acre display a range of products manufactured in the community. Economic diversification is one of the major challenges facing extractrive reserves.

7 On the Mamirauá reserve, floating guardposts are located at the entrance to lake systems to protect valuable fish stocks agianst illegal incursions by commercial boats.

8 These local fishermen were surprised by Mamirauá project personnel as they were fishing in a lake reserved by the community for restocking.

9 At the fourth Mamirauá community assembly, held in July 1995, representatives from the nine sectors discuss the results of scientific research and the zoning implications.

10 The RECA project in Acre, where a variety of NTFPs is grown by frontier colonists, although marketing remains a problem.

11 *A small farmer sustainably harvests heart-of-palm from the* pupunha *tree on an agroforestry project.*

12 On the CAT project near Marabá on the Transamazon highway, a small settler contemplates his new venture into agroforestry. It is hoped that the planting of perennials will provide the income to discourage settlers from practising slash-and-burn agriculture on such a wide scale and enable them to sedentarise production.

13 This flourishing community tree nursery on the Transamazon highway, funded by the ODA, will supply CAT project members with seeds to help them diversify production and introduce agroforestry systems.

southern Brazil (one-quarter in São Paulo alone) and are concerned primarily with urban and industrial issues (*Brazil Report*, 12 January 1995; Viola, 1993). In many respects, they are similar to European and North American 'green movements' in their preoccupation with controlling pollution and addressing physical environmental problems, comparable with the priorities of SEMA during the 1970s. However, a rather different picture emerges in the Amazon region, where preservation of natural resources is closely tied to the challenge of sustaining people's very livelihoods.

In line with trends elsewhere, NGOs in Brazil have followed an evolutionary path (Hall, 1993a). During the 1960s, they were thin on the ground, were staffed by volunteers and concentrated on charitable-type relief and welfare operations to relieve poverty and cope with disaster situations such as the north-eastern drought. In the 1970s and early 1980s, they progressed to a second stage, becoming more systematically involved in promoting material development through agricultural, health, housing and other projects. Such limited concerns were soon complemented by a third phase, based on the use of Freirian-style, awareness-raising techniques (*educação de base*) as the basis for broader action to tackle the root causes of poverty.

Much of this work by NGOs at community level in Amazonia and elsewhere in Brazil was undertaken in close cooperation with an increasingly radical Catholic clergy adopting 'Liberation Theology' as its guiding inspiration, following the Vatican II Council (1962–5) and the 1968 Conference of Latin American Bishops in Medellín, Colombia. This collaboration was critical during the period of military rule in Brazil (1964–85), and was virtually the only channel for action against the adverse effects on the poor of the government's economic modernisation policies, when political opposition was banned and rigid censorship imposed. In a sense, the Catholic church was itself the largest Brazilian NGO working for the alleviation of poverty and for grassroots development.

Following political liberalisation (*abertura*) since the early 1980s, NGOs in Brazil have added a fourth, lobbying or advocacy role to their portfolio. The goal of promoting material development, productive efficiency and community spirit at local level has become almost inseparable from efforts to bring about wider policy changes across a broader front. A stance of open conflict between NGOs and the federal government has been replaced by cooperation in many spheres, enabling such groups to engage in an active policy dialogue with government ministries, and play an instrumental part in bringing about progressive change in favour of previously marginalised social groups. In order to perform this negotiating role, NGOs have had to become more professionalised as organisations, with their own salaried, full-time staff and infrastructure. Understandably, however, mutual suspicions persist and these ancient enemies often remain, to coin a phrase, somewhat 'reluctant partners'.[65]

It may be something of an exaggeration to say that the various ecological groups which have been set up in Brazil make it 'the first Third World country to have an authentic environmental movement' (Castañeda, 1994: 232). Yet in Amazonia, the emergence of a range of organisations concerned with both conservation and socioeconomic development suggest the beginnings of a concerted effort by civic society to address problems which the government alone, even with the best political will in the world, would surely find insurmountable. This has taken place at two levels. Locally, intermediary NGOs have established contacts with communities, assisted in diagnosing their needs and established links with external funding agencies or government bodies to provide longer-term technical assistance to community organisations. There are now dozens of such local NGOs in Amazonia.[66]

A second, much smaller category consists of centrally located voluntary organisations concerned with general advocacy and lobbying on behalf of Amazonia and its peoples. Those such as the Institute of Amazon and Environmental Studies (IEAA) or the Institute of Socio-Economic Studies (INESC), based in Brasilia, may perform a clearly political role, lobbying for changes in public policy: for example, in connection with extractive reserves and in the drafting of Brazil's 1988 constitution. Others comprise branches of international funding bodies such as the World Wide Fund for Nature (WWF) and Friends of the Earth (FOE), which finance specific projects, usually through intermediary NGOs or sometimes directly via community bodies. Globally in 1993, international NGOs channelled $US5.4 billion for overseas development purposes, the equivalent of almost 10 per cent of official bilateral and multilateral assistance (OECD, 1995).

There is a large and growing literature which highlights the effectiveness of intermediary NGOs in being able to address localised problems of poverty and resource degradation.[67] Conventionally, intermediary NGOs have been better placed to enjoy the confidence of local populations and to identify people's needs in a more sensitive fashion when compared with central government bureaucracies. Their physical proximity and socio-political background frequently enable NGO development practitioners to establish a rapport based on cooperation and mutual respect. Intermediary NGOs perform an additional and fundamental role by strengthening grassroots membership organisations of the rural poor (Carroll, 1992). As well as bringing in essential funding from international NGOs and from state bodies, they often have invaluable administrative and managerial skills, which strengthen the combined movement and enable community-based organisations not only to assist in devising local strategies, but also to exert political pressure on the state and even on key outside funding agencies, as has happened in several cases.[68] Their cost-effectiveness and efficacy in executing poverty-focused development projects has led many G7 bilateral aid bodies to channel increasingly large amounts of funding through NGOs. Multilateral agencies such as the World Bank have also sought to establish closer working relationships with international and intermediary voluntary organisations (Cernea, 1988).

Despite these undoubted benefits, however, there are also potential hazards associated with the work of intermediary NGOs, which, unless checked, can easily undermine community efforts. The same financial, technical and managerial resources brought in by NGOs to support local initiatives and speed up the development process can lead to undue dependence, discouraging local collective efforts at resource mobilisation, for example. This is particularly true in northern Brazil, where strong traditions of patron-clientage in social and political life have encouraged the poor to look to individual figures of authority for their salvation: the priest, the messianic leader, the landowner, the local politician, and now perhaps even the NGO worker. Less democratically inclined NGOs might even encourage such dependence as a means of 'capturing' their 'own' portfolios of community projects as a rationale for continuing to receive external aid and the staff positions which this supports. The frequently limited accountability of voluntary organisations, whose performance is often judged on the basis of limited indicators and anecdotal evidence, merely exacerbates this problem.

The middle-class origins and higher incomes of many, if not most intermediary NGO staff members, suggest to some critics that they may not be able to empathise with the poor quite as much as their ideology of *educação de base* sometimes suggests. As Viola (1993: 13) notes: 'Environmental groups have a significantly higher educational level and per capita income than the country and region average.' Berger (1977) in particular has seriously questioned the 'hierarchy of consciousness' assumed by many NGO workers, and the attendant need to 'conscientise' the poor, whose level of awareness is presumed to be inferior to their own.

However, while this last criticism is often valid, it is probably true to say that NGOs working in Amazonia are obliged to place a high priority on harnessing local knowledge as the very basis of productive conservation strategies. Frequently, the only available information on the myriad of ecosystems little known to outsiders is, indeed, in the hands of the local population. In order to stand any reasonable chance of success, productive conservation efforts require that indigenous expertise be respected, consulted and incorporated. Yet while the degree of community participation in the collecting of this knowledge and the way in which it is subsequently used may vary considerably, no resource-preservation exercise in Amazonia can succeed if outsiders presume to hold all the answers and resolutely deny local people decision-making functions.

Since the mid-1980s, Brazil has seen the emergence of a wide range of socio-environmental movements, which comprise both NGOs and grassroots elements (Guimarães, 1991; Viola, 1993). Many of these have been confined to the urbanised south, including neighbourhood movements, occupational health, consumer defence and action by industrial workers. In Amazonia, community groups have joined forces with NGOs to tackle a growing number of specific issues with socio-economic and ecological dimensions.

The longest-standing grassroots action in Brazilian Amazonia has been undertaken by Amerindian groups such as the Kayapó (Pará) and the Yanomami (Roraima) in their centuries-old struggle against the loss of their traditional lands, for demarcated reserves and for their very survival (Davis, 1977; McDonald, 1991).[69] A pro-indian lobby emerged in the mid-1970s, supported by the Indian Missionary Council (CIMI), an arm of the Catholic church, leading to the setting up of the Union of Indigenous Peoples (UNI) in 1981 following a meeting in São Paulo of seventy-three leaders from thirty-two tribes. The massive protest at Altamira in 1989 against the Xingú dam complex, as well as other victories, are testimony to the potential impact of Amerindian collective action at strategic junctures.[70] A comparable or even greater mobilisation of indigenous groups against destructive oil and gas exploration has occurred in the Equadorian and Peruvian portions of the Amazon Basin as well as the Colombian Pacific coast area.[71]

In Brazil, the government's commitment to the demarcation of indian reserves was called into question in January 1996 with the issuing of Decree 1775 (Schwartzman *et al.*, 1996). Following successful lobbying by pro-indigenous groups in the Constituent Assembly, the 1988 Constitution recognised the 'original' property rights of Amerindians. The state was charged with the responsibility of demarcating and protecting their lands, while private land titles in indigenous territories were nullified. The Collor administration committed itself in Decree 22/91 to a policy of quite rapid demarcation. From 1993, however, a number of lawsuits were brought by landowners in the south and north-east of Brazil with claims to indian lands. In the Sete Cerros case, involving the Guaraní, Decree 22/91 was challenged on the grounds that it violated due process of law and denied ranchers the right to contest government action, a right guaranteed by the new constitution. Decree 1775 revised Decree 22/91 and thus allowed interested parties (private, municipal and state) to challenge the demarcation of those reserves identified but not yet fully demarcated, within a three-month deadline.

The Ministry of Justice claimed that Decree 1775 was necessary in order to correct a legal error within Decree 22/91 and protect due process of law for non-indigenous claimants, thus conferring the right of appeal (*contraditórios*) against boundary definitions. However, this stance was itself questioned by indigenous organisations and by the Workers' Party (PT), which raised doubts about its legality and contested it in the courts, alleging that the measure was designed primarily to allow mining and logging interests access to valuable resources in the reserve areas (CAPOIB, 1996).

The outcome of Decree 1775 proved to be something of an anticlimax, possibly due in part to its by now high international profile. By the July 1996 deadline, the National Indian Foundation (FUNAI) had received 419 challenges relating to 34 indigenous areas (from a total of 554 territories in Brazil). Of these, 8 reserves would be the subject of further study by FUNAI and were liable to have their boundaries modified. Yet dissatisfaction with the government's stance on indigenous affairs caused the then head of FUNAI, Marcos Santilli, to resign in March 1996 after only six months in office.[72]

Aside from Amerindians, the best known socio-environmental grassroots movement is that of the rubber tappers, which is discussed at length in chapter three. The *seringueiros*' struggle is arguably the most widely publicised and politically advanced in many respects when compared with other productive conservation groups, and tends to be given prominence in scholarly studies as something of a *cause célèbre* among environmentalists, especially in Europe and North America. In 1989, UNI and the National Rubber Tappers' Council (CNS) joined forces to set up the much-vaunted 'Amazon Alliance of Peoples of the Forest', to campaign for sustainable development policies for the region. However, the organisation has never managed to achieve the desired solidarity between *seringueiros* and Amerindian groups, and, unfortunately, has remained largely ineffective. Be that as it may, the prominence of indians and rubber tappers on the environmental stage should not be allowed to obscure the fact that other players exist. Several active but lower-profile grassroots movements and what might be called 'quasi-movements' have sprung up contemporaneously in response to crisis situations in diverse sub-ecosystems of the region since the 1970s.

An increasingly common form of popular resistance in Brazil has been organised community action in response to threatened eviction and environmental damage due to hydropower development. This has been most evident in the south and north-east, where well-organised populations have successfully mounted strong campaigns for proper compensation and comprehensive resettlement plans. These have dramatically improved the minimalist provisions originally envisaged by the electricity authorities, and caused a major rethink in the power sector on project-planning procedures and resettlement policy (Hall, 1994). In Amazonia, as mentioned above, the Xingú protests of 1989 achieved a similar result, thanks to massive international publicity and intensive lobbying by NGOs against the Brazilian government and the World Bank. Several years earlier, at the Tucuruí scheme on the river Tocantins, local protesters had been less successful. Built to provide subsidised electricity to the Carajás mining and aluminium smelting projects, Tucuruí was the largest dam ever built in an area of tropical rainforest, and displaced up to 35,000 people (Mougeot, 1987, 1990; Hall, 1991). Sporadic public demonstrations during 1980–4 improved measures for compensation and relocation somewhat, but the poor majority incurred severe loss of livelihood. The protest movement did not acquire sufficient political force to achieve more than limited concessions, although displacees have not ceased campaigning for fair compensation.[73]

Perhaps the most pervasive form of rural grassroots action in Brazil has been that of landless farmers to secure productive and property rights. The Landless Rural Workers' Movement (MST) – allied to the PT, the Unified Labour Centre (CUT) and the radical wing of the Catholic church – has been most prominent in southern Brazil. The MST has its own administrative structure, headquarters in São Paulo and a newsletter with a circulation of 30,000. It has a carefully planned strategy based on the targeted occupation of under-utilised estate lands in Santa Catarina, Rio Grande do Sul and São Paulo, with a few interventions in the north-east. By 1988, the MST had already organised over 80 estate occupations involving some 13,000 families (Hall, 1990). The movement has grown rapidly since then, reflecting the hunger for land amongst Brazil's rural poor. It is estimated that, by mid-1996, MST action had resulted in the expropriation and redistribution of almost 8 million hectares of land and the resettling of some 140,000 families on 600 estates, mainly in southern Brazil, with a further 30,000 landless camped at the roadside waiting to take over idle land.[74]

There has been no such systematic or well-structured movement of landless farmers in the Amazon region, where the picture is one of relatively poorly organised action. Small groups of landless farmers have been involved in land conflicts and occupations, sometimes supported by rural unions, church activists or NGOs, but with nothing like the level of support or organisation afforded by the MST to its members in the south. Although carried out with no environmental agenda as such, at least in the short run, family and community-based occupations are common as a means of securing access to land and a livelihood.

During the late 1980s in the states of Pará and Maranhão, for example, some 6,000 families (about 50,000 people) were involved in land occupations. In the conflict-ridden 'Parrot's Beak' area of southern Pará, in the Carajás region, up to 20,000 peasant farmers settled in the 'Brazilnut Polygon', an area of one million hectares divided into large estates leased from the state government in the 1940s by few prominent local families, but illicitly expanded since then (Hall, 1991; Hébette, 1988; Hébette and Colares, 1990). Here, groups of up to 200 hundred landless families at a time, adopting their own 'guerrilla' tactics, took over a total of 200,000 hectares, obliging the federal government to expropriate the land in 1988 under the agrarian reform law. During the mid-1990s, the MST started to organise some estate occupations in eastern Amazonia around Parauapebas in southern Pará, which lead to a massacre of peasants at Eldorado do Carajás in April 1996.[75]

Although, as mentioned above, they had no specifically environmental agenda beyond securing land, many families and communities in the Marabá region have subsequently become involved in the CAT programme of small-scale farming and agroforestry, which is discussed in chapter five. In addition to the community-based action initiated by rubber tappers, Amerindians, hydropower displacees and landless farmers, Amazonian fisherpeople have undertaken some of the most effective and geographically widespread grassroots action to defend their livelihoods and protect natural resources.

Due to the sheer weight of critical attention which has been focused on the aggressive drive to occupy and 'develop' Amazonia since the 1960s, some fundamental misconceptions have arisen. While many recent settlers have for one reason or another been caught up in cycles of destructive activity, at least half of the rural population is actively engaged in efforts to preserve resources as the basis of their livelihoods, in a reasonable state of harmony with their environment. As Nugent (1993b, 1996) has pointed out, such resilience in the face of the post-1964 modernisation onslaught is more typical than extraordinary, although it has tended to be invisible rather than officially acknowledged. The following chapters in this volume suggest, however, that it is from these early experiences that valuable lessons may be learned to guide future productive conservation policies as part of the drive towards a more sustainable Amazonia.

Environment and development

Notes

1 In this volume and in the general literature on the region's development, Amazonia refers to 'Legal Amazonia', which comprises the nine states of Pará, Amazonas, Mato Grosso, Rondônia, Acre, Tocantins, Roraima, Amapá and Maranhão, covering an area of 5 million square kilometres, or 58% of national territory. The north or 'Classic Amazonia' coincides with the forested zone and excludes transition areas of savanna-type grassland (cerrado), embracing only Pará, Amazonas, Acre, Rondônia and Amapá, an area of 3.5 million square kilometres.
2 See, for example, Myers (1984).
3 Forest loss is put at 19,000 square kilometres p.a. for 1988–9, 14,000 square kilometres p.a. for 1989–90 and 11,000 square kilometres p.a. during 1990–1 (Fearnside, 1993).
4 According to press reports, satellite images for 1995 registered 40,000 forest fires in Amazonia, almost five times the figure for the previous year, generating a cloud of smoke which covered an area of 7 million square kilometres. See, 'Inferno na fronteira verde', *Veja*, 8 November 1995.
5 'In the Rainforest', *The Economist*, 7 December 1991. These estimates exclude the state of Maranhão.
6 For example, rancher Pedro Aparecido Dotto from São Paulo owns 2.1 million hectares in Acre, almost 15% of the state and the size of El Salvador. Logger Mário Jorge Moraes owns 1.2 million hectares in Amazonas, an area larger than Jamaica, containing timber reserves valued at $US1.6 billion. Malih Hassan Eumaoula, originally from the Lebanon, has a property of 490,000 hectares, also in Amazonas ('Donos da Geografía', *Veja*, 7 July 1993).
7 See Reis (1982). The original edition was published in 1960.
8 Quoted by Schmink and Wood (1992: 59).
9 For example, Decree 1164 of 1971 which for 'national security' reasons placed under central government control all land within 100 kilometres of existing or planned federal highways, including the *Transamazônica*. For further details, see Schmink and Wood (1992), chapter three.
10 See chapter six for further details on measures announced in July 1996 to curb deforestation in Amazonia.
11 In 1979, SUDAM announced that new incentives would not be granted to projects in areas of 'dense' forest, but only in 'transition' zones. However, as Fearnside (1990) noted, these transition areas are mixed dense forest and scrubland, and ranchers prefer to convert the tree-covered portion to pasture.

In 1988, President Sarney announced restrictions on fiscal incentives for the Amazon region as part of his *Nossa Natureza* ('Our Nature') programme's package of ecological measures. But Law 8167, passed in

1991, limits financial incentives and places greater controls on new projects, but does not prohibit them outright (Fearnside, 1993).
12 Land values in Rondônia tripled in real terms between 1978 and 1986. Potential gains from land speculation can thus be very high for both large and small owners. Small colonists are tempted to seek quick profits by clearing a plot and planting crops or pasture, then selling up and moving on. According to one study, 14 hectares of forest in Rondônia could yield the equivalent of $US9,000 (Mahar, 1989: 38). This phenomenon, compounded by the lack of technical support and sustainable farming systems for the region, helps explain the high rate of colonist turnover on many settlement schemes.
13 Typically, logging companies will offer to bulldoze a track through the jungle to permit smallholders to gain access to their land, and in return be granted the right to extract the more valuable stands of timber, such as mahogany. Farmers will offer felled trunks at very low prices to lumber companies who remove the wood from their land.
14 Mahogany sells for about $US700 a cubic metre. More than 70% of Brazilian production is exported, mainly to the USA and UK (Bonner, 1994).
15 A study of logging in southern Pará found 86 mills in operation, 24 specialising in mahogany and responsible for 90% of the mahogany harvest. Average annual profits for such a company were estimated at $US800,000. Logging companies have opened up some 3,000 kilometres of roads in southern Pará, while all of the area's 15 indigenous reserves have been affected by mahogany-logging (Veríssimo *et al.*, 1995).
16 Research undertaken by Conservation International revealed that the Malaysian timber company WTK acquired control (if not actual legal title) over 1.2 million hectares near Carauari in Amazonas state, while compatriot Sam Ling gained access to a further 50,000 hectares near Itacoatiara as well as 210,000 hectares at São Sebastião do Uatumã (Scharf, 1996).
17 May and Reis (1993) note that the average size of small plots (less than 100 hectares) increased from 17 to 24 hectares during 1975–85, while that of larger farms (over 500 hectares) fell from 4,370 to 3,326 hectares.
18 These included the National Department of Mineral Production (DNPM, 1934), the Vale do Rio Doce Company for iron-ore mining (CVRD, 1945), the Superintendency for Fishing Development (SUDEPE, 1962), the Brazilian Oil Company (PETROBRAS, 1953) and the São Francisco Hydroelectric Company (CHESF, 1953). See Guimarães (1991) and Trebat (1983).
19 The Intermunicipal Commission for Water and Air Pollution Control

(CCPPA) was set up in the early 1960s, precursor to the State Environmental Sanitation Technology Company (CETESB), established in 1975. However, little effective pollution control was effected until the 1980s, under the impetus of a strong state political administration and supported by World Bank funding (Redwood, 1993).

20 UNESCO's 'Man and the Biosphere' (MAB) Programme was established in 1976. The Action Plan for Biospehere Reserves was agreed in 1983 by UNESCO, UNEP, FAO and IUCN and there are presently 324 Biospehere Reserves in 82 countries.

21 Pleistocene Refuge Theory argues that during the drier late Pleistocene period key species retreated to wetter forest 'islands' in Amazonia. Conservation of these areas should, therefore, be a top conservation priority in order to maximise biological protection, while enabling scarce financial resources to be effectively targeted.

Island Biogeography Theory suggests that island species-richness is a function of rates of species extinction and colonisation conditioned by factors such as island size and degree of isolation. While Refuge Theory indicated *location*, Biogeography Theory offered a formula for calculating the size of conservation areas, the general conclusion being that it would be more effective to establish fewer large reserves than many small units. See Foresta (1991, chapter two) for a detailed account.

22 According to Foresta (1991: 89–91), those within the IBDF responsible for developing the plan, '... were careful not to let the theories dominate the selection process: they selected no area solely, or even primarily, because it had been identified as a Pleistocene forest fragment. ... Within the standards of biological value they had established, they let political opportunities determine the regional distribution of conservation energies.'

23 According to Guimarães (1991: 160–1), toxic fumes from a wood-pulp plant sickened residents of the state capital Porto Alegre, including the chief of staff of President Médici, and a decree (no. 73,030) was enacted based on an existing policy statement (E.M. no. 100/71).

24 *Nossa Natureza* was announced in the wake of massive international protests caused by the murder of rubber tappers' leader Chico Mendes just three months earlier, in December 1988. It also followed the Altamira Meeting of February 1989, which galvanised the protests of Kayapó and Xavante indians as well as a myriad of environmental groups from Brazil and elsewhere in what became a world media event against construction of the Kararaô hydroelectric scheme on the Xingú river. The meeting lasted 4 days and brought together 600 indians from 40 tribes.

Due to the adverse publicity, the World Bank temporarily suspended its $US500 million loan, part of a larger $US1.1 billion package to

ELETROBRAS, to fund the first stage of a plan by ELETRONORTE of its 2010 hydropower expansion plan, and the power authority was obliged to drop the Xingú projects (Hildeyard, 1989b; Posey, 1989; Goodman and Hall, 1990).

Press reports on Amazon rainforest loss included a number of dramatic lead stories in the world's media: 'Amazon in Peril', Newsweek, 30 January 1989; 'Bonfire in the Amazon', *The Independent Magazine*, 25 February 1989; 'The Month Amazonia Burns', *The Economist*, 9–15 September 1989.

25 Its full current title is the Ministry of the Environment, Water Resources and Legal Amazonia.
26 IBAMA absorbed the IBDF (forestry), SUDEPE (fishing), SUDHEVEA (rubber) and SEMA.
27 President Collor launched 'Operation Amazonia' in June 1990, three months after his election. Using a quick-response strategy based on the identification of illegal activities through the use of high-definition satellite images, together with the use of helicopters, some 300 IBAMA inspectors sought to catch and prosecute those responsible for illicit logging, forest burnings, deforestation and gold prospecting.

By October of that year, IBAMA had, it claimed, imposed 2,200 fines and closed 88 illegal logging operations. However, the campaign was much criticised for targeting small operators and being biased against the poor settler, while ignoring more politically powerful and larger-scale offenders. Grave doubts were also raised about the effectiveness of IBAMA in collecting fines.

IBAMA claimed that its actions had been responsible for a halving of the deforestation rate in 1990 compared with the previous year, but this was generally thought to have been due mainly to unusually heavy rains in Amazonia, with 'Operation Amazonia' having only a marginal impact. The state of Acre, for example, with over 150,000 square kilometres of forests to be monitored, has only 10 IBAMA staff members for this purpose, who often lack funds to cover even basic transport costs, not to mention political support to enforce the law. See, *O Globo*, 'Ibama prevê êxito na Operação Amazônia', 23 October 1990; *Jornal do Brasil*, 'Muita mata e pouca fiscalização', 2 January 1994).
28 The title of the working-paper outlining the project is 'Development and Security in the Region to the North of the Rivers Solimões and Amazonas'. It started officially with a statement of intent, *Exposição de Motivos* no. 018/85, but was announced to the Congress only in October 1987 (Oliveira Filho, 1990: 155).
29 According to Ramos (1996), the reawakening of the PCN through an emphasis on social and urban infrastructure will reinforce surveillance and regional integration, complementing SIVAM and the Amazon

Cooperation Treaty. It is anticipated that spending will be boosted from a current low level of some $US5 million p.a. (having reached $US47 million in 1989), concentrated around São Gabriel da Cachoeira, home to the fifth jungle infantry battalion.

30 Section VIII, chapter VI, article 225. Paragraph III.4 states that Brazil's 'Amazon rainforest ... shall be utilised within the law to ensure preservation of the environment, including the use of natural resources' (Brazil, 1988: 51).

31 The Rondônia Agricultural, Forestry and Livestock Plan (PLANAFLORO) is funded by loans from the World Bank of $US167 million out of a 5-year budget of $US229 million. PLANAFLORO is designed to support agro-ecological zoning, agroforestry, recovery of degraded pastures, environmental education, extractive reserves, forest management and indian communities.

However, in June 1994, only a year after PLANAFLORO commenced, it was already coming under severe criticism from local groups. The Rondônia Forum of NGOs published an open letter to the World Bank, requesting suspension of loan disbursements on the grounds that attainment of the programme's objectives was being frustrated by several factors, including: opposition from local landowning and logging interests, inability of the state to enforce zoning controls, irregular land-titling activities by the Rondônia Land Institute (ITERON), the state body responsible, and the effective exclusion of NGOs from participation in monitoring the execution of PLANAFLORO (Oliveira and Millikan, 1994; Millikan, 1994).

32 On 21 June 1996, an agreement was signed in Porto Velho by the state government of Rondônia, the World Bank, local and international NGOs. A government/NGO committee was elected to draft a revised PLANAFLORO which would decentralise decision-making powers to community level, while a special $US22 million fund was earmarked for grassroots initiatives (World Bank, 1996c).

33 Brazil's 165 federal Conservation Units cover a grand total of 32,141,280 hectares or 3.7% of national territory. They are currently distributed as follows: (1) *Indirect Use* (total 15,621,734 ha) comprising 35 national parks (9,742,130 ha), 23 biological reserves (3,044,444 ha), 21 ecological stations (2,159,062 ha), 5 ecological reserves (653,070 ha), and 10 areas of special ecological interest (23,028 ha); (2) *Direct Use* (total 16,519,546 ha) comprising 41 national forests (12,604,031 ha), 9 extractive reserves (2,200,755 ha), and 21 areas of environmental protection or APAs (1,714,760 ha).

34 Pig-iron smelters have been required since 1988 to present an Integrated Industry-Forestry Plan (PIFI) to provide for the gradual introduction of charcoal (50% by their tenth year) from sustainably managed

sources rather than virgin rainforest. In 1989, this target was increased to 100% by 1995.
35 Decree 153 of 25 June 1991. This modified Decree 101 of 17 April 1991, regulating Law 8,167 of 16 January 1991.
36 The Coordinating Commission for the Ecological-Economic Zoning of National Territory (CCZEE) was established by Decree 99,540 of 21 September 1990 under the SAE. Its somewhat vaguely worded and ambiguous brief was to undertake studies of Legal Amazonia which would, '... through the macro-zoning of the region, identify the environmental situation and indicate major priorities for government action for the regulation of Amazon territory' (SAE/IBGE, 1993: 7). These studies were contracted out to the Brazilian Institute of Geography and Statistics (IBGE), the Brazilian Foundation for Sustainable Development (FBDS) and the Foundation for Science and Space Technology (FUNCATE).

Under the G7 Pilot Programme's Natural Resources Policy sub-component, $US88 million has been earmarked for IBAMA and Amazon state governments to prepare State Environment Plans and institution-specific Action Plans, including agro-ecological zoning exercises. For further details on the pilot programme, see below.
37 The World Bank would lend $US117 million and the German Development Bank a further $US16 million, or 80% of the total. In its desire to secure Brazilian participation, the Bank reduced counterpart funding to 25%. Of this $US117, some $US56 million was earmarked for training and institutional support for IBAMA and other state-level agencies making up the SISNAMA, almost $US49 million was allocated to strengthening Conservation Units, and $US58 million went to environmental protection.
38 'Brazil pays $US1 million for not using grant', *Daily Telegraph*, 18 February 1992.
39 An evaluation by IBAMA of Brazil's ecological stations, national parks, forests and reserves discovered that only one-third had a reasonable level of infrastructural support for protective purposes. Nationally, it was found that IBAMA had only 548 officials to monitor an area of 300,000 square kilometres of conservation units, one-sixth of the estimated required minimum number, according to the agency. Clearly, however, physical presence on the ground alone would not guarantee accountability in the absence of appropriate political support for environmental policy. See report in the *Jornal do Brasil*, 'Brasil preserva 70% de áreas ecológicas só no papel', 24 March 1991.
40 See *Jornal do Brasil*, 'Reservas ecológicas do País estão ameaçadas', 11 May 1994.
41 FLORAM aimed to replant over 200,000 hectares of degraded lands with non-native tree species.

42 Quoted in Cleary (1991: 73).
43 On 27 February, Lutzenberger had sent out an instruction prohibiting IBAMA from issuing blank forms (*guias florestais*) to logging companies, effectively enabling them to circumvent the law by making their own assessments of commercial timber extraction. He had also openly criticised IBAMA for widespread corruption and had started a number of official investigations into the organisation's activities. See, 'Lutzenberger: madeireiros pressionam Collor' ('Loggers put pressure on Collor'), *O Globo*, 24 March 1992.
44 'O Ministério e a Amazônia', *Jornal do Brasil*, 22 January 1994.
45 'O abacaxí Amazônia', *Isto É*, 29 September 1993.
46 Renamed the Ministry of the Environment, Hydrological Resources and Legal Amazonia, or *Ministério do Meio Ambiente, dos Recursos Hídricos e da Amazônia Legal*. José Seixas Lourenço, former Rector of the Federal University of Pará and head of UNAMAZ, was appointed Secretary for Legal Amazonia.
47 See, for example, the *Eco-Eco* journal, published in Rio de Janeiro by the Rockefeller Foundation. See, also, Margulis (1990) and Almeida (1993). On the Brazilian power sector, see Serra (1993).
48 On *Calha Norte*, see Oliveira Filho (1990). On the Araguaia guerrilla conflict, see Bourne (1978), Dória *et al.* (1978) and Portela (1979). For GETAT, see Wagner (1990) and Hall (1991). For the other cases cited, see Hall (1991) and Wagner (1991).
49 'Military step up presence in the region', *Latin America Regional Reports-Brazil*, RB-94-04, 5 May 1994.
50 For example, the military-backed conference on 'Amazonia – sovereignty at risk', held in Brasília on 7 June 1995. This 'repudiated the subservience of FHC [President Fernando Henrique Cardoso] to the interests of multinationals and the US government', while expressing fears over Brazil's loss of control over 'the largest genebank in the world – Amazonia'. Source: 'Povo Brasileiro Repudia a Traição', *A Semente do Lampadosa*, 1, June.
51 SIPAM is designed to provide, 'a coordinated and integrated structure for the provision of information and action between the various agencies in charge of policies for the Brazilian Amazon ... [and] ... provide surveillance and support mechanisms for the policies on the Amazon's sustained development, (Brazil n.d., a).
52 The Brazilian military had expressed fears that the US military would set up its Southern Command in neighbouring Guyana, following its departure from Panama. There were also worries that Colombian and Venezuelan high-powered radar was for spying on Brazilian activities in Amazonia. See, 'Military step up presence in region', *Latin America Regional Reports-Brazil*, RB-94-04, 5 May 1994.

53 Signed in May 1994, the $US1.4 billion SIVAM contract was not put out to public tender, on the grounds of national security. Details were circulated to embassies and bids from eleven foreign companies were examined. SIVAM became enveloped in rumours of bribery and corruption soon after the US company Raytheon, in conjunction with the Brazilian firm Esca, beat the French Thompson-Alcatel consortium. The contract was annulled in July 1995 due to alleged irregularities, but this decision was later reversed by the Brasilia regional court. Approval of the financing package for SIVAM was blocked by the leader of the senate economic affairs committee, Gilberto Miranda (PMDB-Amazonas).

The subsequent publication of taped telephone conversations between presidential advisor Júlio César Gomes and the Raytheon representative in Brazil, José Afonso Asumpção, on how to overcome this opposition led to the setting up of a senate commission of enquiry into the whole affair. Gomes and the then air force minister Mauro Gandra were both forced to resign as a result. SIVAM's credibility was further undermined by the new air force minister, appointed in November, Brigadier Lélio Lôbo, who in his statement to the commission on 12 December 1995, declared his ignorance of the fact that some twenty air force officials were paid by Esca as consultants.

Retired Brigadier Ivan Frota, who had been involved in initial studies of the SIVAM proposal, further fanned the flames in January 1996 when he publicly declared his opposition to the Ratheon contract, suggesting that an equally efficient system could be built for one-third of the price ($US500 million) by using existing technology, and that the government had obtained approval for the project by, 'buying off senators with concessions and diverse favours'. The brigadier was called to testify before the senate commission, but its president, Antônio Carlos Magalhães (PFL-Bahia), refused to allow him to speak, on the grounds that Frota would not withdraw his accusations against the government.

(Based on reports from: *Jornal do Brasil*, 13 December 1995 and 17 and 24 January 1996; *Isto É*, 20 December, 1995; *Jornal Pessoal*, 131, November 1995; *Latin America Regional Reports-Brazil*, 11 January 1996; and *The Guardian*, 29 December 1995.)

54 Activities under the Pilot Programme are funded through a central $US60 million Rainforest Trust Fund (RTF) as well as bilaterally-pledged funds, of which Germany alone is providing over 50%, with the remainder coming from the European Union, United Kingdom, USA and France. Sub-components of the programme comprise: (1) support for specialised research and major research centres, namely INPA in Manaus and the Goeldi Museum in Belém – $US48 million; (2) small-scale community-based projects – $US30 million; (3) extractive reserves – $US9 million; (4) environmental monitoring and control, including

zoning – $US88 million; (5) demarcation of indigenous lands – $US22 million; (6) forest management – $US19 million; (7) aquatic resources management – $US9 million; (8) rehabilitation of degraded lands – ($US3 million); (9) parks and reserves – $US24 million; and (10) environmental education – $US10 million.

Initial delays in implementation due to the impeachment of President Collor de Mello, as well as bureaucratic and operational complications, were superseded and, by early 1996, the first four sub-components (which together account for three-quarters of total funding) were operational. Sources: World Bank (1995, 1996a, 1996b).

55 The first wave of thirty-seven small projects approved in late 1995 under this component of the Pilot Programme totalled almost $US5 million (World Bank, 1996b).
56 From 4.5 million cubic metres in 1975 to 24.6 million cubic metres in 1987 (Schneider, 1992: 44). Given the extent of illicit logging in Amazonia, it is quite likely that these figures understate the real extent of commercial timber extraction.
57 According to one press report, members of the Guajajara tribe sold 12,000 cubic metres of timber for a sack of rice (Bonner, 1994).
58 See, in particular, Veríssimo *et al.* (1995) for a detailed account of the impacts of mahogany logging in Pará.
59 For further discussion of contextual forces which condition small farmer settlement and production patterns in Amazonia, see Schmink and Wood (1978, 1992) and Collins (1986).
60 For the floodplain or *várzea* agrarian and fishing economies, see Anderson (1990b), McGrath (1993), McGrath *et al.* (1993) and Goulding *et al.* (1996). For sustained small-scale farming and extractivism on terra firma in Amazonia, see Arnt (1994), Anderson *et al.* (1991) and Nugent (1993b). For degraded lands use, see da Silva-Forsberg and Fearnside (1995).
61 According to official census figures, the urban population of the northern region or 'Classic Amazonia', increased from 31% of the total in 1950 to 55% in 1990 (Schneider, 1992: 15). Furthermore, the rate of urban population increase (5.2% p.a. from 1980–90) has been twice that of rural areas (Bogue and Butts, 1989: 51–6). Urban growth rates in Amazonia have outstripped those elsewhere in Brazil. The population of Marabá, in southern Pará, for example, leapt from 10,000 in 1965 to 250,000 in 1990.
62 This figure tallies with a 1987 estimate for the size of the traditional population in Amazonia at 1.5–2 million (Barraclough and Ghimire, 1995: 60).
63 An estimated 2 million people in Amazonia utilise *babaçu* products for their economic survival (Anderson, *et al.* 1991: 9).

64 Under the *Plano Real*, Brazilian NGOs have suffered a loss of spending power due to the combined impact of inflation and an overvalued exchange rate, which has significantly reduced the value of foreign grants. See, 'O miserê das ONGs', *Veja*, 31 May 1995: 93.
65 Farrington and Bebbington (1993).
66 Some of the best-known examples include, for example, the Federation of Organisations for Social and Educational Assistance (FASE), the Centre for Education, Research and Union Advice (CEPASP), the Acre Agroforestry Research and Extension Group (PESACRE) and Saúde e Alegria.
67 See for example: Schneider (1988), (Clark, 1991), Edwards and Hulme (1992, 1995), Carroll (1992), Farrington and Bebbington (1993); Hall (1993a).
68 See Hall (1992, 1994) on the role of NGOs in the case of the Itaparica hydropower scheme in north-east Brazil. See Hall (1991), Redwood (1993) and Millikan (1994) with regard to the POLONOROESTE and PLANAFLORO programmes.
69 It is worth noting with regard to the Kayapó that, in addition to their propensity for collective self-defence, they also have one of the best-documented examples of sustainable indigenous resource management in Amazonia (Posey, 1985, 1989a). Ironically, Kayapó leaders have also become renowned for their commercial dealings over sales of mahogany from reserve areas to logging companies.
70 In 1985, some 200 Kayapó occupied a gold mine near the village of Gorotire in Pará on their tribal territory which had attracted 5,000 prospectors. After taking control of the mine the indians secured overdue fees, negotiated the demarcation of their lands and had the *garimpeiros* removed (Schmink and Wood, 1992). In 1987 in Acre, Kampa, Kulina and Jaminana groups dismantled invading sawmills when the National Indian Foundation (FUNAI) refused to intervene. Aside from these and other individual incidents, Indian and pro-indian groups lobbied the Constituent Assembly to win approval of a law on the granting of prospecting and mineral rights to outsiders on a case-by-case basis.
71 Much of the 2 million acres set aside by the Equadorian government for oil and gas exploration by companies such as Texaco, which arrived in 1964, is on indigenous lands. The Confederation of Indigenous Nations of the Equadorian Amazon (CONFENAIE) was set up in 1980, uniting six ethnic groups to lobby the government for native land rights. The Confederation of Indian Nationalities of Ecuador (CONAIE) was established in 1986 to press for indian rights, and organised a mass occupation of Santo Domingo Cathedral, Quito in 1990. This was followed in May 1993 by a protest march to Quito by 2500 indians against Conoco

and British Gas. Texaco left Ecuador in 1990 after having extracted 1.25 million barrels of oil from 325 wells beneath the rainforest. CONFENAIE and CONAIE have demanded a fifteen-year moratorium on new oil development, while Texaco is the subject of a $US1.5 billion class action lawsuit which, if successful, will oblige the company to clean up the severe pollution it left behind in the forest (Switkes, 1994; Kimerling, 1996).

In Peru, the Coordinating Body for Indigenous People's Organisations of the Amazon Basin (COICA) has assisted and organised local Aguaruna and Huambisa people's resistance movements against penetration by US oil companies in 'Lot 50'. The Interethnic Association for the Development of the Peruvian Amazon (AIDESP), which represents 33 local indian organisations, has prevented Texas Crude Inc. from entering the Pacaya-Samiria national reserve.

In Colombia, indigenous and Afro-Colombian communities in the Atlantic coast Chocó region have mounted a strong campaign to modify current development (read construction and mineral extraction) plans under the 'Plan Pacifico' and channel more benefits towards serving the interests of local communities (Alexander, 1996)

72 A respected activist on indigenous issues within the NGO sector and ex-federal deputy, Santilli gave up his post on 8 March, publicly denouncing the FUNAI 'mafia' and its alleged links with commercial logging interests which, he claimed, were subverting attempts to construct a long-term policy for Indian affairs. See, 'Santilli sai da FUNAI e irrita Jobim', *Jornal do Brasil*, 9 March 1996, and 'Entre a Máfia e o Ministro', *Parabólicas*, 3 (16), March 1996.

73 In May 1996, for example, hundreds of farmers displaced by the dam project a decade and a half previously demonstrated in the town of Tucurui (Report in *Folha de São Paulo*, 28 May 1996).

74 See, 'Olhai as foices dos pobres da terra', *Veja*, 1 June 1995 and 'MST carrega a bandeira da organização, *O Globo*, 19 April 1996.

75 On 17 April 1996, at least 19 people were shot by military police during a demonstration by some 2,000 landless farmers who had been occupying the Fazenda Macaxeira, at Eldorado do Carajás, in the municipality of Curionópolis. The massacre was allegedly planned and financed by local landowners anxious to prevent the MST, which organised the occupation, from supporting further land invasions in the area. The squatters were subsequently resettled on expropriated land elsewhere, a tactic which had been adopted in this volatile region since the mid-1980s through the special government action group GETAT (Hall, 1990, 1991).

Shortly afterwards, in a by now common response pattern, President Cardoso announced the effective reactivation of Brazil's then somewhat dormant official National Agrarian Reform Programme (PNRA). Raul Jungmann, former president of IBAMA was appointed to take charge of the newly created Ministry of Land Policy (Política Agrária), responsible for land reform. It was also announced that 202,000 hectares would be expropriated in twelve states to accommodate 6,000 families (*Folha de São Paulo*, various reports).

3
Extracting a livelihood: the rubber tappers' movement

In the Amazon region, indigenous populations and *caboclos* have long utilised the forest for meeting a range of their basic needs, from food and construction materials to medicines and dyes. While seen as something of an anachronism by some observers, extractivism has, however, demonstrated a remarkable capacity for survival. Extractivism is widely present in Amazonia, from the flooded *várzeas* to the upland terra firma. It has long formed the basis of many people's livelihoods in the region and, nowadays, is combined with other forms of production such as agroforestry, adapting to changing circumstances and evolving ecosystems.[1] In the mid-1990s, in Brazilian Amazonia, as discussed in this chapter, it is estimated that around half (some two million) of the rural population is dependent to some degree upon terrestrial and aquatic extractive activities in order to meet their basic livelihood needs. Although rubber and brazil nuts have enjoyed a politically high profile, altogether some thirty species are actively exploited in the region.[2]

There are two schools of thought regarding the role of extractivism in the regional development of Amazonia: what could be called the 'anti-extractivists' and the 'pro-extractivists'. The first group, epitomised by the work of economist Alfredo Homma (1993, 1994), views development of the extractive economy, including rubber, from a neoclassical perspective. In this conception, all extractive products necessarily follow a unilinear, evolutionary cycle, and the extractive economy is 'doomed to gradual disappearance' (Homma, 1994: 37). Species go through early expansion and stabilisation phases, only to enter into decline due to increased costs of extraction along with a drop in the quantity and quality of the resource, to be replaced by cultivated plantation products and synthetic substitutes. The natural resource base is thus inevitably depleted and former extractivists obliged to migrate to urban centres or convert to agricultural activities. In a similar vein, extractivism has typically been perceived as predatory and backward, '... the most primitive form of subsistence economy', the antithesis of all that is considered 'modern'.[3]

The second, 'pro-extractivist' point of view, questions these evolutionary precepts. From a natural resource economy perspective, it is argued, extractivism performs multiple roles which need to be taken into account within a broader consideration of factors which contribute towards sustainable development. Thus, anthropologist Mary Allegretti (1990, 1994a, 1994b, 1995) highlights the contribution of extractivism to the preservation of biological resources, their diversity and genetic stock, as well as the provision of environmental services in ecosystem regulation. Furthermore, the role of extractivists in protecting and overseeing the forest is of growing significance. In terms of social sustainability, as mentioned above, large segments of the rural population in Amazonia (and elsewhere) depend upon extractivism for their livelihoods, in terms of generating subsistence and commercial products as well as employment.[4] Indeed, she goes so far as to say that 'the social significance of this economy is greater than its economic significance, to the degree that a large part of production is for subsistence' (Allegretti, 1994b: 22).

Despite its importance in ecological and social terms, extractivism has been relatively neglected in regional development policy. Financial incentives have been biased overwhelmingly in favour of environmentally destructive and largely unproductive activities such as cattle-ranching and land speculation. The concept of the 'extractive reserve' is the first major initiative which begins to correct this historical bias. For the first time, the importance of extractivism is being officially recognised and a concerted effort made to protect designated areas against deforestation, while allowing local populations to utilise the natural resource base in a sustainable manner. It epitomises the notion of productive conservation in its attempt to reconcile the preservation of natural assets with the strengthening of people's livelihoods.

The extractive reserve is of crucial importance to the sustainable development of Amazonia for several reasons. Firstly, it is the only productive conservation initiative (as defined above) to be have been formalised under Brazilian federal law, setting a precedent for comparable endeavours in other sub-ecosystems of the region and beyond. Secondly, by virtue of the sheer geographical area covered by official extractive reserve projects at state and federal levels in Brazil (over three million hectares) as well as the size of rainforest population directly involved (some 50,000), no other exercise in marrying natural resource conservation with productive activities comes even close to having such potential regional impacts. If successful, the extractive reserve concept could have a wider relevance for addressing deforestation problems in other parts of the developing world.

The rubber tappers' struggles

Boom and bust

Extractive reserves are the product of over two decades of organised resistance since the 1970s, largely by the rubber tappers of southern Acre in western Amazonia, to the predatory incursions of commercial cattle-ranchers and land speculators. Assisted by generous government financial inducements, these large investors were primarily responsible for rainforest destruction and land conflict, as the frontier moved northwards from Mato Grosso with the extension and paving of the BR364 highway from Cuiabá to Porto Velho and Rio Branco. Before examining the genesis and current situation of the 'movement' in Brazil, however, the origins and social structure of Brazil's rubber economy in the western Amazon region over the past century must be understood.[5]

Although latex from the rubber tree (*Hevea brasiliensis*) had for centuries been employed by indigenous groups in Amazonia for waterproofing, industrial demand became significant only after the discovery of the vulcanisation process in 1839 by Charles Goodyear and the invention of the pneumatic tyre in 1888 for the booming bicycle and automobile industry. The Amazon was opened to international shipping in 1866 and the rush for land was accompanied by rapid penetration of Amazon headwaters, where better quality rubber was to be found along tributaries such as the Madeira, Purus, Jutaí and Juruá. This extended as far as Acre, scene of the modern rubber tappers' struggle, which was annexed from Bolivia in 1903; by 1899, at the height of the rubber boom, Acre supplied 60 per cent of Amazonian rubber. In order to overcome labour shortages, which acted as a bottleneck on rubber production, refugees from orth-eastern droughts during the 1870s and 1880s were brought in by traders, and the traditional rubber estate (*seringal*) was created. Amerindians who were not forcibly incorporated into the estate structure were either exterminated or retreated further into the forest.

Brazil's rubber boom generated great wealth, creating large personal fortunes for a few, and turned Manaus from a remote outpost into one of the most modern cities in South America, with facilities such as piped water and sewage systems, electric trams and street lighting, as well as magnificent private mansions and public buildings, including the opera house. British financial and commercial institutions controlled rubber exports and imports of sought-after consumer goods from Europe, transported by the Booth line's weekly sailings from Liverpool to Belém and Manaus. Wealthy rubber 'barons' controlled a vast network of traders who, in their turn, financed the rubber-estate-owners (*seringalistas*). The rubber tappers themselves (*seringueiros*) were kept firmly in their place by a savage system of debt bondage (*aviamento*), which rendered them virtual slaves.

When it came, the collapse of Brazil's rubber boom was swift. Henry (later Sir Henry) Wickham, a British plantation-owner, helped transport 70,000 seeds from Santarém to Kew Gardens. Although less than 4 per cent eventually germinated, 'the Wickham selection provided the overwhelming genetic stock for the spread of cultivation in the British colonies' (Dean, 1987: 27). Increased production from efficient plantations in Malaya and elsewhere after 1910 led to a large fall in the world price of rubber, the collapse of Brazil's export markets and economic decay in Amazonia. 'Buildings were deserted, elaborate mansions were left vacant, parks and avenues were abandoned, and grass again grew in many streets' (Melby, 1942: 459).

However, the estates continued production to meet internal demand and there were several attempts to revitalise the industry. The most sustained of these came during World War II when the Allies lost control of Malaya and, after the Washington Accords of 1942 between Brazil and the USA, President Vargas launched the 'Battle for Rubber', providing financial incentives and encouraging further migration of north-easterners, who became known as soldiers of the rubber industry (*soldados da borracha*). The father of Francisco 'Chico' Mendes was such a pioneer rubber tapper.

For large rural populations in the western states of Acre and Rondônia, as well as in Amapá at the estuary of the Amazon, rubber tapping remains a mainstay of their livelihoods, although the system has undergone basic changes in the post-war period (Bakx, 1990). Before then, the rubber tapper was closely tied to the estate through debt peonage and coercion. Prohibited from cultivating subsistence crops, the *seringueiro* was obliged to pay the estate-owner's price for goods and accept his price for rubber. In the 1960s, many bosses began to engage in more lucrative, urban-based commercial activities, loosening ties with the rubber tappers, breaking the debt cycle and allowing them more freedom to grow crops and sell their labour outside. Production is now more diversified to include activities such as the production of rice and manioc, brazil-nut collecting and off-farm work.

Despite these transformations in the role of the *seringueiro*, however, most tappers in Amazonia are still dependent on a more benign version of the *aviamento* system. Physical isolation and poor communications mean that, over vast rubber-producing areas, itinerant merchants or *marreteiros* hold a virtual monopoly on the purchase of latex and on the supply of essential consumer goods. It is this vicious circle of dependency, as well as the growing threat of deforestation at the hands of commercial loggers and cattle ranchers, which the extractive reserve is meant to challenge.

The system of wild-rubber-gathering employed in Amazonia has remained relatively unchanged, determined by the fact that, in its natural state, *Hevea brasiliensis* is scattered widely in the forest, usually two or three trees per hectare. The basic household unit (*colocação*) is situated in the forest, either on terra firma or near the river's edge. From here, the tapper will clear up to four trails (*estradas de seringa*), each with up to 200 trees and covering about 100 hectares, spreading out from the house and looping back. One circuit of each trail is made on alternate days to cut the tree and attach a cup to catch latex, while a second round is made to collect the latex. The liquid is then coagulated either by pouring it on to a wooden spit over wood smoke or adding acetic acid and pressing the latex into blocks. Men are responsible for up to 90 per cent of this work. The gathering season usually lasts six months, when rainfall is relatively low and trails passable. These fairly primitive techniques often damage the tree or exhaust it quickly, while the final product is frequently full of impurities. Despite the improvements in rubber quality shown to be attainable from plantations, attempts to cultivate *Hevea* in Amazonia have failed.[6]

Rubber collection is still important, but falling latex prices since the 1980s have led tappers to diversify their economic activities into the areas of brazil-nut gathering, agriculture and some livestock production.[7] Studies have suggested that this diversification has boosted producers' net incomes and that extractive activities compare favourably with, for example, frequently precarious small-scale settler farming.[8] Be that as it may, however, living standards remain generally low and malnutrition is common due to a starch-heavy, unbalanced diet which shows little of the variety typical of the Amerindian's consumption of food. Illiteracy is prevalent and there is a high incidence of communicable diseases such as malaria and leishmaniasis. Under the traditional estate system, provision of health-care and primary education facilities for the rubber-tapping community by their bosses was almost non-existent. Only since the 1980s, thanks to some NGO and local government investment, has the situation started to improve, although formidable problems remain.

Early battles and victories

From the early 1970s, Rondônia and Acre became the scene of intensive, escalating land conflicts as cattle-ranchers and land speculators from the south sought to occupy vast tracts with the aid of official subsidies through SUDAM and BASA. In addition to the clashes among large landowners, small settler farmers and indigenous groups, the *caboclo* population of rubber tappers saw their traditional extractive economy being undermined, as deforestation increased rapidly to make way for pasture and speculative land sales at a time when property prices in the region literally took off.[9] The position of traditional rubber-estate-owners, weakened by a deliberate official policy of withholding credit in favour of the newer and more 'modern' (as well as more profitable) corporatist ranching enterprises, had become even more precarious. Some initially abandoned their domains and their former workers, leaving tappers to fend for themselves. During the early 1970s, however, attracted by the huge rise in land values, many estate-owners returned and tried to wrest control from the tappers in order to sell off large areas to southern *paulistas* or convert them to pasture.

For the first time, *seringueiros* came into open conflict with their traditional bosses as well as with the newer class of ranching entrepreneurs. These clashes were strongest in the most densely populated rubber-producing area of southern Acre, around Xapurí and Brasiléia. Situated close to the federal highways, with easy access for newcomers, settlement commenced in the early 1970s. Further north in Acre, in the rubber zone of the Rivers Juruá, Moa, Liberdade and Gregório, due to its isolation and impassable roads for ten months of the year, the ranching front has barely arrived. The conflicts typical of southern Acre are, therefore, almost unknown here and rubber tapping continues to be based on traditional relationships of debt bondage.

In southern Acre, increasingly violent conflicts drove many tappers and their families from the region, either to the rubber estates of Bolivia's Pando province, or to the urban shanty towns of Rio Branco, Xapurí and Brasiléia, whose populations and social problems rocketed.[10] INCRA's programme of land titling, set up in 1972 to provide deeds to those classed as squatters, had little impact in terms of stabilising the rural population or promoting sedentary, sustainable production systems. Neither did its policy of expropriation to defuse tensions in areas of land conflict, or the setting up of directed colonisation projects (PADs). Faced with official complacency and inefficiency, many tappers decided to make a stand themselves against the land grabbers or *grileiros*.

It was during this period of the mid-1970s that the *empate* or stand-off became widely and quite successfully used against encroaching cattle-ranchers and loggers. The first *empate* took place in Brasiléia on the Seringal Carmen and, by 1988, some forty-five had been organised (Gross, 1989; Arnt, 1994). In one of the most famous of such incidents in 1979 near the town of Boca do Acre, 300 rubber tappers drove out a large group of hired gunmen. The *empate* has been regularly employed since then, and is still an effective tool against deforestation.[11]

Attempts were made during the 1960s to organise rubber tappers politically, but these were frustrated by the 1964 military coup and subsequent repression. The first rural union in Acre was founded by CONTAG, the Confederation of Rural Workers' Unions, in the municipality of Brasiléia in 1975, and in Xapurí shortly afterwards. Over the next few years, they were transformed by leaders such as Chico Mendes and Wilson Pinheiro (the latter having pioneered and perfected the *empate* technique) from conservative, welfare-distribution agencies to radical organisations committed to fighting for tappers' rights.[12] A cruel indication of their effectiveness in the struggle to protect rubber tappers' livelihoods is that both leaders were murdered on the orders of local estate-owners *(fazendeiros)*. Such local landowners claimed large areas defended by the *seringueiros*, but were becoming increasingly frustrated by the effectiveness of *empates* in halting deforestation.

Following the death of Wilson Pinheiro in 1980, the resistance movement in Brasiléia experienced a downturn and Xapurí took the lead in strengthening grassroots organisation amongst the rubber tappers. In 1980 Chico Mendes, assisted by Mary Allegretti[13] and others, drew up a project for schools and rubber producer cooperatives, the *Projeto Seringueiro*, which was funded by Oxfam-UK. Allegretti and a team of community educators from the Ecumenical Centre for Documentation and Information (CEDI) designed a textbook and a methodology based on Freirian principles. Several primary schools and two small rubber tappers' producer cooperatives were set up, which later acquired federal and state government support. Political events in Brazil were unfolding rapidly and, in March 1985, the military handed over to a civilian administration. In May 1985, during the fourth National Congress of Brazilian Rural Workers, the new President of Brazil, José Sarney, announced the National Agrarian Reform Plan (Brazil, 1985). Ostensibly, the objective was to eradicate inefficient and unproductive minifundia and latifundia and encourage the spread of capitalist rural enterprises. However realistic or otherwise this may have been (Hall, 1990), its effect on the rubber tappers was to strengthen their resolve to protect further their own traditional extractive activities.

Organisational efforts now moved for the first time from the local and regional to the national level. For Brazil's policy-makers, the rubber tappers remained 'invisible' and their needs were not being addressed by the agrarian reform proposals. With the assistance of Mary Allegretti and INESC, the first National Meeting of Rubber Tappers was held at the University of Brasilia in October 1985.[14] It was decided to set up the National Council of Rubber Tappers (CNS) to lobby the government for policy reform to protect rubber tappers' land rights and set up development programmes. Soon afterwards, a working group was established to develop the idea of 'Extractive Reserves – the Rubber Tappers' Agrarian Reform', which had arisen in embryonic form during earlier discussions about indian reserves and the need for special provisions to be made for rubber tappers under the agrarian reform plans. The rubber tappers' movement, now seen as a crucial defender of the environment in Amazonia, was receiving intensive media coverage, both in the more democratic climate of Brazil as well as in the United States and Europe.

Simultaneously in the USA, Brazil's official Amazon settlement policies had come under intensive scrutiny by the environmental lobby during its campaign against the World Bank-funded northwest regional development programme (POLONOROESTE). Most of the World Bank's (International Bank for Reconstruction and Development – IBRD) original $US430 million was earmarked for paving the BR364 highway to Porto Velho, while a further Inter-American Development Bank (IDB) loan of $US58 million would extend the asphalt to Rio Branco, Acre's capital and gateway to the rubber estates. Strong NGO lobbying of the Senate Appropriations Subcommittee on Foreign Operations resulted in temporary suspension of remaining bank loan disbursements (over $US250 million) to POLONOROESTE in March 1985, and a reformulation of both IBRD and IDB projects to include environmental safeguards, although their effectiveness has since been seriously questioned (Rich, 1994).[15] During 1987, Chico Mendes made three trips to the USA, to protest to the IDB and lobby US Congress members about the potential social and ecological dangers of paving the BR364 from Porto Velho to Rio Branco. These visits, and the media coverage which accompanied them both in the USA and Brazil, did much to raise the international profile of the rubber tappers and focus world attention on the problem of uncontrolled deforestation in the Amazon.[16] In January 1988, the IDB temporarily suspended loan disbursements for the Porto Velho–Rio Branco stretch of the BR364, although the paved highway was completed to Acre's capital in 1992 and an extension of the asphalt across the Andes is under consideration.[17] In 1987, Amazon burnings had reached a peak, with 350,000 fires detected, and the loss of 48,000 square miles of virgin rainforest, attracting international condemnation.[18]

Matters in southern Acre came to a head in late 1987 when 14,000 hectares of the 60,000 hectare Seringal Cachoeira rubber estate near Xapurí was sold by its owners, frustrated at being prevented from deforesting ('developing') the land. The buyer, Darly Alves da Silva, a rancher from the south of Brazil with a long criminal record, was wanted for murder in his home state of Minas Gerais. Tappers on the estate successfully mounted an *empate* against deforestation and eviction of the population. To avoid further conflicts, INCRA expropriated the land in April 1987 and compensated the owner. During the ensuing months, tensions in Xapurí intensified and several confrontations took place between local landowners, rubber tappers and forestry officials, including an unsuccessful *empate* at the Seringal Ecuador. The Farmers' Democratic Movement (UDR) landowners' lobby group opened an office in Xapurí, while hired gunmen conducted a brazen campaign of intense intimidation against rubber tappers and their families. Two children were injured by shots fired indiscriminately into a demonstrating crowd, while in June a rural union director, Higino de Almeida, was ambushed and killed.

The national protests which these acts of aggression generated caused the federal government to intervene and expropriate four estates, including Cachoeira and São Luis do Remanso, to form the first Extractive Settlement Projects (PAE). These were provided for in 1987 under the aegis of existing agrarian reform (PNRA) legislation, following the recommendations of a working group which had been set up that March and included advisers from the CNS and the IEA. By the end of 1989, ten PAEs had been set up, totalling almost 900,000 hectares and benefiting nearly 3,000 families (see Table 3.1). The conventional INCRA settlement model of sub-dividing the land into regular-sized plots and distributing ownership titles was rejected as inappropriate to the rubber tappers' situation. Instead, the two key notions of 'collective land-use' and 'issuing of usufruct rights' rather than individualised land titles were introduced into the contracts.[19]

The PAE represented only a partial solution to the rubber tappers' problems, however, for they were set up in response to crisis land conflict situations rather than as part of a planned, rational land-use strategy. There were also serious problems with the PAE concept as a lasting solution for extractivists (Allegretti, 1994a). Firstly, it was based on an internal INCRA regulation and could easily be annulled by any future president of that institution. Secondly, the agrarian reform movement had lost much of its political momentum under President Sarney. Thirdly, there were enormous problems in securing the timely expropriation of lands set aside for PAEs. This situation was to change dramatically with the new Brazilian constitution of 1988 and the environmental legislation which followed. On 30 June, the Agro-Extractivist Cooperative of Xapurí (CAEX) was inaugurated, with technical assistance from the IEA and funding from several foreign NGOs.

Table 3.1 *Extractive Resettlement Projects (PAEs) in Brazilian Amazonia*

State	Projects	Area (ha)	Families
Acre	Porto Dias	22,145	83
	Riozinho	35,896	120
	Cachoeira	24,973	80
	Sta.Quitéria	44,000	150
	S.L.do Remanso	39,572	130
	Sub-total	*166,586*	*563*
Amapá	Maracá I	75,000	214
	Maracá II	22,500	94
	Maracá III	226,000	760
	Sub-total	*323,500*	*1,068*
Amazonas	Antimary	260,227	867
	Terruã	139,235	426
	Sub-total	*399,462*	*1,239*
	Total	**889,548**	**2,924**

Source: Menzes (1994: 69).

In spite of these promising advances, the tension in Acre showed no signs of abating and threats against the life of Chico Mendes continued. At his own forty-fourth birthday party, exactly a week before he was murdered, Mendes stoically predicted, 'I don't think I'm going to live until Christmas' (Revkin, 1990: 273). On 22 December 1988, he was shot dead by Darci Alves, son of the union leader's long-standing enemy Darly.[20] Chico Mendes was the ninetieth rural activist to have been murdered in Brazil that year. The previous eighty-nine produced little impact, but his death provoked a massive local, national and global reaction which had lasting repercussions. Over 4,000 people accompanied the funeral cortège in Rio Branco on Christmas Day, while the world news media reverberated with headlines and leading articles examining the events surrounding the murder. In the months that followed, Xapurí itself became a Mecca for visiting journalists and environmentalists.

The murder of Chico Mendes occurred just after the ratification of Brazil's new constitution (Brazil, 1988). The global publicity which his death attracted served to strengthen the growing momentum for changes in Brazil's environmental policies. The constitution mentions the need to set aside protected areas and reserves,[21] and the concept was formally instituted a year later within the framework of the PNMA as one category of direct use 'conservation unit'.[22]

In January 1990, responsibility for administering extractive reserves was passed over to the PNMA under the recently created IBAMA, which set up a working group with INCRA, the CNS and IEA to draw up specific proposals for a decree dealing exclusively with extractive reserves. On 30 January 1990, and following the guidelines set by the working group, President Sarney signed Decree 98,897 which formalises the entirely new concept in Brazil of the '*Reserva Extrativista*' and defines its distinctive attributes in reconciling conservation with natural resource-use on a sustainable basis for specific extractivist groups in designated areas, under the overall supervision of IBAMA.[23]

This represented a major step forward for extractivists, securing a specific policy designed to meet their needs and which recognises the common property element of most extractivist production in Amazonia, including that of rubber tappers, nut-gatherers and others. In order to speed up the implementation process, and in contrast with the PAEs (which co-exist with the new reserves) under INCRA's domain, prior expropriation of lands set aside for extractive reserves was deemed to be unnecessary. In January 1990, President Sarney decreed the first proper reserve in the Juruá valley of Acre, followed in March by three more: the Chico Mendes reserve, also in Acre; Rio Cajarí in Amapá; and Rio Ouro Preto in Rondônia. Several other much smaller extractive reserves, outside of the rubber producing zone, were decreed in 1992 (see Table 3.2). In February of that year, the National Centre for the Sustainable Development of Traditional Populations (CNPT) was set up within IBAMA to provide support and technical assistance.

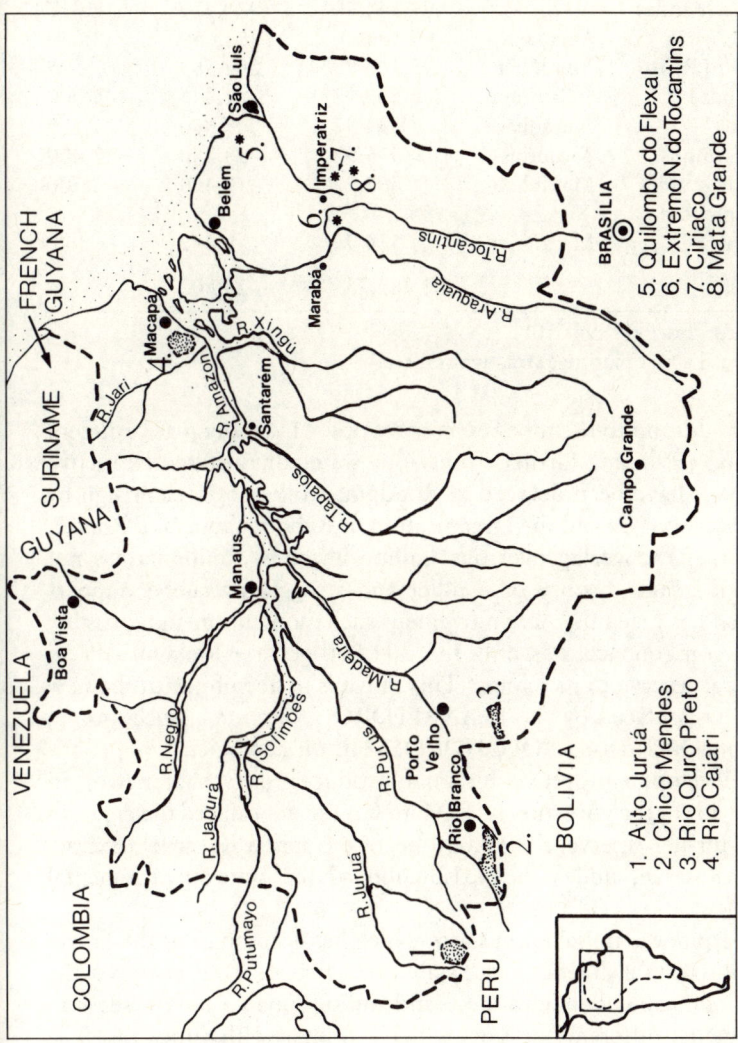

Figure 3.1 *Federal extractive reserves in Brazilian Amazonia*

Table 3.2 *Federal extractive reserves in Brazilian Amazonia*

Name	State	Decree	Area (ha)	Pop.
Alto Juruá	Acre	98,863/90	506,186	5,821
Chico Mendes	Acre	99,144/90	970,570	12,017
Rio Cajarí	Amapá	99,145/90	481,650	3,639
R.Ouro Preto	Rondônia	99,166/90	204,583	775
Pirajudaé *	S.Catarina	533/92	1,444	1,000
Ciríaco	Maranhão	534/92	7,050	1,150
N.Tocantins	Tocantins	535/92	98,280	2,000
Mata Grande	Maranhão	532/92	10,450	1,500
Quilombo do Flexal	Maranhão	536/92	9,542	900
Total			2,289,755	28,802

Source: Brazil (1994: 10).
* Brazil's first marine extractive reserve.

In addition to the nine reserves set up by the federal government during 1990–2, a further twenty-one state-administered extractive reserves have been decreed in Rondônia, following a campaign by the local NGOs and the Organisation of Rubber Tappers of Rondônia (OSR), covering over one million hectares. Rondônia has not had the same history of conflict and struggle by rubber tappers which has given the Acre movement such momentum and, possibly as a consequence, has only the 204,000-hectare Rio Ouro Preto federal reserve to its name.[24] This move is in keeping with the new emphasis placed by the PLANAFLORO programme, successor to the much-criticised POLONOROESTE, on ecologically appropriate development options for small producers (see chapter two). In June 1996, the government of Mato Grosso announced the creation of a further reserve, the 59,000-hectare Guariba Roosevelt Extractive Reserve, under the jurisdiction of the state environmental agency.

Despite the initial enthusiasm which has accompanied the movement to establish federal and state extractive reserves, however, the task of turning them into successful and sustainable enterprises is an altogether different question, which is fraught with difficulties. The concept of extractive reserves epitomises the principle of productive conservation. However, the challenge of generating economic self-sufficiency along with the socio-political unity which is essential for the efficient governance of individual and common property resources within such protected areas is a major challenge which participants are now having to address.

There are three major stages in the process of successfully operationalising the extractive reserve concept: formal request, implementation and consolidation:-

Formal request   The starting point is the presentation of a formal request from traditional extractivists in a given area, which has been duly signed by representative and advisory organisations.[25] This must provide the basic information relating to the topography of the area and to geographical boundaries, history, the land tenure situation as well as to the socio-economic and demographic profile. This basic information (*Memorial Descritivo*) must be accompanied by a clear set of arguments (*Exposição de Motivos*) justifying the request. Once CNPT/IBAMA is satisfied, a recommendation is made to the President of the Republic and the reserve is created by presidential decree.

Implementation   After the initial request has been analysed and agreed to, IBAMA must study the land title situation and either expropriate or agree to let owners stay within the boundaries of the new reserve as long as their activities are compatible with those of the extractivists. When this process is complete, compensation has been paid and the area transferred to IBAMA's jurisdiction, a contract determining usufruct rights (*Concessão de Direito Real de Uso*)[26] is signed between IBAMA and the respective, officially registered Association for a period of at least sixty years. This contract must contain an overall resource-management plan (*Plano de Utilização*) for the reserve, which has to be approved by IBAMA, detailing proposed extractive, agropastoral and agro-forestry activities. Sale or transfer of usufruct rights to outsiders is expressly prohibited; they may only be passed on through inheritance. Within 180 days of this contract being signed, the CNS must submit to IBAMA a population census of the reserve, and, based upon this, either the CNS or the association in question will issue authorisations to individual extractivists (*Títulos de Autorização de Uso*).

Consolidation and development   The official setting up of a reserve and the granting of usufruct rights according to an authorised use plan are, however, only the first steps towards operationalising the new concept. They are necessary but, in themselves, they do nothing to change existing relationships within the extractive economy, which have tended to generate conditions of poverty, deprivation and dependency for the majority. In order to make them a viable concern, substantial investments are needed in the social and economic infrastructure which will diversify and strengthen its productive base, while providing basic services to the population.

During the early 1980s, as the rubber tappers' movement gained momentum and wider recognition, funding for small-scale production, health and education projects came principally from overseas NGOs such as Oxfam-UK, either directly or via Brazilian organisations such as the IEA. Following the establishment of the CNS in 1985 and the subsequent formalisation of the concept, the list of NGOs and of bilateral and multilateral agencies offering assistance has grown considerably to include major bodies such as the Ford Foundation, the MacArthur Foundation, the Canadian International Development Agency (CIDA), the Environmental Defense Fund, the Gaia Foundation, Cultural Survival, Health Unlimited, etc. In addition, many Brazilian institutions such as Campinas University in São Paulo, state planning secretariats and the National Bank of Economic and Social Development (BNDES) have become closely involved in helping to support reserves.

The largest and most significant source of funds for extractive reserves has been the G7 Pilot Programme to Conserve the Brazilian Rainforest, details of which are outlined in chapter two. This $US250 million initiative was announced at the Houston meeting of the G7 in July 1990. Administered by the World Bank, it comprises a central fund (the RTF) of some $US60 million plus co-financing pledges from bilateral donors earmarked for specific sub-components. Under the programme, over $US9 million has been set aside for developing the four largest extractive reserves in Amazonia (Chico Mendes, Alto Juruá, Rio Ouro Preto and Cajarí). These funds (from the RTF, the EU and the Brazilian government) are intended to assist IBAMA during the three major development stages of the reserves: basic socio-economic and biodiversity studies, as well as demarcation work; strengthening of basic infrastructure in the fields of production, transport, health and education; and improving the management capacity of associations and cooperatives responsible for running the reserves.

Managing extractive reserves
The organised struggles of Brazil's rubber tappers in western Amazonia since the early 1970s and their key role in the creation of extractive reserves represents the largest and best-known collective effort to address socio-environmental issues in the region. However, although progress along the road to a more promising future for extractivist populations in Amazonia has been notable, the extractive reserve concept, while highly appealing in theory, remains largely untested in practice. Its economic, political, social and ecological sustainability over the longer term have yet to be demonstrated,

Until now, the gathering of rubber and brazil nuts in Amazonia has been based on traditional forms of production and marketing whose origins can be traced back to the rubber estate and *aviamento* system. Extraction of forest products is through household production. Communities are linked through kinship ties, but are isolated. Any sense of collective solidarity is further undermined by vertical relationships with itinerant traders and merchants, who have gradually replaced traditional rubber-estate-owners as the major outlet for rubber and source of basic household goods. Except for the temporary mobilisation of men, women and children during sporadic *empates* to deal with crisis situations such as the threat of land-grabbing by outsiders, therefore, there has been almost no effort by extractive populations themselves to manage the natural resource base for their collective benefit.

The major challenge for extractive reserves during the 1990s is to install management systems which can ensure their sustainability as productive conservation units. For this to occur, several prerequisites must be met.

Economic viability   The issue of economic self-sufficiency is fundamental. It is not currently known whether extractive reserves will be able to undertake the production, processing and marketing of forest products efficiently enough to generate an adequate economic surplus. This is essential in order to provide not only for the livelihood needs of households in which extractive activities are an important component, but also for the reserves eventually to become largely independent of external support such as the G7 Pilot Programme.

Conservation The question of natural resource protection is equally vital: can monitoring and surveillance mechanisms be instituted, which will permit the effective defense and conservation of fragile rainforest ecosystems by their inhabitants against hostile outside forces such as commercial loggers and land-grabbers?

Collective action To a large extent underpinning the above issues of economic viability and resource conservation is the broader challenge of fashioning from these highly individualistic systems a degree of socio-political solidarity. It is suggested here that, in order both to strengthen the likelihood of achieving economic sustainability, as well as for the purpose of protecting common property resources, the formation of an active 'movement' is not only desirable but essential.

As highlighted in chapter one, such a productive conservation strategy or movement will depend for its formation and continued existence on two sets of factors: firstly, instrumental calculations by participants of net economic benefits and costs accruing from particular strategies, as well as, secondly, less tangible factors arising from shared experiences and community solidarity which may develop, for example, in response to external threats to the natural resource base which underpins people's livelihoods and socio-cultural identity. It is therefore pertinent to ask whether the rubber tappers' movement, as it is so often referred to, can be legitimately described in these terms. In order to answer this question, a good starting point is to repeat the definition of a social movement offered by Scott (1990: 6) as, 'a collective social actor constituted by individuals who understand themselves to have common interests and, for at least some significant part of their social existence, a common identity'. Although a succinct definition, which is also appropriate for conservation movements, it still begs the question of how much and what type of collective action, common interests and identity are required for the label 'movement' to apply.

Until the 1970s, the rubber tappers of Amazonia had not been politically organised in any sense. Isolated on their traditional estates and bound to landowners or merchants by long-standing ties of debt bondage and patron clientage, *seringueiros* had little opportunity to question the system or seek changes to improve their livelihoods. Over much of the region, this situation still predominates, even in areas already decreed as extractive reserves but where estate-owners have not been expropriated, and/or where the merchant (*marreteiro*) may still exert a strong influence through trading and personal relationships. As already mentioned, this situation started to change dramatically in southern Acre during the 1970s and early 1980s, as rural trade unions were set up in Brasiléia and Xapurí, and dynamic leaders such as Wilson Pinheiro and Chico Mendes introduced the *empate*.

The setting up of the CNS, which arose from the first Rubber Tappers' Congress in 1985, followed on closely from these early struggles in western Amazonia. The CNS was born from the struggles of rubber tappers and brazil-nut gatherers in the western states of Acre and Rondônia, but has, since then, broadened its mandate to include other extractive groups in the eastern states of Pará, Tocantins, Maranhão and Amapá. Four of the eight reserves decreed in the northern region of Brazil, while covering a relatively small area, are situated in eastern Amazonia (see Table 3.2 above). The rubber tappers' cause is now officially viewed by the CNS as merely one component in the general move to extend the concept 'as part of the struggle for agrarian reform in Brazil, which originally arose as a solution for land conflicts in the River Acre valley ... [but which] ... from the beginning, took account of the diversity of land use practised by the peoples of Amazonia'.

The CNS now claims to represent the interests of all practitioners of extractivism in the Amazon region, in its role as general defender of the forest and promoter of extractive reserves, as the basis of a 'a new development model for Amazonia' (CNS, n.d.: 3–5). However, there are serious grounds for doubting the extent to which the extractivists' struggle can be considered an authentic 'movement', as defined above. Serious questions may be raised on the grounds of fragmented organisation and purpose as well as possibly unrepresentative leadership.

Despite any superficial appearance of uniformity when viewed from outside, Amazon rubber tappers emanate from a large, geographically and culturally diverse area, with contrasting local conditions and political histories. Even within western Amazonia itself, birthplace of the extractive reserve, it is possible to observe contrasting attitudes towards the setting up of reserves and the nature of people's involvement in carrying forward this process. The reserves of Chico Mendes in Acre and Ouro Preto in Rondônia illustrate this divergence.

The Chico Mendes reserve can be said to enjoy a substantial grassroots involvement; in terms of the 'coverage' of community participation (using the categories outlined in chapter one above), it has a high aggregate participation ratio (APR). While the differential participation ratio (DPR) varies by gender and geographical distribution in particular, as discussed further below, its high APR reflects the fact that the Chico Mendes reserve has been at the leading edge of the rubber tappers' struggles since the 1970s, and arose as the result of confrontations with land-grabbers and the resulting political campaigns which brought about policy innovation. Brasiléia and Xapurí, which cover most of the Chico Mendes reserve, were the first rural unions to be set up in western Amazonia, in 1975 and 1977 respectively. They were born of the early struggles and *empates* and this is reflected in the relatively high level of union membership within the reserve enjoyed by these two organisations, which have had active and committed leaders, not least of all Wilson Pinheiro and Chico Mendes themselves (Brazil, 1994).[27]

This strategy included a broadening of the scope of local participation in the movement via alliances with lobby groups such as INESC and the IEA in Brazil, and influential NGOs in the USA and Europe. Further weight was given to the Acre tappers' campaign by the fact that the CNS chose to set up its headquarters in the nearby capital, Rio Branco, where it had direct links with the reserve's unions until 1992, when a state-level council branch was established, also based in Rio Branco.[28] With regard to the 'intensity' of participation, therefore, the Chico Mendes area forest-dwellers have always been highly proactive, taking the initiative in defending their territory by barring entry to ranchers and speculators, while helping to police the reserve and demarcate the boundaries of this vast area of almost one million hectares.

Other extractive areas, from different biological, geographical and socio-political contexts, are not characterised by the same degree of collective involvement. The Juruá reserve, for example, (the first to be officially decreed) in northern Acre, is not served by a tarmac road and land access is cut for much of the year (Whitsell, 1994; Almeida and Menezes, 1994). Social relations of production here are more heavily conditioned by vestiges of the traditional *aviamento* system. It has proved extremely difficult for the newly formed reserve association (ASAREAJ) to recruit an active membership with a view to implementing a resource conservation plan. However, this has also been attributed to an incomplete communications strategy on the part of the leadership, which marginalised many less accessible areas.

The Rio Ouro Preto reserve in Rondônia also fits this mould and contrasts with the Chico Mendes situation. Located near the border with Bolivia, away from the ranching frontier on lands which are partially submerged for six months of the year during the wet season (November to May), Ouro Preto has not had the same history of violent confrontation typical of southern Acre. Chico Mendes visited the region in October 1988, two months before his murder, to help organise the first meeting of local rubber tappers at Guajará-Mirim, which eventually took place in February 1989. Before then, however, there had been no history of political organisation amongst *seringueiros* there, who lived under the traditional estate system, although by then absentee landowners were merely renting out *colocações* to individual families and ceding control over production to the tappers, at a price.[29] Although the meeting was well attended and gave rise to a long list of grievances,[30] there is some doubt as to how much real pressure was exerted by the grassroots movement and to what extent the state government seized the initiative for its own political ends.

The state government of Rondônia was anxious to placate the World Bank after the POLONOROESTE fiasco and accelerating deforestation of the 1980s, to rebuild its image and obtain new loans under the PLANAFLORO scheme. As part of the PLANAFLORO zoning exercise, the state was divided into six areas and Zone IV, which includes Ouro Preto, was designated for extractive activities. In 1989–90, the Rondônia State Forest Institute (IEF) bypassed both tappers' organisations and NGOs, and set aside over 204,000 hectares for the Rio Ouro Preto reserve, which was officially decreed in March 1990, without the direct involvement of either the CNS or the local population (Wawzyniak, 1994). The Guajará-Mirim Rubber Tappers' Association (ASGM) was set up only in March 1991, with technical assistance and funding for health and education infrastructure investments from a range of Brazilian NGOs such as the IEA, ECOPORE and INDIA, and overseas agencies including Misereor, WWF and Oxfam, as well as state and municipal governments.

Although the setting up of the extractive reserve on state initiative coincided with rubber tappers' interests, it could be labelled an exercise in 'passive' local participation since, in the first instance at least, the population affected had little or no say in how the process was conducted. This involvement may become more proactive at the later implementation stages when capacity-building and policing roles become more pronounced. For example, the OSR, set up in 1991 independently of the CNS, has been putting pressure on ITERON to involve reserve inhabitants in the boundary demarcation process at Rio Ouro Preto.

The strong influence of continuing traditional social and commercial links with merchants and estate-owners at Ouro Preto has resulted in lower levels of participation in the ASGM compared with the Chico Mendes reserve. The association started in 1991 with 40 members, but three years later had only 85 of a population of about 125 families. While the APR superficially seems quite healthy, however, only a small part of the membership is paid up and the ASGM has insufficient working capital, on top of which suggestions of maladministration have been made.[31] This has created something of a vicious circle, which means that one-third or more of rubber production is sold privately to local merchants, denying profits to the association, which remains in debt to local commercial lenders despite the injection of outside funds.

The above examples show that areas in Amazonia embraced by the extractive reserve differ greatly in their cultural and political histories, and this has led to contrasting forms of internal organisation, including styles and levels of grassroots participation by rubber tappers in this process. Diversity may be a source of strength, to the extent that locale-specific solutions are developed to deal with the problem of reconciling production and conservation activities. However, there is a danger that such divergence may generate political rifts within the reserve movement amongst regions which undermine its broader ability to forge a common purpose, secure policy change and capture the necessary resources to sustain a long-term strategy for Amazonia. This said, however, another potential source of conflict which threatens to undermine the influence enjoyed by the rubber tappers since the late 1980s lies in the role of the CNS as their political representative.

The CNS was set up in 1985 to support rubber tappers all over Amazonia in their desire for protected areas and for other policy changes to strengthen their livelihoods as extractivists. Such a support role has to some extent been undermined by two related factors: the expansion of its remit to include non-rubber tappers, and internal political divisions. By the time of the third Rubber Tappers' Congress, held in Rio Branco in 1992, there were strong pressures from the NGO community in Brazil as well as left-wing political organisations such as the PT and the allied trade union federation CUT, to include other, non-rubber tapper groups of extractivists as well as landless rural workers under the CNS umbrella. Significantly, the president of the CNS for 1992–5 was not a rubber tapper in the traditional mould of those who had pioneered the early struggles in southern Acre, but a small farmer from eastern Amazonia who had worked with local development organisations in Pará.[32]

The CNS has taken on the broad mantle of representing 'the struggle for survival of those groups which traditionally inhabit Amazonia' (CNS, 1992: 1), rather than just the interests of rubber tappers. Thus, in addition to supporting the formation of the four major rubber tappers' reserves, the CNS has taken up the cause of babaçú extractivists in Tocantins and Maranhão and the setting up four babaçú reserves (see Table 3.2), whose future is highly uncertain.[33] Furthermore, the political message of the CNS is now more strongly couched in terms of radical agrarian reform than ever before, linking extractivists and small farmers as 'the main forces responsible for agrarian reform in Amazonia and Brazil' (CNS, 1992: 1). To be able to respond more effectively to specific needs, the CNS has set up six regional offices and has moved its headquarters from Rio Branco to Brasilia.[34]

There is clearly a certain political logic to the CNS policy of joining forces with other groups of rural producers in the struggle to introduce more appropriate development policies for Amazonia, and decentralising its operations to state level accordingly. Yet there are several associated dangers which threaten to undermine the unity and, hence, the effectiveness of the CNS as an authentic representative of rubber tappers' interests. Tension within the movement and the CNS is apparent between those from the heartland of the tappers' movement in Acre and Rondônia on the one hand, and newer activist members from eastern Amazonia on the other. Traditional *seringueiro* leaders express resentment at what they regard as the diluting of their efforts, as the CNS has expanded its political base to encompass the cause of Amazonian populations as a whole, with whom they may in practice have little in common. In addition, many rubber tappers dislike what they see as the cooptation of the CNS leadership by outside political interests, such as the PT.

These political conflicts are undoubtedly underpinned by the frequently stark contrast between extractivists and small farmers in their relationship to the land and their use of natural resources. Rubber tappers and other extractivists have learned to place a strong emphasis on preserving forests as their major means of livelihood. Small farmer settlers, on the other hand, see ownership of the land itself as their primary concern. Forest preservation is often a minor preoccupation for small farmers. Firstly, the law requires that prospective landowners convert forest to arable use or pasture as proof of 'productive' use.[35] Secondly, the logic of itinerant, slash-and-burn agricultural practices places emphasis on cultivation of short-cycle crops for immediate benefit. Thirdly, such incentives to remove forest cover may well be compounded by farmers' desire to capitalise themselves through land speculation, in a situation where the market adds value to converted jungle.

Internal political-ideological tensions within the movement have also been exacerbated by institutional and personal rivalries amongst participant organisations. A major clash occurred in 1992, for example, between the IEA[36] and the CNS. This resulted in a permanent rift between the two organisations, essentially over the sharing of power and rights to leadership roles within the rubber tappers' movement.[37]

Amazon rubber tappers and their institutional allies have made formidable progress in securing a place for extractivism within Brazil's legal and development policy framework and in getting concrete projects started. Be that as it may, however, there is a danger that the political cohesion and sustainability of the movement is being compromised. The notion of a collective 'movement', already problematic due to the diversity of local situations and socio-political histories within Amazonia's areas, is being further undermined by an inappropriate leadership-style through the CNS. The council's own perceived hegemonic role as promoter of land reform for Amazonia and representative of all regional groups which pursue any form of extractive activity, together with growing signs of internal political conflict as it expands its remit and coverage, threaten to dilute its power as an effective vehicle for promoting rubber tappers' interests. There is a very real danger that these developments may serve to weaken that role and subsume it to other concerns not directly connected with the rubber tappers' agenda for action.

Extractive reserves: prospects for a sustainable future

Chapter one argued that productive conservation movements should be viewed as a rational response by resource-user groups to growing environmental pressures which threaten their livelihoods. In the case of Amazonia's rubber tappers, a crucial challenge to be faced by planners and policy-makers is the creation of economic and non-economic incentives which will allow non-destructive uses to become viable, long-term options for rainforest populations. Fundamental issues which are unresolved and are likely to remain so for a while are firstly, whether rubber tapping and other productive activities, extractive or otherwise, can become economically viable enough to provide forest-dwellers with an adequate level of income to guarantee their long-term presence as custodians of the forest reserves, and secondly, whether appropriate management systems be set up which build upon existing solidarity and cooperation to encourage a shared, collective sense of responsibility to preserve the forest as a common property resource.

If extractive reserves are to form part of a viable productive conservation strategy for Amazonia, both of these questions must be satisfactorily answered. In order to halt or even reverse the present tendency towards depopulation of the *seringais*, extractive reserves must provide the means for rubber tappers and their families to sustain their livelihoods.[38] Economic sustainability would provide tappers with an incentive to retain and diversify their traditional sources of income, while at the same time giving them an interest in preserving the forest. Discussions and initial efforts to improve the income-generating capacity of extractive reserves have focused on two areas. In the first instance, this has consisted of improving product quality and support services for existing rubber and brazil-nut industries. In addition, however, it will also be necessary to diversify the range of productive activities to include sustainable forest management, agroforestry and use of other non-timber forest products (NTFPs) such as medicinal plants.

For most of Amazonia's *seringueiros*, rubber-tapping and brazil-nut gathering still form the mainstay of their livelihoods, complemented by subsistence farming and hunting.[39] Throughout the

1980s, however, government subsidies for domestic rubber were gradually withdrawn and cheaper Malaysian imports encouraged, while synthetics also became increasingly popular. In 1980, the rubber tapper received $US1.80/kg latex, but by 1995 this figure had fallen to under $US0.50 (Almeida and Menezes, 1994; Silberling and Franco, 1995). Furthermore, *seringueiros* themselves usually receive less than the official price when they sell to intermediaries. In 1990, a special tax on cheap imported rubber (TORMB) was withdrawn, reducing funds available for supporting rubber production in Amazonia, which declined from 85 per cent of national output in 1985 to 28 per cent by 1992.[40] In response, the CNS organised a demonstration in Brasilia by 150 rubber tappers on 30 March 1993 (billed as an '*empate* against hunger and destruction of the forest'). An interministerial group has since been studying the TORMB issue with a view to creating an investment fund for Amazonia rubber tapper's, a measure which the CNS and IEA have long called for.

While reforms are undoubtedly necessary in order to guarantee minimum prices for rubber producers, substantial investments will also be required in the areas of production and marketing. Efforts are under way to improve the quality of Amazonian latex by encouraging the production of smoked rubber sheets (PBD), which have fewer impurities and command a price 40–70 per cent higher than the rubber traditionally produced in the area.[41] The CNPT/IBAMA has been distributing special kits to some *seringueiro* families and training tappers in the new techniques, and there are plans to extend this scheme significantly under the Resex component of the G7 Pilot Programme. Another linked initiative has been the production of high-quality 'plant leather' (*couro vegetal*), which was pioneered on the Alto Juruá. This is being sold to private companies for the manufacture of shoes, bags and other items for sale on domestic and international markets, with an estimated global potential of some $US2 billion.[42]

In an attempt to help revive Amazonia's rubber industry, the cooperative in Xapurí (CAEX) has built a processing factory to serve 2,600 tappers, producing high-quality rubber annually for the internal market.[43] Similar plants are planned for the Juruá and Ouro Preto reserves. It remains to be seen, however, whether a sufficiently large slice of Brazil's market for rubber can be captured to make the operation viable. Given the lower price of imports from Malaysia, government subsidies will almost certainly be required. These are, arguably, regardless of their direct economic significance, justified in terms of the environmental and social roles performed by extractive reserves.

Efforts have already been made to increase the added value of brazil nut production accruing to rubber tappers, but with little success to date. The experience of CAEX, which serves the Chico Mendes reserve, underlines the potential difficulties inherent in attempting to develop independent, alternative processing and marketing arrangements.[44] CAEX was set up by the CNS for three reasons: firstly, to replace long-standing 'exploitative' exchange relations between producers and *marreteiros*, or middlemen traders, in the purchase of brazil nuts and rubber; secondly, to establish a consumption cooperative for basic goods; and thirdly, to increase the added value of nut sales by processing them and selling directly to national and overseas purchasers, thus undermining the monopsony over finished nuts in Brazilian Amazonia which has been held for generations by the Mutran family.

Cultural Survival initially provided seed money for a small brazil-nut factory at Xapurí, which was inaugurated in November 1989, less than a year after the death of Chico Mendes. In this heady atmosphere other donors were quick to lend their support to an environmentally friendly and politically correct project, which promised to create jobs while conserving the rainforest. In the space of five years, CAEX and its nut factory attracted over $US1.6 million in overseas grants, a considerable achievement by any standards.[45] Yet in spite of the high hopes held out for CAEX and the large volume of funding secured, results have so far been disappointing. This has been due to a combination of factors ranging from international competition to sheer mismanagement and bad planning by the cooperative itself (Hecht, 1994).

When the brazil-nut factory opened in 1989, production was centralised in the town of Xapurí, but serious problems soon became apparent. Productivity was much lower than anticipated due to high rates of absenteeism on the part of the female labour force and the use of inefficient technology for opening and processing nuts. This was exacerbated by late payments to workers, whose wages were rapidly eroded by a 600 per cent annual rate of inflation. Severe overstaffing at CAEX and the obligation to meet social security obligations (equal to 65 per cent of the wage bill) also proved a heavy burden. All these factors increased production costs and placed CAEX at a severe disadvantage on the international market, where the price of nuts from Bolivia, currently the world's largest producer, was 42 per cent lower. The cooperative's problems were epitomised by its failure to meet contractual obligations for supplying brazil nuts to 'Ben and Jerry's' ice-cream factory in the USA. In order to produce its highly publicised 'Rainforest Crunch', the company was eventually obliged to purchase nuts from commercial suppliers such as the Mutran family. This, of course, rather defeated the social purpose of the exercise, which was to provide additional support for traditional tapper groups working with the cooperative.[46]

The solution encountered for CAEX's production problems was to decentralise a large part of nut-processing activities to four rural, 'mini-factories' (*Projeto Castanha*). Ostensibly, this was for technical reasons of reducing transportation expenses and nut losses as well as to raise producers' incomes. Yet a prime motivation appears to have been to cut labour costs through the change from a waged to a piecework system, which did not require social security payments to be made.

Initial attempts at decentralisation seem to have met with limited success. Productivity is much lower than anticipated and payments to workers correspondingly reduced. It was expected that women would provide the main labour force for nut-processing, as in the central factory. However, CAEX took no account of major competing demands on women's time in agricultural activities (rice-harvesting, manioc-planting, processing and land preparation), which compete directly with the early part of the brazil-nut processing cycle. This meant that children and adolescents, who also form a significant part of the agricultural labour force, were employed in nut-processing instead. Thus, not only did children allegedly miss out on schooling, but production fell far short of anticipated levels, with only eleven of twenty working days per month being devoted to the mini-factories. Furthermore, what additional rural income has been generated through decentralisation has been concentrated in the hands of a relatively small group of households loyal to the CNS.

The future of decentralised brazil-nut production at Xapurí thus looks somewhat uncertain. Serious management problems within CAEX have also undermined the cooperative's early experiments in production and marketing of the nuts.[47] These problems have since been addressed and the future remains uncertain, although there is still optimism with regard to the potential for expanding production. At Cajarí, for example, the state government of Amapá, the CNS and the WWF are providing strong technical, political and financial support to the association in setting up a processing and marketing infrastructure. A brazil nut processing plant at Brasiléia, to be administered by the already existing Consortium of Producer Associations for Brasiléia and Epitaciolândia (CAPEB), will also commence production in early 1997 to serve the local area, including that portion of the Chico Mendes reserve.[48]

Whatever potential exists for increasing revenues from rubber and brazil nut production, the viability of extractive reserves will also depend heavily on diversification into non-traditional activities such as agroforestry and a range of alternative NTFPs, and even sustainable logging. The urgent need to lessen dependence upon rubber and brazil nuts was clearly established at the first major international seminar to discuss economic options for rubber tappers, held in Rio Branco, Acre (IEA, 1991). Another study also concluded that future efforts on market diversification should be concentrated on agroforestry, while research be continued into finding new uses for NTFPs (Afsah, 1992). In principle, there is great potential to expand output of foods, spices, fruits and fodder crops, as shown in what is now a growing number of detailed surveys of forest products.[49] *Couro vegetal* production at Alto Juruá and a heart-of-palm project for Rio Cajarí are two examples of diversification into new markets. Fish nurseries are also being supported for their income-generating potential.

However, while it is a significant achievement to document forest plants' economic potential in principle, little is known about the actual capacity of domestic and overseas markets to absorb them in large enough quantities to make them economically attractive as part of an overall development strategy.[50] Plans under the G7 Pilot Programme to introduce and expand cultivation of non-traditional forest products will, therefore, include marketing studies as well as training in agroforestry systems and management. Difficulties currently being experienced by nascent associations in setting up financially viable marketing systems for rubber and brazil nuts underlines the need for major investments into infrastructure and management training in this field.

Commercial timber extraction has been ruled out within Use

Plans *(Planos de Utilização)* as an option until it can be clearly demonstrated that sustainable logging is viable. Although what appear to quite successful extractive-based experiments are taking place elsewhere in the Amazon region, such as the Yanesha Forestry Cooperative in eastern Peru (Hartshorn, 1990), Brazilian Amazonia has little such experience to call upon, and current research in this area is still at a highly embryonic stage. One pilot experience in sustainable forest management, including agroforestry and selective timber extraction, is taking place at the Porto Dias PAE in Acre.[51] In view of the past battles between *seringueiros* and invading commercial loggers there is, understandably, a strong reluctance to permit the possibly irreversible destruction of tappers' natural capital.

A significant breakthrough in the provision of official support for rubber tappers occurred in June 1996 with the setting up of a Commission for the Assistance Programme for the Development of Extractivism (PRODEX), the first credit line specifically to support extractivism in Amazonia. This is earmarked from the existing $R224 million Constitutional Fund for the North (FNO) credit line for small borrowers, instituted earlier by the government through the BASA, following massive popular political pressure by small farmers in the region.[52] PRODEX reached the statute books largely due to the commitment to the rubber tappers' cause of Marina Silva, PT Senator for Acre and herself the daughter of *seringueiros*.[53]

Another government proposal would streamline the PAE, originally introduced as a stopgap measure in the 1980s, and gear it towards sustainable forest production.[54] It would provide an alternative model to the conventional INCRA settlement project (PAD), based on individual private ownership and agricultural techniques imported from outside the region which ignore local aptitudes. Despite the many economic problems which remain, these new initiatives reflect a greater government commitment to introducing measures consistent with new development policy guidelines for Amazonia, discussed in the final chapter.

Debates over the economic future of extractive reserves have thus become highly contentious. Some observers are cautiously optimistic about the commercial potential of agricultural and forest products (Anderson, 1992; Schwartzman, 1994). Others, for a variety of reasons, remain sceptical that extractive reserves can ever become economically viable or self-sufficient enterprises, viewing their activities as doomed to becoming marginalised and insignificant in the Amazon context of expanding commercial agriculture and ranching (Browder, 1992; Homma 1993). Given the current state of ignorance in this field, much more research is required to gauge the genuine potential, nationally and globally, for forest products.

The provision of greater economic incentives for rubber tappers to exploit the forest in a non-destructive manner will go a long way towards creating the instrumental rationale for users to preserve their individual and common property resources. Yet providing the right market signals will be of little consequence unless the social structure and people's consequent relationship to the land is also conducive to conservation. For example, under the traditional estate system, absentee owners demanded maximum production of latex from their dependent tappers, who were thus obliged to adopt destructive practices, leading to declining yields and the death of many rubber stands. Such disincentives to conserve natural resources must be replaced with positive inducements.

The expropriation of rubber estates to set up extractive reserves and settlement projects has broken once and for all the grip of the *seringalistas* upon rubber tappers' lives. Similarly, the gradual substitution of the *marreteiro* by formal associations and cooperatives, if properly executed, will begin to weaken long-standing relationships of dependency and debt-bondage. However, the motivation to conserve natural resources is also closely tied to the issue of property rights.

Under the management system currently being set up, collective usufruct rights (*concessão real de uso*) will be granted by IBAMA to the new tappers' associations. This does not signify collective use of the land as such, since the associations will, in turn, assign usufruct rights to individual families on their own *colocações*. In practice, this is merely confirming *de jure* a situation which already exists *de facto*, since families have for many years claimed or 'bought' trails from departing owners or occupants.

Nonetheless, according to research carried out on the Rio Ouro Preto reserve, this legally more secure situation encourages tappers to adopt conservationist extraction methods and take better care of their assets (Wawzyniak, 1994). Conversely, it has been noted elsewhere that insecurity of tenure leads extractivist populations to adopt destructive practices. On the São Luis do Remanso PAE in Acre, for example, threats from ranchers and INCRA itself to take over land have led the resident population to practise highly destructive shifting cultivation and convert land to pasture, deforesting 15 per cent of the reserve, in order to maximise short-term gains (Anderson, 1992; Rodrigues, 1991).

On the grounds of instrumental rationality, therefore, there is no inherent, immutable tendency for extractivist populations to conserve their natural resources. The 'defenders' of the forest will only do so if it serves their livelihood interests. Production and marketing incentives must be conducive to sustainable forest use, and a sense of individual responsibility encouraged through rights of usufruct or ownership.

Yet such individualistic calculations of benefits and costs are only one side of the productive conservationist coin. An additional and perhaps equally important foundation for the motivation to pursue non-destructive strategies in the interests of the collective welfare, thus avoiding the 'freerider' problem, lies in shared group identity and perceptions. Such commonality of interests has never characterised Amazonia's rubber-tapping economy, which has been organised very much along vertical lines of dependency and indebtedness between tappers on the one hand, and estate-owners or merchants on the other. Despite some ties of extended kinship and godparentship, rubber tappers have no significant tradition of collective organisation.

The beginnings of such joint action were forged in those areas such as southern Acre where *seringueiros'* livelihoods were directly threatened by cattle-ranchers and land speculators, giving rise to the *empate*. However, translating this reactive, defensive stance into a more proactive, long-term management strategy for extractive reserves is a major challenge. Research quoted in chapter one into the sharing of common-pool resources suggests that cooperation is more likely in groups which are small and homogeneous and whose members are in frequent contact with each other. Although superficially homogeneous, extractive reserves are often quite socially and geographically diverse, with a history of inter-community separation and infrequent contact. They are invariably large, both geographically and demographically; the Chico Mendes reserve is almost one million hectares in size and has a population of some 12,000, which is widely scattered, much of it severely isolated.

The challenge now faced is how to overcome the consequences of this history of individualism to build up new management structures

The rubber tappers' movement

which will further a sense of shared identity and collective responsibility over and above calculations of personal benefit. This is likely to be easier in those areas with a history of collective struggle against land-grabbers and, hence, a common purpose. However, other factors are probably as important, if not more so. The efficiency of management in the hands of newly formed extractivist associations, for example, will play a key role in winning or losing rubber tappers' confidence. Furthermore, it will be important to set up consultative procedures as well as education and training programmes in order to involve and inform the grassroots more actively.

By late 1996, some two years after the project became operational, significant progress had been made in establishing participatory reserve-management structures. Tappers' associations had been established in all four Resex and reserve-use plans approved.[55] Their management capacity, in collaboration with local institutions such as rural trade unions as well as the CNPT/IBAMA and state authorities, will only reveal itself with the passage of time. It remains to be seen how well these organisations can engage the rubber tapper population in reserve management, and how they can enhance project efficiency and effectiveness.

Environmental monitors (*fiscais colaboradores*) have been relatively successful in eliminating illegal logging, preventing the worst excesses, although some connivance still exists between rubber tappers and commercial loggers. Furthermore, the issue of appropriate remuneration has threatened to undermine their commitment to the task. Issues of productive potential, economic diversification and marketing of forest products are also being prioritised. Additional problems which await resolution included finalising the land tenure and concessional status of some reserves (notably Cajarí and Rio Ouro Preto), as well as matters relating to the provision of affordable extension services by a decentralised technical assistance and rural extension company (EMATER), and the availability of counterpart funding for working capital.

The four major extractive reserves for rubber tappers referred to in this chapter have benefited from access to earmarked funds within the G7 Pilot Programme. This has, despite the remaining problems, enabled a significant start to be made in setting up appropriate infrastructure and support services. Yet the other four much smaller federal reserves in Amazonia (Ciríaco, Extremo Norte do Tocantins, Quilombo do Flexal and Mata Grande – see Figure 3.2) have not been so privileged. Based on other NTFPs such as babaçu and buriti as well as subsistence agriculture and fishing, the land tenure situation is more complex and permanently conflict-ridden (von Behr, 1995). Social organisation of the extractivist populations here is undermined by land struggles and internecine conflicts based on divisive religious and party political affiliations. With no clear overarching collective structures, no beneficial economic policies and little investment in these less high-profile areas, much needs to be done before they are liable to become sustainable productive conservation units.

Extractive reserves have made a promising start, but their future remains uncertain. They are a pioneering innovation upon which forest-dwellers, the Brazilian government and international donors are pinning great hopes. Studies are under way for the formation of more federal reserves.[56] Yet the economic, political, social and ecological challenges faced are formidable by any measure. In terms of their participatory basis, there is a very real danger that new forms of paternalism and patronage will substitute more traditional structures, a recurrent theme in Brazil. In one reserve area, for example, the new association president stands accused of having taken on the merchant's role during the leadership campaign, and paying artificially high prices for latex in order to win tappers' votes, depriving the official *seringueiro* association of business.[57] In Xapurí, as described above, the CAEX cooperative has had to deal with serious financial and managerial problems. There is a risk that, in the eyes of many *seringueiros*, reserve associations and their leaders will be perceived as the new bosses or *patrões*, seeking to manipulate members and share the burden of costs, while denying them full economic returns or decision-making powers to participate effectively in the running of the reserves.

Any extractive reserve policy must remain sensitive to local variations of ecology and social relations of production. The temptation to impose a uniform model should be avoided, given the biotic diversity of areas to be protected and their often contrasting traditions of social participation. The mere existence of a conflict with outsiders over natural resources should not lead planners to assume an automatic, collective commitment to long-term conservation on the part of users. Building upon local circumstances and initiative, alternative forms of economic activity and collective socio-political as well as managerial organisation are required to eliminate traditional dependency ties without creating new forms of exploitation or impoverishment. Consultative procedures and educational programmes will be necessary to help inculcate a sense of confidence, legitimacy, mutual obligation and responsibility amongst reserve members. Continuing government support over the long term will be necessary if extractive reserves are to survive the eventual withdrawal of overseas funding. Given the huge quantity of government funds poured into almost totally worthless enterprises such as cattle-ranching in Amazonia, subsidisation of the more productive and socially equitable Extractive Reserves is a perfectly reasonable use of official funds.

Many ambitious claims have been made for the potential of extractive reserves to address problems of environmental degradation in Amazonia. It may be somewhat over-optimistic, for example, to expect that 'extractive activities can be the point of departure for a reordering of the regional economy'.[58] Yet it is to be hoped that the pioneering efforts of rubber tappers are not wasted and that Chico Mendes will not have died in vain.[59] While no panacea for Amazonia's problems, this on-going experiment will surely yield vital lessons for the sustainable development of large portions of Amazonia, both in Brazil and beyond.

Notes

1 Near Manaus, for example, as pasture formation and agricultural production lead to deforestation, rubber tapping and brazil-nut gathering are being replaced by the harvesting of fruit from palm trees which grow on fallow land (Lescure *et al.*, 1994).
2 Lescure *et al.* (1994).
3 Cited by Allegretti (1995: 2).
4 In Acre, Amazonas and Amapá, for example, census data show that some 43, 26 and 19% respectively of the rural population is engaged in plant extractivism (Allegretti, 1994b: 27–8).
5 See Hall (1991), Gross (1989).
6 A range of explanations from inappropriate economic and political conditions to labour constraints have been blamed for the failure of rubber plantations in Amazonia such as those of the Ford Motor Company in the 1930s and 1940s at Fordlândia, near Belém, and Belterra, near Santarém. Dean (1987), however, attributes this problem to the prevalence of the South American Leaf Blight (*Microcyclus ulei*) in plantation rubber.

7 A survey of the Chico Mendes reserve, shortly after it was decreed, documented the following production values: rubber 35%, brazil nuts 25%, subsistence agriculture (manioc, rice, beans, corn and fruits) 29% and livestock 9%. See CNS/FUNTAC/CIDA (1992).
8 A study of the Cachoeira and São Luis do Remanso extractive reserves in Acre found, for example, that producers enjoyed an annual net income of $US348 from extractivism and agriculture, representing a 21% return on investments. This surplus allowed cash remittances to be made to relatives living outside the reserve, although good communications by river and road were an advantage in this instance (Rodrigues, 1991).
9 From 1970 to 1975, for example, land prices in Acre rose by 2,000% close to the federal highways (BR364 and BR317) and by 1,000% generally. During this period, 5 million hectares changed hands, or over 30% of the state's land area (Bakx, 1990: 52).
10 For example, the population of Rio Branco, Acre state capital, rose from 36,000 in 1970 to over 92,000 in 1980 and over 200,000 today.
11 The *empate* is a localised confrontation between groups of men, women and children and invading ranchers or their hired hands. They are usually organised during the dry, 'burning' season from August to October, before the onset of rains in November which prevent further deforestation until the following year. It is claimed that, during the 1980s, such 'stand-offs' prevented the destruction of over 1.2 million hectares of rainforest (Gross, 1989). For some graphic accounts, see Revkin (1990).

There are many recent recorded cases of such resistance. During mid-1993, for example, a series of stand-offs were held to prevent the illegal extraction from the Chico Mendes extractive reserve of valuable mahogany logs (*Boletim do CNS*, July 1993). In June 1994, the CNS reported that the community of Nova Esperança in Xapurí had organised a peaceful *empate* to prevent the deforestation of 450 hectares by a local rancher and the cutting down of over 1,000 rubber trees.
12 Wilson Pinheiro became president of the Brasiléia union in 1978 and was assassinated by hired gunmen in 1980. An attempt to kill Chico Mendes at the same time was thwarted by his absence from Xapurí. In view of the failure of local police to act, the tappers took justice into their own hands. One of the landowners who was alleged to have ordered the killing was summarily tried and executed, provoking a rapid and violent police response (Gross, 1990).

Chico Mendes was elected onto the Xapurí municipal council for the opposition MDB (Brazilian Democratic Movement), later becoming president of the Xapurí rural workers' union and an active member of the PT. He was murdered on 22 December 1988.
13 Mary Allegretti, an anthropologist from Curitiba in the southern state

The rubber tappers' movement

of Rio Grande do Sul, had done her Master's dissertation on the rubber tappers of Acre and became a close friend of Chico Mendes. She played a central role in the organisation of 'Projeto Seringueiro' and, working for INESC, the Brazilian NGO, and was instrumental in organising the crucial first National Meeting of Rubber Tappers in Brasilia in 1985. Later, she set up the IEA, which continued to play a major part in researching into and lobbying for the creation of extractive reserves, as well as publishing studies on broader issues concerning development policy for Amazonia, until it closed down in 1995. See Revkin (1990, chapter 9) for further details.

14 At the meeting, 130 rubber tappers from Acre, Rondônia and Amazonas states were brought together, many of whom had never travelled outside their home areas. They met with officials from the Ministries of Education, Agriculture, Health, Agrarian Reform and Culture, as well as Congress members. A final document listed sixty-three demands, which centred on the need for an appropriate development policy for rubber tappers.

15 As an initial response, the Bank funded a series of compensatory measures under the Programme for the Protection of the Environment and Indigenous Communities (PMACI). This was later complemented by a revised and more 'sustainable' successor to POLONOROESTE, – PLANAFLORO. See chapter two for further details.

16 See Revkin (1990, chapter 11) for an account of these visits. In 1987, Mendes was awarded the Global 500 prize by UNEP and the Better World Society Protection of the Environment Medal.

17 Extension of the BR364 through Cruzeiro do Sul, connecting to Pucallpa and on to Lima, is the start of one of two proposed trans-Andean routes. The other route under consideration is through southern Acre (where it becomes the BR317) via Xapurí to Maldonado and the Peruvian port of Matarani. The second alternative appears to be favoured by the Brazilian federal government on the grounds that it is much shorter and could even be funded by domestic funds, although it is understood that both Japan and the IDB have been approached as possible sources (Shankland, 1993).

In June 1996, environmental groups in Acre protested at governor Orleir Camelli's resumption of paving of the BR364 and BR317 without environmental impact assessments (EIAs) having been carried out. This led to IBAMA imposing a temporary embargo on work along certain stretches, pending completion of these EIAs.

18 See Revkin (1990: 232–3), whose figures are based on data from the Brazilian National Institute for Space Research (INPE).

19 Respectively, *'exploração condominial'* and *'concessão real de uso'* (Gomes and Felippe, 1994).

20 Darly Alves da Silva and his son Darci were eventually arrested and charged with the murder. They were each sentenced to nineteen years in gaol, but later escaped from their Rio Branco prison in mysterious circumstances. Darly was recaptured by federal police in July 1996 at Medicilândia on the Transamazon Highway (see Figure 5.1), although his son fled. They had managed to purchase a large plot of land from INCRA to set up a cattle ranch, and had even managed to secure two subsidised loans from BASA.
21 Chapter VI, article IV, states that it is necessary to 'create territorial spaces, specially protected by federal, state and municipal powers, of relevant ecological interest and extractive reserves'. (Brazil, 1988).
22 Law 7,804 of 24 July 1989 defined the system of 'Environmental Conservation Units' (*Unidades de Conservação Ambiental*).
23 Article I states: 'Extractive reserves are territorial spaces designated for the self-sustaining use and conservation of renewable natural resources by extractivist populations.'
24 According to local sources, the state government of Rondônia is keen to establish its own extractive reserves as much for political as for conservationist reasons. Under legislation passed in the 1970s designed to give the central government control over lands for settlement projects along federal highways in Amazonia, much of the state comes under federal jurisdiction. Establishment of state extractive reserves by Rondônia would revert control over much of this area back to regional government.
25 The procedure is laid down by Decree 98,897 of 30 January 1990, and IBAMA regulation no. 51-N of 11 May, 1994.
26 This concept originated in Decree 271 of 28 February 1967.
27 The third union, Assis Brasil, was established in 1988 and is considerably weaker, with only 30 active members of a total 620 within the reserve.
28 The CNS Regional Vale do Acre-Purus or CNS/RVAP.
29 Under the old system, the entire rubber production belonged to the landowner, who exchanged it for over-priced basic consumption goods which the tappers needed. *Seringueiros* were not allowed to grow subsistence crops or engage in any other income-generating activities.

From the 1970s, as the *seringalistas* became indebted, rubber trails were rented out for 50 kg of latex per year. At the same time, a new class of merchants (*marreteiros*) travelled the area, purchasing rubber in full or partial exchange for household goods. These verbal contracts are often made a year in advance, thus placing the rubber tapper in permanent debt. This system led to over-production of rubber, the use of damaging extraction techniques and the physical exhaustion and ill-health of tappers (Wawzyniak, 1994).

30 At the meeting, 278 rubber tappers were present, 167 from the Rio Ouro Preto area. The difficulties identified included delayed payments for rubber, instability of tenure, non-existent health and educational facilities, low rubber prices and exorbitant prices charged for consumer goods (Wawzyniak, 1994).
31 Members are required to pay 3 kg. of rubber per month in subscriptions. When discussions were held with ASGM staff in June 1994, no member had handed over the 100 kg of rubber to become a shareholder and provide much-needed working capital.
32 Atanagildo de Deus Mattos ('Gatão') worked for many years during the 1970s with FASE, a well known NGO with *educação de base* projects all over Brazil. Julio Barbosa de Aquino, successor to Chico Mendes as leader of the Xapurí rural union, was elected vice-president of the CNS for 1992–5, after which he took charge of the Xapurí cooperative (CAEX).
33 The CNS supported the creation of four small reserves, decreed in 1992: Quilombo do Flexal, Mata Grande and Ciríaco in Maranhão and Extremo Norte do Tocantins. By mid-1994, the two-year deadline for regulating the land tenure situation had expired and they were threatened with becoming void. IBAMA alleged lack of funding to carry out the necessary demarcation and expropriation work (*Jornal do Brasil*, 7 May 1994).
34 These are located in Acre (Rio Branco and Cruzeiro do Sul), Rondônia (Porto Velho), Amapá (Macapá), Maranhão (São Luis) and Pará (Marabá).
35 As evidence of economic activity and in order to become eligible for a property title, INCRA requires that settlers deforest a portion of the land claimed and either cultivate crops or sow to pasture. Such indications of 'productive use' are also sufficient to exempt farms from the risk of expropriation under Brazil's agrarian reform law of 1985 (Hall, 1990).
36 This was renamed the Instituto de Estudos Amazônicos e Ambientais, or Institute of Economic and Environmental Studies (IEAA), but closed down in 1995.
37 It is worth briefly outlining the background to this episode, since it reveals much about the potential latent conflicts which can damage seemingly strong coalitions. Since the 1970s as a postgraduate researcher and, later, as a member of INESC in Brasília, anthropologist Mary Allegretti has played a key role in the strengthening of the rubber tappers and the heightening of their international profile. She set up the IEA as an NGO to lobby in favour of rubber tappers' interests, forging links between the embryonic movement and Western environmental and development NGOs during the 1980s, and she was instrumental in

helping to arrange the first national rubber tappers' congress in 1985.

In May 1992, the IEA and a representative of the rubber tappers signed an agreement with a Curitiba-based food company, Nutrimental, to produce a cereal bar ('Chunk') which would include brazil nuts bought from extractive reserves. This new initiative was to be launched during the Earth Summit in Rio de Janeiro in June that year. In addition to offering a regular outlet for nuts, Nutrimental would donate 2.5% of net profits from the operation to the rubber tappers' movement, to be used in social and economic development projects as decided by a committee comprised of representatives from the IEA, CNS and WWF.

Two months later, the agreement was publicly denounced by the CNS, which accused the IEA of wanting to usurp the leadership of the rubber tappers' movement and to promote its own interests at the expense of the council. The IEA, in its turn, published a detailed repudiation of these accusations. Whether indicative of a power struggle over hegemony within the movement or of personal rivalries, or both, this incident broke the long-standing working relationship which had existed for several years between the CNS and the IEA.

38 This trend has been documented in many extractive reserve areas and rubber-tapping zones generally in Amazonia, and has been attributed to the decline in official prices of latex as well as the lure of expanding regional towns and cities (Bakx, 1990; Arnt, 1994). In Acre, according to census figures for example, the working population employed in extractivism fell by 11.2% from 1960 to 1970, and a further 6% by 1980 (CNS/FUNTAC/CIDA, 1992).

39 A recent study of reserves in Acre found that 62% of production was based on extractivism, including 35% from rubber and 25% from brazil nut gathering (CNS/FUNTAC/CIDA, 1992: 43). Another survey of the Cachoeira and São Luis do Remanso PAEs in Acre found that rubber production averaged between 590 and 670 kg per *colocação* p.a., giving a mean annual income of some $US440 (FUNTAC, 1991).

40 The Tax on the Organisation and Regulation of the Rubber Market (TORMB) is a tax on cheap imported rubber designed to level the price to industrial consumers with that of Brazilian rubber. In 1989, the TORMB raised $US49 million, but this fell to an estimated $US2 million in 1992. It is alleged that these funds were not used to benefit rubber tappers but were instead channelled to estate- and plantation-owners as well as industrial processing plants (*Informativo IEA*, 2 (2), March–April 1993). It is also alleged that TORMB revenues were illicitly used to cover the administrative costs of IBAMA (which absorbed SUDHEVEA, the state rubber authority).

41 This is known as *Cernambi Virgem Prensado*, or Pressed Virgin Rubber (CVP).

42 In this system, latex is treated with special chemicals which prevent the rubber from hardening. Framed sheets of cotton are then coated in latex and smoked intensively in small ovens, after which they are soaked in water. Finally, the rubber sheets are vulcanised by the contracting company.

This initiative started in 1991 when two Green Party activists, designer Beatriz Saldanha and businessman João Fortes, encouraged and financed the production of 3,000 sheets of *couro vegetal* on the Alto Juruá extractive reserve in Acre to produce goods for sale at the UNCED in Rio de Janeiro the following year. A company was set up, Couro Vegetal da Amazônia S.A. (CVA) and, with funding from the BNDES, the scheme has expanded to involve some 200 rubber producers in four areas, including Alto Juruá, the Inavini National Forest and the Kaxiwaná and Yawanawá indigenous reserves.

These groups are under contract to supply 150,000 sheets of 'plant leather' by the year 2000, under the 'Treetap' logo. Conservation International is assisting in developing a marketing strategy, while efforts continue to improve product quality, the inconsistency of which has been a problem. In May 1996, this market received a boost when Mercedes Benz announced that *couro vegetal* would be used in upholstering its vehicles. (Benedicto, 1995; Silberling and Franco, 1995; Franco, 1996).

43 This was built with a $US150,000 grant from IBAMA. It is expected that the factory will produce 1,650 tonnes of high quality rubber balls (GEB) for mixing with imported rubber, and will generate over $US92,000 net income annually. See CAEX, CNPT, IBAMA (1993).

44 The following account is based on Hecht (1994) and the author's field visits.

45 Funds were provided for working capital, purchase of equipment and buildings, and technical support. Donors included the government of Austria ($US700,000), Ford Foundation ($US335,000), NOVIB ($US110,000), Inter-American Foundation ($US160,000), IDB ($US$80,000), Cultural Survival ($US76,000) and WWF ($US21,000). See Hecht (1994).

46 Cultural Survival set up a company to market nuts and fruits, called CS Enterprises (CSE), while Ben and Jerry established Community Products Inc. (CPI) to supply entrepreneurs wishing to make 'rainforest friendly' products. CPI was due to give 60% of its profits to charity, a third to Cultural Survival to cover project costs and a 5% 'environmental premium' for harvesters. Thus, 'socially responsible business' in support of the tappers and the rainforest would be encouraged.

As events turned out, however, CPI was unprofitable and did not make the full envisaged payments to Cultural Survival, while over 95%

of Ben and Jerry's brazil nuts for 'Rainforest Crunch' have been supplied by monopoly commercial companies since it was launched in 1989 (Entine, 1995).

47 In late 1993, in order to qualify for a loan of $US700,000 from the Bank of Brazil to set up a rubber processing plant, the cooperative used funds provided by the Austrian government to fire all the Xapurí nut factory female workers and cut costs, paying off the long-standing social security debt at the same time.

However, this was only a small part of the problem. The cooperative had also been charging its own huge overheads to the factory, so that in fact CAEX staff accounted for three-quarters of the total bill and the productive female nut-crackers only one quarter. When crisis point was reached, however, the productive labour force was the first to be sacked. By mid-1994, CAEX had ceased nut processing altogether and, somewhat ironically, sold the unprocessed brazil-nut harvest to its arch enemy, the Mutran family.

48 Funded through the small projects (PD/A) component of the G7 Pilot Programme.

49 Less familiar forest products from Brazilian Amazonia with known, if unquantified, commercial potential include: (i) Food crops – cupuaçú (*Theobroma grandiflorum*), açaí (*Euterpe sp.*), pupunha (*Bactris gasipaes*), graviola (*Anona reticulata*), coffee (*Coffea arabica*), black pepper (*Piper nigrum*), guaraná (*Paulinia cupania*), coconut (*Cocos nucifera*), and avocado (*Persea americana*); (ii) Fruits – jack fruit (*Artocarpus integrifolia*), sorva (*Couma macrocarpa*), araçá-boi (*Eugenia stipitata*), araçá-pera (*Psidium acutangulum*), sapota (*Quararabea cordata*), caçarí (*Myrciaria dubia*), sapoti (*Manikara zapota*) and mapati (*Pourouma cecropiae folia*); (iii) Extractive – copaíba (*Copaifera duckei*) louro-de-óleo (*Ocotea sp.*) and the babaçú palm (*Orbiqnya phalerata*); (iv) Fodder crops – gliricídia (*Gliricidia sepium*) and leucena (*Leucaena leucocephala*). See Brazil (1994), Lescure *et al.* (1992), May (1992), FOE (1992), IEA (1991, 1993a) and Smith *et al.* (1996).

50 Some marketing initiatives have got under way. For example, the First Exhibition of Acrean Forest Products (FLORA I) was organised in Rio Branco in 1994, followed by FLORA II in 1995 and FLORA III in 1996.

51 In this 22,000-hectare PAE, 100 hectares will be managed in small plots by some twenty members of the local association. A forest inventory will be taken and training given to colonists in timber extraction and processing to increase its added value. The project is supported by the Acre state government (FUNTAC) as well as a local NGO (CTA), with $US210,000 funding from the G7 Pilot Programme under the small projects (PD/A) component.

52 See chapter five for further details on the FNO.

53 See Silva (1996). PRODEX became law through Decree 1,930 of 17 June 1996.
54 While only a draft proposal at the time of writing in late 1996, it aims to adapt agrarian reform settlement projects to Amazon conditions and biodiversity preservation, rather than its destruction. It seeks to reduce levels of burning and emphasises rational forest management (Brazil, 1996).
55 These are as follows: (i) Associação dos Seringueiros da Reserva do Rio Cajari (ASTEX/CA), (ii) Associação de Seringueiros e Agricultores da Reserva Extrativista do Alto Juruá (ASAREAJ), (iii) Associação dos Serigueiros de Guajará Mirim (ASGM), and (iv) on the Chico Mendes Reserve – Associação de Moradores da Reserva Chico Mendes na região de Xapurí (AMOREX), Associação de Moradores da Reserva Chico Mendes na região de Brasiléia (AMOREB), and Associação de Moradores da Reserva Chico Mendes na região de Assis Brasil (AMOREAB).
56 It was announced in June 1995 that the Brazilian government was undertaking studies for the setting up of a further six extractive reserves, in addition to the existing four federal units. These would be situated in the Middle Juruá (Acre), on the Guariba and Roosevelt rivers (Rondônia), Tucuruí (Pará), Alto Araguaia (Tocantins) and Alto Paraiso (Goias).
57 Author's field visit to Rio Ouro Preto, 1994.
58 Allegretti (1995: 165).
59 See Hall (1996).

4
Fishing for a future

The importance of fish as a global resource is reflected not just in the size of the fishing industry and level of international trade, but also as the basis of people's livelihoods. It is estimated, for example, that about 100 million men, women and children depend on fishing for their sustenance (*The Ecologist*, 1995). The world's total fish catch rose steadily from the mid-nineteenth century, but levelled off during the 1970s and has since been subjected to increasing pressures, especially from commercial fleets.[1] Marine coastal grounds and, latterly, deep-sea areas have received the most publicity in connection with the 'fishing crisis' and ensuing conflicts between competing nations over the rights of access to dwindling reserves. However, estuarine and inland fishing grounds in floodplain zones comprise a major livelihood resource in many countries and have themselves become subjected to similar pressures. This is certainly the case along the River Amazon and its tributaries, where freshwater fish provides up to 90 per cent of animal protein, as well as being a major source of employment and income for the *caboclo* population.

Fishing is especially important in the nutrient-rich, white-water rivers and the floodplain (*várzea*) lakes they serve, such as those embraced by the Mamirauá project, considered in this chapter.[2] The seasonally flooded *várzeas* cover an area of some 180,000 square kilometres, or between 2 and 3 per cent of Amazonia.[3] With its complex aquatic systems and high species diversity, together with relatively easy access and low population density, these wetlands have, since the 1970s, become increasingly attractive to outside commercial fishing interests.[4] Such pressures have been responsible for a substantial decline in the size and yields of the most important commercial fish, such as tambaqui and pirarucu. Other causes of fish stock depletion include gold-prospecting as well as disruption of fish migration cycles due to dam construction. Extensive deforestation along the lower and middle reaches of the Amazon has also led to a marked loss of terrestrial and aquatic biodiversity (Goulding *et al.*, 1996).[5] This crisis has been facilitated by the lack of an overall government fisheries conservation policy for Amazonia.[6]

The fishing crisis in Amazonia

The floodplain of the River Amazon has always played a central role in the regional economy. Early accounts of the exploration indicate that the Amazon floodplain used to support far more people than today, possibly over one million.[7] Local populations have been supported by a combination of subsistence farming, fishing, extraction of forest products and some cattle-raising. Since the 1970s, the livelihoods of the *várzea* rural population (otherwise known as *ribeirinhos*, or riverbank-dwellers) has been put under increasing strain, and resource-management strategies have undergone major changes. In the Lower Amazon, owing to the decline in jute production, the major cash crop and basis of the local economy since World War II, *ribeirinhos* have switched from agriculture to commercial fishing. Government incentives for cattle-ranching during the 1970s and 1980s as part of its mainstream regional development policy, along with its concomitant neglect of small-scale farming, have generated additional pressures on land.

However, while fisherpeople along the River Amazon have become more dependent on artisanal fishing to meet their basic needs, they have at the same time been subjected to severe competition for access to fish stocks from commercial enterprises which supply both rapidly expanding urban markets in Brazil as well as overseas demand, especially the USA (McGrath, 1993).[8] This was facilitated by the building of a highway network in the 1970s which connected Amazonia with the rest of the country, as well as by the introduction of more efficient fishing technology (including the use of gill nets, better seines and polystyrene ice-boxes) and the setting up of refrigerated plants in the region's major cities.

Although commercial fishing had long been established in the region, serious expansion commenced from Belém and Manaus in the late 1960s and early 1970s respectively, as a result of growing demand and improved technology. During this time, confrontations between indigenous fishing communities and commercial vessels from Manaus brought about the so-called 'fish wars', which led to violent conflicts and several deaths. The best-known cases are those of Lago Janauacá, upstream of Manaus, and Lago Grande de Monte Alegre, near Santarém, which experienced face-to-face conflicts as early as 1966.[9] By 1980, Manaus fishing boats had pushed beyond the River Solimões to affluents such as the Purus, Juruá, Negro and Japurá in the north and west, as well as the Madeira, Marmoré and Guaporé on the southern axis, extending the fish wars in the process. By the early 1980s, Goulding (1983: 191) could confidently declare that 'the fisheries frontier of inland Amazonia is now history'. According to research carried out by Hartmann, by 1989 forty-four Amazonian lakes in Brazil had experienced major confrontations between local fishing communities and outsiders.[10]

The 'tragedy of the commons' denied – popular resistance and productive conservation

Given the relative indivisibility of fishing grounds and general lack of individual tenurial rights in seas, rivers and lakes, fish are often considered the common property resource (CPR) *par excellence*. Explanations for the root causes of overfishing, as different users compete over access, are often sought in the 'tragedy of the commons' model (McGoodwin, 1990; *The Ecologist*, 1995). This theory implies that, once the growth in competition for fish results in declining yields, individuals will try to maximise their catches in the short term and ignore the collective interest, leading to depletion and eventual destruction. According to this perspective, there is a direct contradiction between 'rational' individual behaviour based on extracting as many fish as possible as fast as possible, and the collective interest, which is better served by a more measured and conservationist strategy that attempts to strike a balance between individual and group requirements.

In this view, only outside intervention to implement preventive measures can avert the 'tragedy'. Conventionally, therefore, policy for preserving such CPRs should comprise either direct government control or privatisation of common property fisheries (McGoodwin, 1990). State intervention, it is argued, would allow strict vigilance and regulation of fishing activities. Alternatively, conversion of presumed 'open-access' fisheries to private property would, it is thought, provide individual owners with a greater incentive to conserve stocks, as well as making them responsible for bearing the costs of management. Yet while these may seem attractive options for policy-makers, there are a number of basic flaws in the proposals for either public or private control of fishing.

Firstly, governments on their own generally lack the technical capacity and financial resources effectively to monitor and control the huge geographical areas involved. Furthermore, the power of the state to act may be constrained by political factors such as alliances of decision-makers with strong vested interests. Secondly, it cannot be assumed that private property will automatically be conserved by its owners, many of whom seek to extract economic rent and other benefits, with little or no regard for the environmental consequences. The history of livestock, agricultural and logging activities as pillars of Amazon development policy since the 1970s and major causes of deforestation, discussed in chapter two, bear ample witness to this flawed assumption.

A third objection to the 'tragedy of the commons' model lies in ascribing the cause of resource degradation to the nature of the common property rights regime itself. External pressures on resources associated with modernisation strategies, such as the industrialisation of fishing technology, are generally held to be a far more important source of strain upon Amazonian fish stocks than endogenous pressures arising from competition amongst artisanal fisherpeople.

A fourth major criticism of the 'tragedicomedy of the commons' model, as the theory is so aptly renamed by McGoodwin (1990: 89), concerns the assumption that common property is necessarily open access, and that users have little or no control over its use. Studies of supposedly open-access commons all over the developing world have shown that this assumption is usually flawed and based on outsiders' ignorance of local circumstances (Bromley and Cernea, 1988). Fishing communities often develop their own cooperative systems for avoiding or mitigating over-exploitation of stocks. Thus, the history of fishing and evolution of social norms governing fishing practices will vary considerably depending on specific cultural-political contexts. Many examples may be cited from around the world which show how collective action has been taken by fishing populations to resist threats to their resource base.[11]

Inhabitants of Amazonia's wetlands have also evolved relatively balanced resource-management strategies to manage their vital fish stocks. In both Brazil and Peru, the cosmology of Amazonian fisherpeople has traditionally favoured conservation, discouraging overfishing and stimulating diversification of catches (Sternberg, 1995; Hiraoka, 1995). In the face of growing threats since the 1970s, however, fishing communities in the region have been left with little choice to become more proactive in defence of their livelihoods and the natural resource base, as these are threatened by commercial penetration. Rivers accessible to migratory fisherpeople are generally far more vulnerable to uncontrolled extraction than enclosed lakes and channels. Given the open boundaries and transient nature of populations, both fish and human, controls are difficult to impose. However, in many lakes which serve sedentary Amerindian and *caboclo* communities, groups have developed mechanisms to control and regulate both production and access. This would appear to be a highly rational strategy, given the central importance of fish in the diets and livelihoods of riverine populations. The Cocamilla people, who live in the Achual Tipisca community on the Huallaga River in the Peruvian Amazon, allow only subsistence fishers to use their lake in order to prevent overfishing by outsiders (Stocks, 1987). Similarly, on the Tamshiyacu-Tahuayo Communal Forest Reserve near Iquitos, set up in 1991, access by commercial fishing boats is carefully regulated by the community (Coomes, 1995).

In Brazil since the 1970s, as fishing has become an increasingly important source of income for the wetlands population, a growing number of fishing communities along the Amazon have set up lake reserves (*reservas de lago de várzea*). Such units have much in common with the rubber tappers' extractive reserves, discussed in chapter three. According to figures released by the church land commission (CPT) for Amazonas, local communities monitor access to some 160 lakes in that state alone, or 15 per cent of the total, confronting invaders in aquatic *empates*.[12] Water-based reserves have been set up under local legislation (*lei orgânica municipal*) in a number of Amazonian municipalities. Use of the *empate* is officially supported in at least seven municipalities along the middle and upper reaches of the Amazon, including Tefé, which embraces Mamirauá.[13] However, since *várzeas* are the property of the Brazilian Navy and subject to central government jurisdiction, which guarantees open access to wetlands, such moves are in fact illegal under federal law.

Notwithstanding such legal niceties, however, local police forces and judges have often been persuaded to intervene alongside communities in defence of local resources, in an attempt to set precedents for changes in federal law over the longer term. Reserves are intended not only to prohibit or limit access by larger, outside vessels, but also to regulate the growing volume of commercial fishing undertaken by the local population itself. Techniques employed include limiting extraction during the low-water period when fish are physically more concentrated and thus highly vulnerable, restricting the size of boats and prohibiting the use of gill nets, or allowing only traditional methods such as the harpoon, line and bow-and-arrow. Commercial vessels are confronted and asked to depart, but, if they refuse, are seized and handed over to the authorities.

As the above account suggests, no government fisheries conservation policy exists for Brazilian Amazonia, and neither does federal law protect local natural assets. Rather, communities have been obliged to take the initiative in defending the aquatic resources which form the mainstay of their livelihoods. During the 1990s, however, two major initiatives have been sponsored by a combination of government and NGOs which are attempting to change this situation: the Iara and Mamirauá projects in the middle and upper reaches of the Amazon respectively. Before discussing the Mamirauá project, the Iara scheme will be briefly described.

The Iara[14] research project was set up in 1990 as a collaborative exercise among several institutions. These include the National Institute for Amazonian Research (INPA) in Manaus, the Goeldi Museum in Belém, the Agricultural Science Faculty of Pará (FCAP) and the environmental control agency IBAMA, with the German government as providers of technical assistance and major funding. Based in Santarém, it covers a 400-kilometre stretch of the Amazon between Itacoatiara in Amazonas state and Almeirim in Pará. It has focused on one of the major conflict zones of the fish war, Lago Grande de Monte Alegre, currently a closed reserve to which only local groups have access. Over a ten-year period, and with cooperation between scientists and fisherpeople, Iara aims to carry out a range of multi-disciplinary studies of the biology, ecology, technology, economy and social organisation of fishing in this region. It is hoped to feed back information to assist fishing communities, in conjunction with NGOs, local authorities and other interested groups, to design resource-management strategies, while also exerting pressure on central government to introduce a fisheries conservation policy for Amazonian wetlands.

Iara is undoubtedly an important undertaking which promises to yield valuable data about the still little-understood *várzea* ecosystem and economy. The Mamirauá project is similar, but has as its main objective not just the collection of information but the design and implementation of an integrated management plan for a large area of Amazonian wetlands. As a case-study, it thus offers a clearer illustration of the potential and limitations of community involvement in a production-conservation approach which seeks to harness directly local participation as an effective and powerful tool of longer-term environmental policy.

Mamirauá: defending, using and preserving wetland commons

The Context

The Mamirauá project comprises a total area of 1,124,000 hectares of *várzea* or seasonally flooded rainforest, located in a triangle formed by the white-water (nutrient-rich) River Solimões and the black-water Japurá just north of the city of Tefé in the western portion of Amazonas state. It was designated an Ecological Station in 1990, under Amazonas state law, and constitutes the only official conservation area in Brazil located within flooded *várzea* forest.[15]

Project activities are presently concentrated in a much smaller area of 200,000 hectares, which has over 600 lakes, although the aim is eventually to expand activities to encompass the whole reserve (see Figure 4.1). Water levels in this part of the Amazon Basin fluctuate by up to eleven metres a year, being highest from May to June and lowest during September to October. At maximum flooding, the high ground is covered by up to one metre and lowest-lying areas by more than eight metres of water. An extensive network of oxbow lakes and channels are connected at high water, but become self-contained or isolated during the drier period, forming ideal fishing and breeding grounds. Behind the natural levees associated with these waterways, the terrain slopes downwards to back swamps (see Figure 4.2).

The dynamic interaction of local topography and hydrology has produced a complex mosaic of five major types of habitat (Polshek, 1993; Ayres, 1993). These consist of high *restinga* and low *restinga*

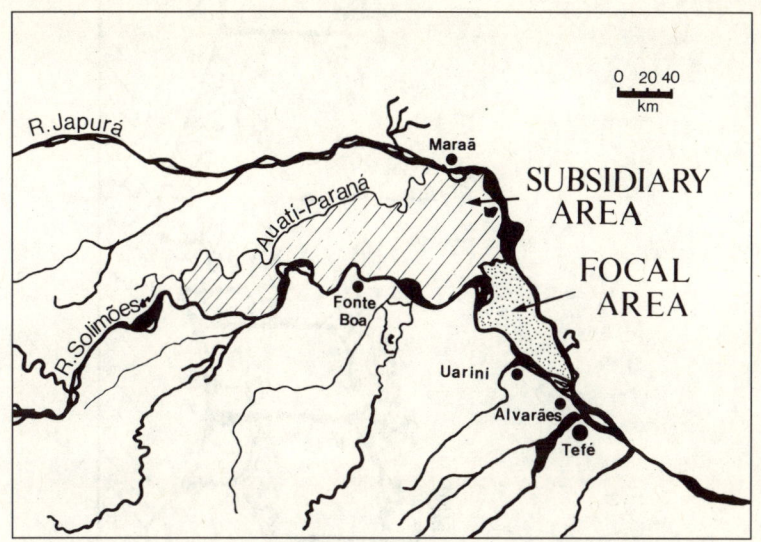

Figure 4.1   *Mamirauá project area*

forests along the levees, transitional shrubland called *chavascal* in the swamps, seasonal grasslands and open water areas. High *restinga* forest is similar to terra firma forest, but is submerged for two to four months a year and comprises some 12 per cent of the forested area. Low-lying *restinga* and *chavascal* constitute over 85 per cent of the forest, being inundated for 4 to 8 months of the year.

The area is rich in biodiversity with a high degree of endemism (Ayres, 1993). The hydrological cycle limits the diversity and distribution of most animal groups, particularly terrestrial, which includes six species of primates, two of which are endemic,[16] many bird species and an abundance of fish and aquatic animals, including two species of freshwater dolphin, as well as alligators. In fact,

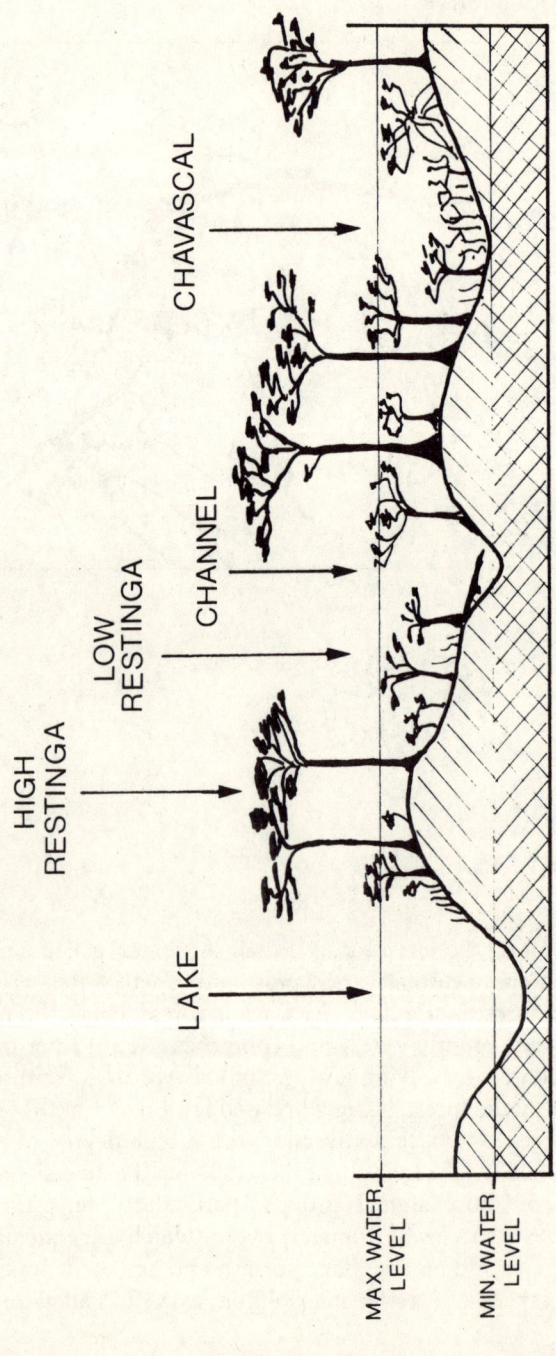

Figure 4.2 Cross-section of upper Amazon várzea

Mamirauá is said to house the richest aquatic system on earth. A striking feature of the *várzea* plants is their mechanism of seed dispersal, relying on frugivorous fish which enter the submerged forest, including the commercially valuable tambaqui and the pirarucu, the project's symbol.[17]

This part of the Amazon Basin was first settled by Spanish and Portuguese missionaries in the early 1600s. A combination of territorial disputes, use of Amerindian labour and assimilation has led to the extinction of most indigenous groups in the area. According to the accounts left by early Western travellers and missionaries, the *várzeas* once supported a substantially larger population than is the case today. Yet unlike other areas of terra firma and *várzea* in Pará, Acre and Rondônia, the wetlands of Mamirauá have not experienced massive human contact induced by intensive immigration and colonisation, with its resulting deforestation and altered land use.

The Mamirauá reserve population is predominantly *caboclo*, descendants of white and indigenous peoples, who live mainly on the river margins in houses on stilts as protection from flooding. Some 5,300 people use the resources of the focal area, about 1,700 of whom actually live within its boundaries in seventeen major communities and several smaller settlements. They have no formal land titles, since all wetlands in Amazonia are the property of the navy, although squatter laws allow tenancy rights to be acquired. Average annual household (seven members average size) income is estimated at $US900 and, although people do not show visible signs of the acute malnutrition evident in some other parts of Amazonia, they lack health and educational facilities as well as technical assistance for agriculture. Poor health and other social indicators reveal serious problems which belie the romantic image often held by outsiders of fisherpeople's supposedly idyllic Amazonian lifestyle.[18]

The local economy is based on subsistence agriculture (especially manioc), fishing, timber extraction and minor forest products. Small traders are responsible for most of the commerce between Tefé and Mamirauá, operating a system of informal credit, comparable with but less severe than the traditional *aviamento* common amongst rubber tappers. Farming is limited to the low-water period on fertile sediments, which are vulnerable to seasonal flooding and can prove disastrous for the domestic economy during especially wet years (as happened in 1993). Logs are cut in the dry season and floated downstream during the high water period, a practice which goes back half a century. However, extraction levels are still low and this method is much less destructive than the clear-felling techniques employed elsewhere on terra firma.

Fishing is most intensive during the dry season, when fish are concentrated in cut-off channels and lakes. Mamirauá residents use a variety of methods such as gill nets, cast nets, bow-and-arrow, harpoon and handline. Research carried out so far suggests that about 70 per cent of fishing by users of Mamirauá is for subsistence purposes, with the remainder for commercial sale.[19] In common with other *ribeirinho* populations in the middle and upper Amazon reaches, both in Brazil and Peru, Mamirauá users have over the years acquired a detailed understanding of the area's complex biotopes and seasonal fluctuations. This has led to the development of locally adapted fishing and resource-management strategies which have on the whole been well balanced and non-predatory.[20]

Early struggles for survival and the church
The major threat to this dynamic equilibrium and, as a consequence, people's livelihoods, has stemmed from growing commercial exploitation of the reserve by large vessels from Tefé and as far away as Manaus, about 800 kilometres downstream. As already mentioned, the Amazon has seen a rapid expansion of commercial fleets since the 1970s to meet growing domestic urban and export demands. These boats employ large, fine-mesh gill nets and have considerable storage capacity. Research indicates that such pressure has already resulted in severe overfishing, especially during the drier season when fish are concentrated in cut-off lakes, reducing populations and size classes of the most valuable species such as pirarucu and tambaqui.

Mamirauá experienced these problems as early as the mid-1970s, when the 'fishing frontier' moved westwards from the middle reaches of the Amazon around Santarém and Manaus. The prelacy of Tefé adopted Liberation Theology in 1970 and turned its attention towards some of the social and economic problems encountered by the population. Spearheaded in its work with fishing groups by a dynamic priest, the late Irmão Falco, the prelacy organised religious groups (CEBs), and held its first contacts with communities in 1976 about problems with invading fishing vessels.[21] By 1986, the first direct confrontations with commercial boats were registered and a general community assembly was organised to discuss the problem.

The Mamirauá region was divided into several sub-sectors, each with its own fishing committee (*comité de pesca*), responsible for monitoring the situation and organising resistance. Incoming boats were challenged in a series of aquatic *empates* or stand-offs involving men, women and children. Local police were called in to confiscate fishing tackle, although, as explained, there was no strictly legal basis for such punitive action, merely the goodwill of local authorities to assist the population. A Preservation and Development Group (GPD) was set up, with two representatives from each of eighteen communities, also involving the fishing committees. Closely advised by the diocesan Movement for Basic Education (MEB), the GPD still encourages the formation of local associations and strengthening of rural unions with a view to boosting agriculture and artisanal fishing and to oversee conservation measures.

As mentioned above, according to Brazilian federal law (1934), wetlands belong to the state, administered by the navy, and anyone is allowed to fish there.[22] Clearly, there is a direct clash here with the Amazonas state government's declaration of Mamirauá as an Ecological Station, which prohibits all productive activity in the area thus decreed. Municipal legislation designed to protect local resources, such as that introduced in Tefé and other areas during the 1990s, is, as mentioned above, incompatible with federal law. The new Brazilian Federal Constitution of 1988, which highlights the need to conserve valuable ecosystems, also runs counter to the 1934 civil code.[23]

In 1987, the prelacy of Tefé was at the forefront of an attempt by the CPT for Amazonia-Roraima partially to rectify this anomaly. A change in state and municipal law was sought in order to bring about an 'aquatic reform' (*Lei de Pesca*) which would have allowed lakes to be designated for specific, controlled uses (breeding, subsistence and commercial production) by the population. However, the attempt encountered strong political opposition from regional vested interests and was resoundingly defeated in the state legislative assembly.

The Mamirauá project

Following church initiatives during the 1970s and 1980s, it was proposed that a protected reserve be established under the aegis of existing Amazonas state legislation, at least as a stop gap measure until federal law could be changed to overcome the contradictions outlined above. Moves in this direction were led by Dr Márcio Ayres, a Brazilian primatologist who had worked in the area for several years on a study of the white uakari monkey. Following a long campaign, the Lake Mamirauá Ecological Station (EELM) was officially decreed by the Amazonas state government on 9 March 1990.

Mamirauá falls under the jurisdiction of the Environmental Protection Institute of Amazonas State (IPAAM), which has an official agreement with the National Council for Science and Technology Development (CNPq) and the MMA, covering project management, infrastructural support and scientific research as well as the introduction of conservation and management measures. Between 1992 and 1996, the first official funding phase, the project acquired overseas support of around $US3 million from a range of organisations, including (principally) the British Overseas Development Administration (ODA) as well as the WWF and Wildlife Conservation International (WCI). The main objective of this initial phase was to prepare a management plan for the 200,000-hectare focal area of the reserve, which will permit the conservation of its biodiversity alongside the productive use of natural resources by the local population.

Mamirauá was the first project in Brazil to attempt to reconcile biodiversity preservation with livelihood maintenance in an integrated programme within a legally protected 'conservation unit'. The hope is that such a methodology could be replicated in other wetland areas of Amazonia where fisherpeople's livelihoods are being placed in jeopardy by the growing threats to their natural resource base. The Amazon basin has 200,000 square kilometres of flooded forest in its middle and upper reaches, and the bulk of the region's rural population is concentrated along its waterways. The potential for such a productive conservation approach to be attempted elsewhere is thus considerable.

Mamirauá's original legal status as an Ecological Station signifies that, in theory, 90 per cent of the area should remain completely untouched by humans, while the remaining 10 per cent may be set aside for scientific research only. As already mentioned, however, this was considered a temporary legal solution, pending attempts by the project to bring about changes in federal law which will permit both conservation and productive use within an officially decreed 'direct use' conservation unit.[24] One of the project's aims has been to help introduce legislation which will allow preservation and sustained extraction for subsistence and commercial purposes. Towards this end, on 12 July 1996, Mamirauá was declared Brazil's first 'Sustainable Development Reserve' under Amazonas state law.

The project seriously challenges the notion, still popular in some quarters, that it is possible to preserve fragile ecosystems by excluding resource-users altogether. In contrast, underpinning Mamirauá is the notion that a successful conservation strategy is highly dependent upon the 'effective participation of reserve inhabitants and those within its direct area of influence, supported by a broad research programme designed to manage existing resources' (Ayres, 1993: 68). Like the rubber tappers' extractive reserves, Mamirauá is based on the principle of the Integrated Conservation and Development Project (ICDP). As will be detailed below, community participation is a key component of the management strategy in several respects. The feasibility of the ICDP concept rests to an overwhelming degree on the nature and extent of local people's involvement during all stages of design and implementation.

After the reserve was formally established, an NGO was set up to run the programme, based in Tefé, the Mamirauá Civil Society (SCM). The project is divided into five sub-programmes with distinctive functions and staffing.[25] The 'core operations' division is responsible for overall project administration and coordination of the management plan. 'Information systems' has the task of constructing a database of all information collected in the reserve area to allow data analysis, cross-referencing, modelling and geographic information systems (GIS) analysis essential for the full zoning of the reserve.

The 'aquatic systems' sub-programme is concerned with the conservation and management of fish and aquatic animals. Fish is the major exploited natural resource in the area. It provides some 85 per cent of all animal protein in the local diet, while the project zone itself supplies 10 per cent of fish marketed in Tefé.[26] Rational fisheries management thus forms a major pillar of the resource-management strategy at Mamirauá. Scientists from the INPA in Manaus and the Goeldi Museum in Belém are carrying out biological studies of major species of fish such as tambaqui and pirarucu, as well as research into *várzea* fish communities and mammals such as the pink river dolphin (*Inia geoffrensis*), the grey dolphin (*Sotalia fluviatilis*) and Amazonian manatee or *peixe boi* (*Trichechus inuguis*). Inventories of aquatic flora and fauna are being undertaken, while studies of the soil and hydrology will enable a map to be produced to support the zoning process. The cooperation of subsistence and commercial fishermen is sought in allowing access by researchers to fish catches for measurements to be taken as part of the survey process. This information will contribute directly to the setting up of a fish-management strategy for the reserve, which will permit sustainable extraction without causing harm to the aquatic ecosystem.

The 'terrestrial systems' sub-programme deals with research into commercially hunted species as well as on the economics and environmental impacts of logging. Work on the vulnerability of hunted animals will be used to determine appropriate wildlife-management techniques, to prevent the killing of endangered species and to encourage the sustainable utilisation of game by the local population. Assessments of the density and diversity of fauna are required for the zoning process, and inventories are being undertaken of a number of representative genera and species, including fish, caiman, birds, mammals and invertebrates. Research on timber extraction by local communities is being carried out with a view to monitoring the process and encouraging the adoption of sustainable forest-management techniques. Although logging occurs only on a relatively small scale at Mamirauá, the tendency is for such activities to increase, as inhabitants seek to supplement their incomes based on agriculture and fishing. Wide-scale deforestation at Mamirauá could have potentially disastrous consequences and throw the delicate ecosystem into a state of imbalance.

As on the other projects considered in this volume, at Mamirauá serious thought is being given to exploring the economic potential of agroforestry and non-timber forest products. Research shows that the inhabitants of Mamirauá practise complex and diverse agricultural and agroforestry systems; in three villages, no fewer than twelve agroforestry management techniques were employed at household level, each adapted to its specific micro-environment (Vasquez *et al.*, 1995). These observations match and reinforce the conclusions of existing research, which demonstrates the complexity of *várzea* agro-ecosystems in the Amazon estuary (Anderson, 1990b). Extension work is being undertaken to disseminate flood-resistant plants as well as more common varieties such as oranges and cupuaçu (*Theobroma grandiflorum*). Efforts are also being made to save the sapota tree (*Quararibea cordada*), which has been used locally for 2,000 years and to introduce camu-camu (*Myrciaria dubia*) trees into settlements.

Finally, the 'community participation and socio-economic' subprogramme is intended to gather information on the relationship between the inhabitants of the Mamirauá area and its natural resources. A survey team (comprising anthropologist, socio-economist, ethnobiologist and nutritionist) carries out surveys to accumulate economic and social baseline data for long-term monitoring of changes within the project area. Attention is being given to ways of increasing the economic returns from fishing and other natural resources, consistent with the conservation aims of Mamirauá. An extension team (consisting of a rural extensionist, nurse and education officer) is responsible for enhancing the provision of community services to the population, in collaboration with the local authorities, such as basic schooling, health-care and environmental education. This group has the key task of helping to consolidate a Mamirauá community association and facilitating the close involvement of Mamirauá inhabitants in the design and execution of a management plan for the 200,000-hectare focal area.

From the outset of the project, socio-economic issues have been strongly emphasised in the multi-disciplinary approach adopted at Mamirauá. Due in large measure to the hitherto prominent role played by anthropologist Dr Deborah Lima Ayres, the human dimension has been recognised as crucial to the successful implementation of a long-term management plan. This is so not only because of the perceived need to understand the interrelationships between the Mamirauá population and its natural resource base in the water and on land. As will become apparent, it is also vital because of the central role played by the human population in the creation, administration and enforcement of a management plan for Mamirauá. Without such involvement, the chances of success are greatly reduced, possibly close to zero.

Socio-economic research has been systematically undertaken since 1991 in order to produce a database for the purpose of analysis and monitoring. This started in 1991 with a census of 253 households (of a total of some 400 within the reserve area), complemented by a 20 per cent sample economic survey of household units within and outside the project area. These provide solid demographic data such as population size, sex ratio, education, religious and ethnic diversity, settlement and migration patterns. In addition, some information on major economic activities was collected, including agriculture, fishing and timber extraction. A longitudinal survey has also been undertaken to gather more data on household production and consumption patterns, using self-monitoring by 39 households, which will facilitate analysis of key issues such as income levels and the structure of the household economy itself. These data will be essential for understanding the role of natural resources in livelihood strategies.

Anthropological studies have also been carried which reveal the dynamic and adaptive nature of *várzea* communities. A study of fourteen locations through oral histories has revealed the high level of geographical mobility and the numerous reasons behind this phenomenon, including physical factors such as land movements and flooding as well as socio-political causes linked to land conflicts and religious features.[27] A subsequent study of individual family movements has revealed how, due to unusually heavy flooding since the 1980s, *várzea* communities have declined and terra firma settlements have expanded. These kinds of information will be vital in determining demographic dynamics within the Mamirauá area and will have to be taken into account when defining settlement zones in the management plan.

Environmental education at Mamirauá adopts a two-pronged, somewhat conventional approach aimed at children and the wider public. The first of these targets primary school children through specially designed modules in the curriculum, which teach pupils about the wetlands ecosystem and warn about the dangers of the over-exploitation of resources such as fish and timber. Teachers have been trained for this purpose, while several settlements closest to Tefé have themselves been involved in the design and pilot-testing of tailor-made primers, as the basis of a full programme in the fourteen largest communities.[28]

The second part of the environmental education programme has been directed at the general adult population of Mamirauá through talks and meetings. It adopts a similar stance, condemning 'bad' practices which carry heavy ecological costs, and encouraging 'good' methods, those considered not to be destructive of the resource base. As a complement to the project's other activities, the environmental education programme does seem to have achieved a degree of success in disseminating knowledge about the project and encouraging wider debate about the need to combine resource extraction with conservation measures at Mamirauá. However, the usefulness of environmental education at Mamirauá could perhaps be enhanced if it were more directly integrated into resource management, a theme which is discussed below.

Another 'socio-economic' sub-programme comprises various activities in the field of health and nutrition. Community health centres have been built and equipped, while health workers have been trained to deal with minor injuries, give vaccinations, monitor the health situation and provide basic health education. Together with the Amazonas state secretariat of health (SESAU) and the prelacy of Tefé, the project has helped to set up a number of health posts with trained local attendants. A major socio-epidemiological survey carried out in 1993 of 300 households revealed a higher-than-average infant mortality rate at Mamirauá, due largely to preventable causes such as diarrhoea. The study also showed evidence of malnutrition-induced stunting of children at weaning age. Further activities in the programme have included public education during 'health weeks' on matters of hygiene and preventative medicine, as well as trials of community water supply and sanitation installations. It is hoped that improved health-care facilities and training for medical staff will be provided through collaborative initiatives with the local authorities.

Such health and nutrition activities are often criticised by outside observers as standing outside the ICDP logic, which is based on the conservation, management and productive use of natural resources by local communities. According to this reasoning, a successful project of this nature should itself create the incentives necessary for participants to address any problems which may threaten the human or natural resource base. Yet health and education inputs may occupy a crucial role in the early phase of the project, when it is important to win the confidence and support of local people. Not only should this strengthen relationships between resource-users and project staff for the purposes of research and planning; these initiatives also serve to strengthen the resolve of communities in their demands upon local authorities for basic health and education services. Thus, activities which are apparently marginal to conservation efforts per se may be vital in building up local participation. This is important in a situation such as that of Mamirauá which, as will be seen in the following pages, may have its apparent unity of purpose undermined by a number of potentially divisive factors.

Arguably, the most important responsibility held by the socio-economic division of the project is that of setting up and strengthening participatory mechanisms to facilitate the design and implementation of a long-term environmental management plan for Mamirauá. In addition to the agricultural, health, nutritional, environment education and social research activities discussed above as vehicles for encouraging people's involvement in the project, a number of other mechanisms have been set up. Two local men with a long history of grassroots work with the prelacy have been hired as community outreach workers, whose job it is to travel the EELM and encourage dialogue within and amongst settlements over the mutual problems faced and proposals for tackling them. Regular meetings are organised in each of the eight geographical sub-sectors, while an annual general assembly is held to resolve major issues concerning the management plan.

This strategy, which builds very much upon pioneering work undertaken in the 1980s by the prelacy of Tefé, entails three major stages: firstly, reaffirming the rights of access to common property fishing grounds traditionally enjoyed by *ribeirinhos* but which have, since the 1970s, come under threat, both external and internal; secondly facilitating cooperation between scientists and Mamirauá inhabitants in the longer-term process of zoning the 200,000-hectare focal area of the EELM which will balance subsistence and commercial needs with conservation of stocks; and thirdly, helping to create a new legal category which will offer federal legislative protection to wetlands fishing areas.

The first general meeting organised by the Mamirauá project for reserve communities took place in September 1992, when it was agreed that the area would be organised into eight (now nine) sub-sectors, based largely on the division previously employed by the prelacy in its work with fisherpeople.[29] At this encounter, affirmations of common interest were made in terms of conservation and decisions made about basic organisation, such as the election of sector and community representatives. The second general assembly took place in February 1993, and was attended by about 120 people, mainly representatives from some forty of the total fifty-two settlements involved with the EELM. For many, this was the first opportunity they had enjoyed to discuss common problems. Predictably, discussions centred around the growing threats posed by commercial fishing vessels. An initial, tripartite zoning exercise was carried out, which allocated the lakes of each community for reproduction, subsistence use and commercial exploitation.

At the third general assembly in July 1993, the zoning process was advanced and six different types of areas defined. The categorisation allowed for reproductive, domestic and commercial use, as well as setting aside 'urban lakes' for fishermen from the local towns of Tefé, Uarini and Alvarães. This went a long way towards resolving the long-standing conflicts between Mamirauá's artisanal fisherpeople and urban-based fishermen (such as the Tefé fishing 'colony') who supply the towns by fishing in the ecological station but which are not part of the EELM. As will be detailed below, however, these clashes of interest have by no means ceased.

The fourth meeting (now organised on an annual rather than a six-monthly basis) was held in Tefé in July 1995, principally to disseminate the major results of aquatic and terrestrial research programmes to the communities, as well as to debate the health and educational components. These conclusions indicated the varying degrees of success achieved by the project so far in providing and encouraging the adoption by resource-users of various guidelines on fishing and hunting, consistent with overall productive conservation aims. Discussions were also held about procedures for drawing up a first draft of the management plan, which was completed in mid-1996. This incorporated proposals for the inclusion of scientific data to guide zoning, since the current designation of protected and non-protected lakes is based solely on community judgement and takes no account of biodiversity patterns and dynamics. At the time of writing, the final management plan proposal still had to be properly discussed with the communities involved, and agreement reached on the zoning of Mamirauá into diversified use areas. In order for the plan to be effectively implemented during a second phase, a balance will have to be struck between, on the one hand, conservation goals informed by scientific criteria and, on the other, the perceived livelihood needs of Mamiraua's fisherpeople.

From resistance to productive conservation
Alternative theories of common property resource-use considered in chapter one challenged the 'tragedy of the commons' thesis advanced by Hardin and others. Over-exploitation of natural

resources can be avoided, it was argued, if users perceive an interest in their preservation and are supported in their pursuit of such goals. Evidence suggests that this perception is likely to be based on a combination of two broad sets of factors. Firstly, individuals' self-interest in terms of how non-predatory resource-use will improve their own livelihoods. Secondly, collective responsibilities felt towards fellow producers, expressed in the conscious foregoing of short-term advantage in order to guarantee longer-term sustainability, both of natural resources and the livelihoods which they support.

In only a few years, Mamirauá has taken major strides towards the goal of defining and executing a sustainable CPR management strategy. Since the project became operational in 1992, Mamirauá has achieved a commendable degree of success in excluding commercial boats and implementing a lake-zoning policy, building upon but substantially expanding the pioneering efforts of the Tefé prelacy during the 1980s. Although the official project-holders, through the SCM, have given scientific direction to the enterprise and have been responsible for obtaining vital funding and technical support, the productive conservation strategy which is being attempted would not be feasible without the close cooperation of the resource-user population itself.

The Mamirauá project will depend for its ultimate success on successful community participation even more strongly than in the cases of other groups of small-scale producers. This is because, unlike the rubber tappers and small farmers discussed in this volume, for example, the population of Mamirauá is more heavily dependent upon a single resource. Whereas *seringueiros* in western Amazonia and small cultivators along the Transamazon highway tend to diversify their income sources and be more closely involved with the urban informal sector, the *caboclos* of Mamirauá still rely overwhelmingly on fish for a living. Fishing accounts for 72 per cent of Mamirauá's annual market income of $US2.36 million. This is quite apart from internal consumption by resource-users, estimated at a further $US2 million p.a. (Mamirauá, 1996). It is therefore imperative that common property aquatic resources be extremely carefully managed. For this to be achieved, people's participation is not merely useful; it is absolutely essential in several critical respects.

At Mamirauá, such involvement is being manifested in a number of distinctive and important ways. For such a large area, the scope of people's involvement across the 200,000-hectare focal region of the Ecological Station has been substantial, if patchy at times. Although the APR is difficult to measure, reports from community and sector meetings as well as attendance records at the annual general assemblies suggest that about two-thirds of the population is involved in the planning-conservation process, directly or indirectly. However, while participation in the bi-monthly sectoral and annual general meetings is quite high, interest in the monthly community meetings varies considerably. In addition, some fishers remain outside the project structure altogether. Frequent mention is made at community meetings, for example, of those 'isolated' fishermen (*isolados*) who cannot be persuaded to cooperate with the management process. Continuing abuses of zoning regulations by internal users bear witness to this on-going problem.

However good the overall level of involvement, it may hide crucial divisions within the population which reduce the scope of participation and can undermine the collective unity required for a successful conservation strategy. The relative socio-economic homogeneity of the population means that class divisions, unlike in other areas of Amazonia, are not significant at Mamirauá. However, the small size and geographically scattered nature of fishing settlements render close contacts difficult, and place major demands on the project in terms of transportation and logistics. Horizontal links amongst communities may also be undermined by the continuing strong tradition of debt-dependence on merchant traders or *regatões* who ply the reserve in their boats, buying fish, while selling other basic foodstuffs and consumer items at inflated prices.

According to research undertaken by project social scientists, a gender division of labour exists in which women fish to meet the subsistence needs of the family, while men are more concerned with commercial sales, often having to travel some distance in order to find valuable pirarucu and tambaqui. Although most formally elected community representatives are men, women are said to exercise a major influence on decision-making within the project through 'informal' channels via the household.[30] Research results so far do not indicate that gender divisions as such undermine the propensity for collective action at Mamirauá.

A more significant source of conflict amongst Mamirauá's users is religious in origin. The EELM project has included within its ambit a number of Protestant (Pentecostal) communities, which did not take part in the church's earlier programme. While these form only a small minority of the total user population, they are a source of mistrust and suspicion. Their respective community and religious leaders resent the project's attempt to challenge predatory fishing and destructive logging techniques, which appear to threaten their own local leadership as well as their economic vested interests in trade and commerce in these items. Project extensionists have thus had an uphill struggle persuading some settlements to cooperate with the overall strategy.

If the scope of participation is substantial but variable at Mamirauá, its effectiveness in terms of objectives and its strength is no less significant. Community involvement is critical in a number of less proactive dimensions to the success of the project. For example, in cooperating with researchers to supply scientific information on aquatic and terrestrial systems, which is essential for understanding the dynamics of biodiversity on the EELM; and helping to share the cost burden of community dialogue and mobilisation.

In other, more active ways, the capacity of fishing communities to discuss conservation issues and organise themselves has been enhanced via the system of representative participation set up to create a forum for the discussion of reserve issues. This has resulted in the local population acquiring a forceful voice in the definition of zoning arrangements and internal regulations. To the extent that this mechanism is giving fisherpeople greater control over the environment as it affects their livelihoods, it undoubtedly reflects a process of at least partial popular empowerment, notwithstanding the broader constraints under which the local economy and society is obliged to operate.

The potential strength of local participation has been most visibly and graphically illustrated by the vigilance system set up by the project to exclude commercial fishing vessels. As noted earlier, fishing communities in the region have, since the mid-1960s, been confronting outside commercial vessels which have 'invaded' their areas in large (up to forty tonne) boats, using high extraction methods such as large, fine-mesh gill nets. Men, women and children in canoes have literally formed human chains, barring the entrances to lakes, emulating the *empates* of the rubber tappers in Acre. The crews of commercial boats have been asked to leave or face retaliatory action; they have either been reported to IBAMA or, more usually, had their fishing tackle and even their vessels seized and handed to the authorities for the infractors to be dealt with. Mamirauá was, in fact, closed to large Manaus boats and smaller Tefé vessels in February 1993. While the Manaus commercial fleet has accepted this ban, however, local boats from Tefé have been reluctant to do so and some continue to fish in 'prohibited' areas, although the incidence has been lower than for many years.

Setting up a proper system of community vigilance has been a major first step in the overall management strategy. It represents a significant advance from a purely reactive strategy against incursions by outside vessels to a preventive approach which discourages such abuse, internally as well as externally generated, in a more systematic and proactive fashion. This has been facilitated by placing eight floating 'guardposts' (*flutuantes*) at the entrances to key lake systems along the River Japurá, which are home to valuable fish stocks. *Flutuantes* are equipped with a searchlight and solar-powered shortwave radio, allowing communications with each other, with project headquarters and with the IBAMA office in Tefé. Each post is permanently staffed by an environmental monitor, which is recruited from the community, given special training by IBAMA and paid a basic salary by the state government.

The aim is to extend coverage to the whole focal area, with a *flutuante* for each sector, including the more exposed River Solimões side of the reserve. Along the Japurá, this approach has been quite successful in keeping out commercial vessels, but in more exposed Solimões sectors, such as Horizonte and Liberdade, incursions by Tefé boats have been common and communities have felt powerless to intervene. In some Solimões sectors such as Ingá and Liberdade, the problem of overfishing is compounded by demographic pressure, which has resulted in the invasion of lakes set aside for preservation purposes.[31] Proactive commitment to the management plan is also reflected in the fact that nearly all the settlements at Mamirauá have agreed, as the result of discussion at community meetings and the annual general assemblies, on a preliminary zoning of lakes and channels for subsistence, commercial and conservation purpose, pending finalisation of the formal management plan.

In the early phase of preservation activities at Mamirauá, attention was focused on threats posed by external 'enemies'. Subsequently, however, the need to tackle internal abuse has been underlined. People's active participation has thus entailed a growing awareness of the need to stamp out infractions by Mamirauá's local users themselves. Initial findings are promising in this regard. Research results presented at the fourth assembly in 1995 suggest, for example, that although 25 per cent of pirarucu fishing trips in 1994 took place in non-designated areas, this figure dropped to 11 per cent a year later. The proportion of fish landed at Tefé market taken from the reserve has fallen from 13 per cent to around 9 per cent, which is indicative of increasing project effectiveness in implementing controls. A measure of agreement has also been reached amongst local people over the need to ban the use of gill nets in some areas for hunting valuable pirarucu and turtles, in order to lessen the risk of overexploitation.

Despite major progress, however, surveys by the project have shown that about one-third of all fishing trips within the EELM still take place in lakes set aside for reproduction and preservation. Related to this fact, the vigilance system has also collapsed in some communities. Consensus on the designation and use of lakes is thus still far from complete. As already mentioned, people's active and passive participation in a number of dimensions is absolutely crucial for the success of Mamirauá's productive conservation strategy. Without such public collaboration in the execution of a management programme, fish stocks would be rapidly depleted. Persistent shortcomings in the scope and strength of participation are attributable to a number of project-related and contextual factors.

Communication amongst the geographically scattered settlements within the 200,000 hectares so far covered by the project is difficult at the best of times. The distances which have to be covered are great, while community representatives are often overburdened, lacking the time and money to do their work effectively. Contact with communities is easier in the more densely populated areas around the local towns of Tefé, Alvarães and Uarini (see figure 4.1 above) and along the busier Solimões, while more isolated areas along the Rivers Japurá, Aranapu and Panauã tend to be less well integrated into the project.

Regular flooding has also destabilised settlements, as the ground, quite literally, shifts beneath them. This leads to a pattern of high internal mobility within the reserve, making attendance at project meetings logistically far more difficult.[32] The urban 'pull' factor is also quite strong amongst small rural producers who, through kinship ties, seek a wage income as well as access to better health and education facilities. This has led to a significant level of rural-urban mobility at Mamirauá.[33] At the same time, however, they recognise the frequently precarious nature of urban life and the food insecurity risks involved (Alencar, 1993; Ayres *et al.*, 1995). As in the rest of Amazonia, however, urban-based informal sector employment is increasingly combined with rural activities in the formation of livelihood strategies.

If physical obstacles to collective participation and communication are significant, the socio-political structure of *caboclo* society at Mamirauá does little to help. 'Communities' are often quite small settlements of a few households, based on the nuclear family and extended kinship. Aside from the aquatic *empates* mounted against commercial fishing vessels, there has been no tradition of broad-based collective action or political organisation. This could be attributed to the lack of socio-economic differentiation amongst Mamirauá's local users, and the relative lack of internal class conflict, compared, for example, with other Amazon frontier regions. Furthermore, ties of debt-dependence with itinerant traders in the reserve serve to reinforce vertical relationships at the expense of any potential for collective cooperation. That said, however, joint action may be favoured by the importance attached to horizontal kinship ties which incorporate living relatives in resource-sharing. The relative absence in the *várzea* of the notion of individual private property and inheritance is thought to discourage divisive, vertical kinship structures (Ayres *et al.*, 1995).

In this less than favourable situation, considerable resources need to be allocated for encouraging development and consolidation of the participatory mechanisms needed to underpin any longer-term management plan. However, the project's community programme has been run by only three people: a coordinator and two locally recruited extensionists. Although the two community workers have years of experience working for the prelacy with the local population, they cannot adequately cover the vast reserve area with its sixty separate settlements of lake-users. The environmental education teacher, health extension worker and scientific researchers provide some extra support, but it is still clearly inadequate given the sheer scale of the task. In this advanced stage of project preparation, a greater presence on the ground is required to get the productive conservation message across and support the population more effectively in its organisational efforts.

Mamirauá: lessons for Amazon fisheries conservation

Since the mid-1970s, fisherpeople at Mamirauá have been involved in actively defending their livelihoods, progressing from the use of spontaneous or reactive protests against commercial boats to a more systematic approach which envisages the longer-term, comprehensive management of their resource base. First, under the aegis of the Catholic church and, more recently, through the Mamirauá project, the defence and more sustainable use of common property natural resources has advanced substantially. While this can be rightly hailed as a major achievement, the design and successful execution of a management plan for the reserve will require some changes in community participation strategy in order to galvanise popular support more effectively. In terms of the theoretical discussion contained in chapter one, such changes are important for persuading individual users that conservation is in their own (instrumental) interest, as well as for generating a more powerful sense of group (collective) identity and responsibility.

At present, in spite of major progress in encouraging reserve users to take part in the Mamirauá programme, there is a continuing and perhaps inevitable clash of interests and perspective between project management on the one hand and the local population on the other. This separation of project and community at Mamirauá is exemplified by current procedures adopted for developing a reserve management plan, which has been carried out independently at two distinct levels.

Community zoning has been based on local needs and perceptions of the areas currently designated for subsistence, commercial and conservation purposes within areas controlled by sectors. Science-based project-mapping of the whole focal area, on the other hand, centres on the distribution of major habitats with a view to identifying areas which are critical both to the preservation of biodiversity and for maintaining or boosting production. The final management plan will need to reconcile these two visions following consultation between resource-users and scientists, adjusting community-defined zones in accordance with the results of scientific research on habitat distribution and estimated productivity, as defined in Phase II of the project.[34]

At a series of general assemblies, in addition to the already mentioned informal zoning of Mamirauá, communities introduced a number of measures designed to protect valuable resources: for example, on the extraction of logs beyond the legal limit (45 centimetre diameter), the restricted hunting of manatees for subsistence use only, prohibition of nets near turtle-breeding grounds and a ban on the taking of eggs and young birds. As part of Phase II, Mamirauá scientists have proposed a range of new restrictions on hunting and fishing of key species such as tambaqui, manatees, turtles, alligators and birds which will have to be discussed and negotiated with the communities, and which are likely to be contested in many instances.

That a conflict should exist between the preservationist priorities of natural scientists and the more immediate livelihood concerns of local groups is only to be expected. While this process could generate irreconcilable conflict, it offers a golden opportunity to all those involved in Mamirauá to construct a more durable and participatory system for reserve management over the longer term.

At one level, the problem of non-compliance or 'freeriding' in a CPR governance situation such as Mamirauá may be addressed by increasing project staffing in order to provide better coverage. This would enable information about the project to be disseminated more effectively, dispelling the hostile rumours which sometimes circulate, and for closer links to be established amongst otherwise isolated settlements.[35] More attention could also be given to strengthening community-level organisation and leadership training. Other extensionist activities could include, for example, training in conflict resolution, assisting communities in mapping natural resources and preparing local management plans, as well as technical advice in extractive and agroforestry activities to supplement fishing and logging. There is little doubt that, at Mamirauá, the community participation programme is presently underfunded compared with other scientific research components, and especially considering the critical importance of resource-user involvement for the success of the long-term management strategy. It is therefore incumbent upon Brazilian and overseas funding organisations to provide appropriate financial support to enable more qualified extensionists to be recruited and for a more effectively structured programme of community involvement to be initiated.

In addition to the question of understaffing, there is another, perhaps more fundamental matter which has to be considered. This concerns the extent to which communities are directly and actively involved in the provision of information for resource management and in subsequent decision-making. The project has undoubtedly been sensitive to the potential dangers of simply transferring the results of scientific research to the local population as the basis for a 'blueprint' plan. At the same time, it has helped set up a structure of representation through which communities can be involved in decision-making, for example, about informal zoning. Individual residents on the reserve are also involved in a broad spectrum of project research activities, supplying information for aquatic and terrestrial scientific programmes, as well as taking part in socio-economic and health-monitoring aspects.

Yet in some respects this is essentially a passive process, in which information supplied by the community will subsequently be used by others on the people's behalf. There appears to be little direct participation by resource-users in research undertaken by the project. Thus, there is the risk that local or indigenous knowledge will be marginalised; that sufficient community collaboration will not be sought in the highly critical area relating to the generation and analysis of information upon which management decisions should ultimately be based.

Such direct participation in research by resource-users could be facilitated by their closer involvement in local resource management. For example, rather than promoting conventional environmental education in which practices are categorised *a priori* as 'good' or 'bad', training could be provided in community resource-mapping and monitoring, encouraging users to understand their relationship with the environment as well as the limits of resource exploitation. In spite of the richness of indigenous knowledge in many respects, research suggests that *caboclo* fisherpeople have a tendency to overestimate resource availability. In an authentically participatory research and management process, it is more likely that residents would acquire the means to understand the implications of different production patterns, identify problems and be able to propose solutions.

Closely linked to the need for greater community initiative in defining a research and management agenda is the need for a strong reserve association which would be capable of taking on more independent responsibility for reserve management. At present, community representation is quite loosely structured and has no formal leadership above the sectoral level. Overall coordination of community affairs within the focal area of the EELM is undertaken by the Mamirauá project management. It is uncertain whether project leaders are fully committed to the idea of setting up an independent body or association to take charge of reserve management and community activities. This is understandable in terms of fears relating to the risk of political infighting amongst sectors and communities for leadership or the dangers of cooptation by outside interests, as well as concerns over the possible fragmentation of project authority and decision-making. It is likely, however, that the longer-term organisational sustainability of Mamirauá will require a greater degree of local governance and closer community involvement in active decision-making.

In development projects of this nature, there is always a risk that the holders might become new patrons, paternalistically dispensing benefits while retaining overall control. Yet just as fisherpeople and peasant farmers have developed passive forms of resistance to traditional bosses, so project beneficiaries may covertly resist project authority if they feel that they are being manipulated. They are likely to pay lip service to conservationist goals without changing their own behaviour substantially. It is essential that participants have a vested interest in pursuing the productive conservation approach. Resource-users will only be able to do this if they feel that they are masters of their own destiny and not mere pawns in a programme dominated by outsiders. One way of enhancing such perceptions is to facilitate the establishment of a relatively autonomous reserve association alongside project management, possibly under a broader organisational umbrella.

The potential of such a participatory, productive conservation approach for protecting resources and livelihoods in Amazonian *várzeas* could be considerable. Its replicability will, however, depend upon a range of factors. As already discussed at length, the nature and degree of community involvement will be a critical variable in any such strategy. In addition, however, planning must be informed by systematic research into the biological and social dynamics underlying wetland ecosystems. Following the example of Mamirauá, information will be required on the composition and movements of fish stocks and aquatic mammals, as well as data on rural–urban migration of the *ribeirinho* population and the role of agricultural as opposed to fishing activities in the household economy.

Many critical questions remain largely unanswered, principally because the Mamirauá experience is still at an early stage in its evolution. It has to be demonstrated, for example, whether a productive conservation fishing system can be set up to stabilise the *ribeirinho* population and prevent excessive out-migration. Also to be investigated are the complementary and diversified economic activities that are necessary to supplement community fishing in order to generate additional household income. Furthermore, in view of the growing dependence upon fishing as a basis of livelihood in the region, whether a sustainable balance be struck between subsistence and commercial extraction amongst fisherpeople themselves, even if outside vessels are effectively banned.

Phase II of the Mamirauá project (1997–2001) is building upon its initial success, while addressing some of the key issues raised which are critical for its longer-term viability. These proposals (Mamirauá, 1996) recognise the need to involve resource-users more closely in the decison-making on management of the reserve. Thus, it is suggested for example that communities play a more decisive role in the selection and dissemination of alternative economic strategies (agroforestry, sustainable logging, ecotourism) for Mamirauá, in an attempt to reduce pressures on existing natural resources such as fish and timber. It is also proposed that participatory studies be made of the household economy and biodiversity within Mamirauá, with a view to revising present zoning and management rules as necessary.

Most importantly, a revised management structure has been put forward which will address the above-mentioned problem of resource-users not being significantly involved in management decisions above local sector level. A nineteen-member Deliberative Council would be set up, including nine community representatives (one from each sector) alongside researchers and other involved parties. Its purpose would be to inform a new management committee, responsible for the day-to-day running of the reserve. Major decisions would be taken jointly by both groups, and subjected to approval by the annual general assembly. At the same time, more resources would be invested into extension work in order to provide greater project coverage and contact with the local population. In principle, this new set-up would go a long way towards involving resource-users more effectively in reserve management at Mamirauá. However, it remains to be seen how far the new structure will facilitate community empowerment.

In Amazonia, the attention of the world's media, academic researchers, government policy-makers and international donors has tended to be focused on the problems of deforestation, land conflicts and settlement on terra firma, as exemplified by the cases of the rubber tappers and small farmers along the *Transamazônica*, discussed in the next chapter. The crucial importance of addressing aquatic conservation and livelihood issues has been highlighted by the reaction of fishing communities against the threat of commercial depredation, as well as by the establishment of pioneering projects such as Mamirauá and Iara. If such a strategy can be successfully implemented and replicated across Amazonia's wetlands, building upon the knowledge and adaptive strategies developed by local indigenous and *caboclo* populations, there is a real possibility that major degradation can be averted and the artisanal fishing economy preserved. If not, the future of regional fishing looks bleak.

This alternative scenario may already be observed on the island of Marajó, situated at the mouth of the River Amazon (McGrath, 1993; McGrath *et al.*, 1993). Here, *ribeirinhos* have not been able to assert control over their resource base, allowing commercial fishing and cattle-ranching to expand virtually unchecked. As a result, catches have declined substantially and local fisherpeople have been relegated to an increasingly marginalised role, with only the most highly capitalised being able to earn good incomes. At the same time, *várzea* lands have become concentrated into the hands of larger cattle-ranchers, who also appropriate adjacent lakes and exclude locals, selling off fishing rights to outside entrepreneurs.

The situation on Marajó island is being reproduced upstream, as livestock rearing and deforestation spread. Problems on the *várzeas* now increasingly parallel those on the terra firma frontier in Amazonia, characterised by frequent conflicts between an essentially predatory, monopolistic minority of landowners and an increasingly marginalised class of small producers trying to eke out an existence in the face of a declining resource base. Yet regionally, although some depletion has taken place, the wetlands resource base is more or less intact.

The importance of floodplain habitats in Amazonia is underlined not just by their more global role in preserving biodiversity, but also by their economic and social functions. It is estimated, for example, that the food chain leading to perhaps 75 per cent of the total commercial catch in Amazonia begins in flooded forests such as Mamirauá (Goulding, 1981). The time is thus ripe for concerted action to prevent further destruction of Amazonia's rich and productive *várzea*. Although many problems have still to be faced, Mamirauá offers a pioneering example of how productive wetland resource-use and environmental management may be effectively reconciled.

Notes

1 International trade in fisheries products grew at a rate of 18% p.a. in the 1970s, falling to 10% p.a. in the 1980s. The FAO estimates that 70% of global fish stocks are depleted, while 9 of the world's 17 major fishing grounds are in serious decline or have been fished out altogether. The crisis is not limited to the North-West Atlantic and North Sea, but is becoming increasingly common in developing country grounds, such as the Gulf of Thailand, India and the North-West Pacific (McGoodwin, 1990; *The Ecologist*, 1995).

Its causes have been attributed to a combination of factors; the enclosure of local fishing grounds by commercial interests at the expense of indigenous populations, the creation of global markets for fish and processed fish products, the expansion of industrial fishing fleets and the new law of the sea, which has added to the pressure on developing country fish stocks.

The new law of the seas has increased such pressure in two ways: (i) by extending Exclusive Economic Zones or EEZs to 200 miles, thus increasing the jurisdiction of industrialised countries – the USA, France, Australia, New Zealand and Japan now control 33% of EEZ area; and (ii) by permitting developing countries to license foreign fleets to extract 'surplus stocks' (*The Ecologist*, 1995).

2 The rivers of Amazonia may be divided into three broad categories. Most (such as the Solimões, Japurá, Purus and Madeira) are muddy or *white-water* rivers whose headwaters lie in the Andes, where the diverse geology and volcanic soils provide a rich sediment load. Waters which rise in the rocky Brazilian central highlands to the south or Guyana highlands in the north are nutrient-poor, *clear-water* rivers (Tapajós, Xingu, Tocantins) which may be either acidic or alkaline. *Black-water* rivers (such as the Rio Negro) are also free from heavy sediments, acidic and black in colour due to organic overload arising from the inability of sandy soils to decompose organic matter. All types of floodplain have

their own distinctive ecosystems which are high in biodiversity. For further details, see Goulding *et al.* (1996).
3 The *várzeas* border the River Amazon and its tributaries, running from Pucallpa in Peru to the sea, with an average width of 20–100 kilometres (Barthem, 1995).
4 It is calculated that the Middle and Upper Amazon have a potential fish production of 217,000 tonnes p.a., and over 385,000 tonnes p.a. for its estuary, accounting for 63% of national production. Of an estimated 1,300 plus fish species in the Amazon Basin, at least 30% have still not been classified (Barthem, 1995).
5 Of 1,300 known fish species (possibly rising to 2,000) in Amazonia, over 230 have been exploited, the most commercially important of which have been tambaqui (*Arapaima gigas*) and pirarucu (*Colossoma macropomum*). See Moran (1993) and Barthem, (1995).
6 In the Amazon estuary, the fisheries authority (SUDEPE) – now absorbed by IBAMA – has imposed restrictions on industrial fishing, but these have proved ineffective.
7 The population of the lower Amazon floodplain in 1500 is estimated at twenty-eight people per square kilometre, compared with a current figure of four to seven people per square kilometre (Moran, 1993). Although archaeological investigations are providing new evidence of larger populations in the Amazon floodplain, accurate estimates are difficult to reach due to the shifting nature the river network and the destruction of remains (see Goulding *et al.*, 1996, chapter two).
8 From 1960 to 1990, for example, the population of Belém tripled to 1.2 million, and that of Manaus increased six-fold to 1.1 million. While domestic demand increased rapidly, in 1980 exports accounted for about 90% of the total catch of Belém's fleet, notably catfish (Goulding, 1983).
9 At Lake Janauacá in 1970, six people were killed in the 'fish war' (*Jornal do Brasil*, 27 February 1992). In Monte Alegre, fishing communities had for some time been protesting about the use of predatory extraction methods such as gill nets and explosives. Violence finally erupted in 1966, when over 100 men attacked refrigerated fishing boats in the lake, destroying two and confiscating nets. This series of confrontations culminated in the death of a *ribeirinho* in 1989 (McGrath, 1993).
10 Cited in McGrath, 1993: 112.
11 Several of the better-known cases may be briefly mentioned to illustrate this point. The Marovo of the Solomon Islands, Moluccans of Indonesia and the Cree in Canada place control over the allocation of fishing rights in the hands of leaders and councils. Among the Ponam of Manus Island in Papua New Guinea, marine tenure of inland fisheries is held by a small number of patrilineal leaders as trustees for, and answerable to,

the wider group, and each is responsible for allocating rights in separate ecological zones of the reefs and seas (Carrier, 1987).

The Kaiama people of Lake Oku in southern Nigeria open their grounds for a two-day period once every seven years, obliging outsiders to pay a fee (Fairlie *et al.*, 1995). Recent research on inland fishing in Bangladesh and Sumatra has shown how access rights are determined by a system of leasing by auction of fishing units. The same study demonstrates how fishing rights in Thailand are allocated by agreements negotiated among villagers and village heads with no need for coercion (Heady *et al.*, 1994).

In India, the reaction of coastal fishermen to commercial overfishing has been more broadly based. Since the 1960s, they have formed a social movement which has undertaken collective action to safeguard their commons against commercial fleets, through mass demonstrations and road-blocking. In 1994, this culminated in a strike by an estimated one million fishworkers along a coastline of 7,500 miles in protest against government fishing policies which encourage heavy foreign investment in this sector by multinational companies (Kurien, 1992, 1993, 1995).

12 *Folha de São Paulo*, 20 June, 1993.
13 'Empate é lei de preservação em 7 municípios amazônicos', *Jornal do Brasil*, 27 February 1994. The municipalities which 'legalised' the aquatic *empate* were Silves, Parintins, Tefé, Itapiranga, Anori, Urucurituba and Itacoatiara.
14 Iara signifies 'mother of the waters' in Tupi-Guarani Indian language.
15 The Ecological Station of Anavilhanas and the Jaú National Park have large flooded forest areas, but under black water. The Pacaya-Samiria reserve in Peru, which is over 20,000 square km in size, is only partly seasonally flooded.
16 The squirrel monkey (*Samiri vanzolini*) and the white uakai monkey (*Cacajao calvus calvus*).
17 This process is well illustrated in the beautiful BBC television documentary, filmed at Mamirauá, 'The Flooded Forest'.
18 For example, the infant mortality rate is 85 per 1,000 live births. Some 40% of under-fives suffer from respiratory ailments, 30% or more from dysentery and intestinal parasites. Of 200 mothers surveyed, 38% had lost at least one child before reaching the age of five (Mamirauá, 1996).
19 Information supplied by Mamirauá project researchers (field visit, July 1995).
20 For further details on the development of informal resource management amongst Amazonia's *várzea* fishing population, see Moran (1993, chapter four), Goulding (1981, 1990), McGrath (1993), Barthem (1995).

Fishing for a future

21 This account is based on discussions with Dom Mário Clemente Neto, Bishop of Tefé, during field research carried out by the author in July–August 1995. Additional information is taken from Faulhaber (1987) and Derickx and Trasferetti (1993).
22 *Código das Aguas*, Decree 24,643 of 10 July 1934.
23 Section VIII, Article 225 of the 1988 Constitution (Brazil, 1988).
24 Extractive reserves (RESEX), national forests (FLONAs) and areas of environmental protection (APAs) are considered 'direct use' conservation units under federal law, permitting the presence of human groups making their livelihoods there through the restricted use of local resources. No form of human exploitation is permitted in Ecological Stations, which are considered 'indirect use' conservation units under current environmental legislation.
25 The total staff on the Mamirauá project numbers some sixty-five including field assistants and postgraduate students attached to collaborating institutions such as the CNPq.
26 About 200 tonnes of the 2,000 tonnes landed annually at the Tefé fish market originate in the Mamirauá area.
27 See Alencar (1993).
28 The primers are published under the title of *Coleção Mamirauá* by the Federal University of Pará, Belém.
29 These sectors are: (i) along the river Japurá – Mamirauá, Tijuaca, Jarauá and Boa União, and (ii) along the Solimões – Aranapu, Ingá, Liberdade, Horizonte and Barroso. Each sector has two coordinators and each community two representatives. Sectors are encouraged to meet on a bi-monthly basis.
30 Conclusions drawn by Dr Deborah Lima Ayres in fieldwork on the project.
31 Numerous declarations to this effect have been made by representatives at community and sector meetings as well as the annual general assemblies. For historical reasons, population density in the Ingá and Liberdade sectors is much higher than elsewhere in the reserve; 9.0 and 6.4 persons per square kilometre, compared with a level of 0.6 to 2.0 in other sectors (Mamirauá, 1996: 21).
32 The average period of residence in a given locale at Mamirauá is reported as 6.6 years.
33 A project survey found that 75% of heads of household at Mamirauá had also lived elsewhere from time to time, mainly in towns and cities (Mamirauá, 1996).
34 Phase II (Mamirauá, 1996) defines two major zones: (i) 'protected zones', where only scientific investigations are allowed, intended solely for biodiversity conservation, and (ii) 'sustainable use zones', governed by norms established by communities and agreed at general assemblies.

In addition, 'special management zones' would be identified for specific purposes (ecotourism, fish, turtles, aquatic mammals, etc.).

35 In the early phase of the project, for example, a rumour circulated that foreign interests were behind Mamirauá and that the real plan was to extract all the fish there for export overseas. In its most ludicrous version, a pipeline was to be built which would suck fish from the lake and transport them directly to the USA. Such rumours were actively encouraged by those regional and local economic groups directly opposed to the conservation project.

5
Survival on the Transamazon highway

The previous two chapters have focused on rubber tappers and fisherpeople, groups which are pioneering the development of distinctive productive conservation strategies in Amazonia. However, the high-profile nature of struggles such as those of the *seringueiros* in western Amazonia has tended to obscure the much broader and numerically far more significant needs of small farmers in the region. About two-thirds of Amazonia's rural population of some seven million depend primarily not upon forest extractivism or fishing, but on agriculture, although in practice these activities often supplement each other quite closely.

A growing body of research evidence suggests, furthermore, that links are increasing between these more traditional activities and informal sector occupations such as gold-prospecting and urban-based commerce.[1] These occupations can no longer, therefore, be conceived of as being mutually exclusive or their practitioners as sedentary. They are, rather, complementary endeavours which involve rural Amazonia's inhabitants in increasingly diversified and complex livelihood strategies. This is coupled with a large degree of geographical mobility, much of it seasonal and rural–urban rather than being confined to expanding rural frontier zones, as conventionally perceived.[2]

Violence, land and livelihoods

The history of Brazilian rural development in general, and that of recent Amazonian settlement in particular, has been strongly predicated on modernisationist belief in the ability of large landholdings and industrialised agriculture as the key to economic and social progress in the countryside. This ideological justification, together with reinforcing political, strategic and commercial factors, introduced a strong policy bias from the mid-1960s against small farmers. In Amazonia, despite its pioneering role in pushing forward the physical frontier, and whatever its perceived role in the political economy of development, small-scale agriculture has been largely excluded from sharing in the generous subsidies which have been extended to other politically influential groups such as cattle-ranchers and commercial loggers. Although many of these economic incentives have now been withdrawn in the context of financial austerity and tightened fiscal control, as well official embarrassment over their inefficacy (see chapter two), the allocation of what resources still exist in the form of rural credit, for example, is still biased heavily in favour of large landowners and corporate enterprises.

However, in spite of indifferent or hostile government policy towards peasant farmers in Amazonia, and despite growing urbanisation in the area, it does not seem likely that small settlers will be relegated to a residual or marginal status within the evolving regional economy. Just as *caboclo* rubber tappers and fisherpeople have seized the initiative and become active participants in the pursuit of sustainable livelihoods, so migrant farmers are faced with a similar challenge. That is, how to modify and complement existing production techniques to provide adequate and relatively stable incomes, while avoiding the destructive practices which have so far predominated, striving to maintain the natural resource base upon which this set of activities will increasingly depend. Small farmers have only been able to survive and stake their claim in the regional economy because they have been prepared, quite literally, to fight for their livelihoods against powerful competing interests. In some instances, as with official INCRA settlement schemes on the Transamazon highway, land and minimal support have been provided by the state. Yet in the vast majority of cases (99 per cent of settlers), incoming northeasterners (*nordestinos*) and southerners (*sulistas*) have had no such support. The struggle to secure access to land has therefore been the most evident manifestation of this proactive stance by the peasantry. As noted in chapter two, large areas have been effectively secured for small-scale production through these tactics, especially by the MST in southern Brazil, as well as in the north-east and in the Amazon region, and subsequently formalised under agrarian reform legislation (Hall, 1990).

The cost in terms of personal trauma, injury and death has, however, been considerable.[3] Pará alone accounted for one-third of the national total of deaths from rural violence during the 1980s. The infamous 'Parrot's Beak' area, so named due to its distinctive shape, which embraces southern Pará, south-west Maranhão and northern Tocantins, accounted for no fewer that 1,017 land-conflict-related murders during 1982–92.[4] The eastern Amazon region, home of the Carajás mining complex, witnessed a number of major peasant massacres during the 1980s.[5] As new state highways such as the PA70 (now the BR222) and the PA150 were constructed in southern Pará, as well as in longer-settled areas such as the 'Brazilnut Polygon' around Marabá, peasant farmers developed quite sophisticated 'guerrilla' tactics in their confrontations with *fazendeiros* in land struggles. The radical Catholic church in the Marabá area was instrumental in forming and strengthening the movement of rural trade unions, or STRs (Araújo, 1991; Peixoto, 1991). Initially sporadic and fragmented protest has been transformed into well-organised resistance, although in Amazonia this phenomenon has not reached the scale of land occupations in southern Brazil organised by the MST.[6] Well into the 1990s, rural violence continues to be a depressingly familiar part of daily life in Eastern Amazonia.[7]

Although not apparent at first sight, this conflictive history has had important repercussions for current attempts to develop more sustainable agroforestry and farming systems in the region. This is true both with regard to gaining access to land as a basic factor of production, as well in terms of forging at least on a partial basis the group solidarity required for productive conservation to be viable. Although the intensity of land conflict has diminished since the most violent period between 1975 and 1985, and many land claims have been legalised, underlying tensions in the region are still strong. They reveal themselves in continued, if less frequent, overt land conflicts and outbreaks of rural violence (Amnesty International, 1988; Human Rights Watch, 1991). Such latent conflicts are also evident in the growing phenomenon of slave labour, as the landless engage in activities such as forest clearance for large cattle-ranching enterprises, gold-prospecting and charcoal production linked to the Carajás mining complex and associated pig-iron smelters (Sutton, 1994; Tavares, 1995).

Resistance to land-grabbing, as well as more active land seizures, have constituted perhaps the first important steps in a 'self-help' strategy adopted by small-scale producers to secure for themselves a more permanent stake in Amazonia. However, as many a disillusioned settler will testify, land on its own is of limited productive use unless it is complemented by other factors of production such as credit, more appropriate production technologies and marketing outlets. Where such support is not available to cash-strapped farmers, the temptation is always to capitalise through non-productive means such as pasture formation and land speculation.

The almost total lack of official assistance offered to small farmers has, as noted, obliged them to diversify livelihood strategies by engaging in complementary income-earning activities such as gold-prospecting and street-vending within the urban informal sector. The ability of small, pioneer settlers to secure stable, sedentary livelihoods in the region has been severely constrained by their dependence upon slash-and-burn, short-cycle food crop production. In virgin frontier areas with a low population density, this system works in the short run, although the ecological cost may be high in terms of lost forest cover. In areas of relatively intensive occupation, however, such as those of southern Pará and the Transamazon highway discussed in this chapter, the carrying capacity of landholdings where such techniques are used has often been reached or exceeded. The inability to rotate land has led to rapid deforestation, short fallow periods, soil degradation and declining crop yields, inducing farmers to sell up and seek new lands elsewhere, where the cycle will be repeated (Fearnside, 1990).[8] The added incentive to engage in land speculation in order to capitalise themselves further encourages a short-term perspective on the part of peasant farmers, which is incompatible with resource-conservation objectives.

Once land has effectively (either *de facto* or *de jure*) been acquired, therefore, the challenge for farmers and their allies is to devise the means through which agricultural and related production may be strengthened to provide subsistence farmers with higher and more stable incomes, while conserving the natural resources upon which such activities depend, to a large extent, for their success: namely, the land itself as well as its forest cover, soils, flora and fauna. Amazonia is currently home to a growing number of locally based projects and initiatives which are attempting to reconcile these two objectives. That is, they are trying to strengthen people's livelihoods, while breaking the destructive cycle associated with the usual pattern of settlement and land-use in frontier and post-frontier situations in Amazonia. These initiatives usually try to balance the short-term subsistence and income needs of small cultivators with longer-run considerations of sustainability. That is, they attempt to diversify current practices which revolve around the use of slash-and-burn farming methods, short-cycle crop production and timber extraction, with their harmful ecological and social impacts. These are complemented or replaced by agroforestry and forest-management practices designed to limit deforestation and which, if successful, enable the sale of higher-value agricultural and non-timber forest products.

Indigenous groups and *caboclo* peasant farmers have a long tradition of living in relative harmony with their environment, even with population densities substantially higher than those witnessed today, especially in floodplain or *várzea* regions. Amerindian groups, 'have subsisted for millennia by the effective use of diverse resources and without grossly degrading the environment ... [whereas] ... contemporary land development is often unstable in character' (Eden, 1990: 63). With Amerindian population density in lowland Amazonia limited by factors such as poor, leached soils and the availability of animal protein, groups have developed mechanisms which help avoid environmental degradation (Meggers, 1954; Gross, 1975). Many indigenous populations have maintained or successfully adapted these long-established practices, combining subsistence cropping with fishing and managed extraction of forest products for a range of food, medicinal and other purposes.[9] The far more numerous, mixed-race *caboclo* peasant population in Amazonia has built upon these traditions.

Although the number of such initiatives is still quite small in relation to the scale of the problem, research from both lowland floodplain areas as well as terra firma locations shows how groups of rural dwellers have developed situation-specific systems of rational land-use which meet their needs while preserving the local ecosystem.[10] Pioneer farmers from the centre-south and north-east of the country have also set up a range of local projects designed to put in place sedentary forms of farming, forest management and agroforestry which break the destructive cycle associated with imported slash-and-burn farming. Although most of these schemes have been in existence for only a few years, and many problems still have to be faced, they do reveal the potential for diversification of production systems within the rainforest environment, based on a combination of subsistence, short-cycle agriculture and commercial agroforestry.[11]

Perhaps the most long-standing and commercially successful is that of Tomé-Açu in Pará, set up in the 1920s. However, Tomé-Açu cannot be considered in any way representative of immigrant farmer initiatives in Amazonia. Not only does it have a distinctive socio-economic background, but it has also proven its sustainability over time.[12] Other schemes, started in the 1980s and 1990s by smallholder settlers, include the adjacent Mixed, Economic and Concentrated Reforestation Project (RECA), the Association of Victorious Rural Producers (ASPRUVE) and the Agricultural Cooperative of Extractive Producers (COAPEX) projects in southern Acre,[13] the Granada initiative, also in Acre,[14] community agroforestry in the Paragominas area of Pará,[15] small settlers along the Cuiabá–Santarém highway in the Tapajós National Forest,[16] *ribeirinhos* in many locations, including near Maracá in the state of Amapá, Combú Island adjacent to Belém and on the River Tapajós near Belterra,[17] the community of Uraim on the Belém–Brasília highway just south of Paragominas,[18] projects supported by Poverty and Environment in Amazonia (POEMA) on Marajó Island and near Abaetetuba, as well as peri-urban agroforestry initiated by the municipality of Rio Branco.[19] The remainder of this chapter will examine two linked programmes along the Transamazon highway in the state of Pará, which are attempting to develop their own productive conservation alternatives to the slash-and-burn farming normally practised by new settlers in Amazonia.

Centro Agroambiental do Tocantins (CAT)

The Agro-Environmental Centre of the Tocantins (CAT) was set up in 1988 as a unique experiment in inter-institutional cooperation for promoting sustainable rural development in one of Amazonia's most violent and ecologically degraded areas, the notorious 'Parrot's Beak' region of southern Pará. It grew from the realisation by a committed group of small farmers, united by their land struggles in the region, that 'their habitual cultivation methods were destroying their livelihoods, as well as the precious legacy of future generations, the Amazon rainforest' (Matheson, 1996: 103). Subse-

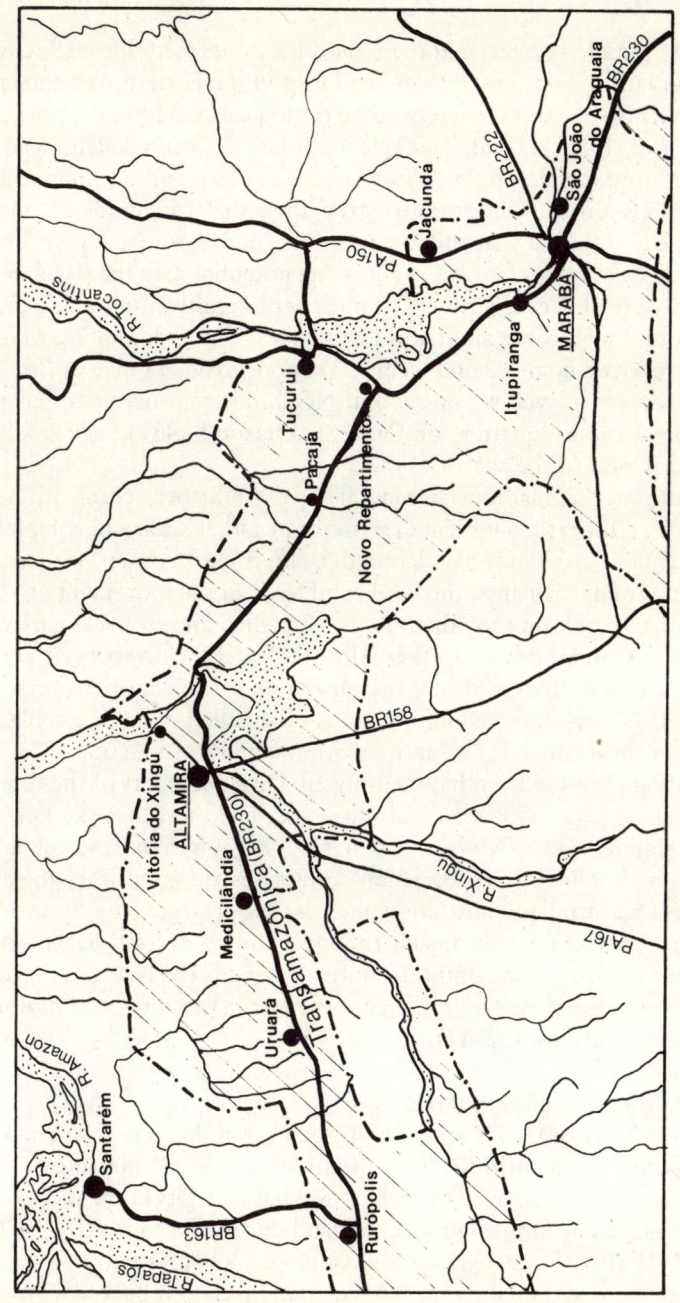

Figure 5.1 *Areas covered by the CAT and PAET programmes along the Transamazon highway*

quent detailed research in the region has confirmed this instinctive observation, 'that present-day land uses in the Eastern Amazon are frequently not sustainable from an ecological standpoint' (Almeida and Uhl, 1995: 1,745). This refers not just to uncontrolled logging or pasture formation, but also to intensive slash-and-burn farming.

CAT's aim is, therefore, to strengthen the livelihoods of small pioneer settlers by introducing farming and agroforestry systems which offer greater income-generating potential than the slash-and-burn agriculture which typifies most settler cultivation, while preserving forest cover and natural resources. The programme, which has received financial and technical support from a range of Brazilian sources as well as official and NGO aid from overseas, has its impressive headquarters on the Transamazon highway, seven kilometres west of the city of Marabá.[20]

Although similar in its broad objectives to the projects mentioned above, it differs from them in terms of its larger scale and complexity. CAT is essentially a collaborative enterprise between two major groups of participants: the local rural trade union movement on the one hand and, on the other, official Brazilian and overseas agricultural research bodies together with the Federal University of Pará. Thus, it was envisaged that the efforts of peasant farmers, technicians and academics could be jointly channelled towards establishing a new model of 'agro-environmental' production. CAT's guiding philosophy is that the only effective defenders of the forest are those who live there and work the land, and that the key to developing a successful strategy lies in, 'organisation, research and training'. The CAT programme comprises three basic elements: firstly, a central administration and training centre; secondly a rural union arm which coordinates the involvement of local STRs – the Agrarian Foundation of the Tocantins-Araguaia (FATA); and thirdly, the agricultural research branch – the Socio-Economic Laboratory of the Tocantins (LASAT).

The farmers' association (FATA)
At the heart of CAT's approach is the notion that a well-organised peasantry must form the basis of any process of sustainable development in the region. This perception has its roots in the proactive role played by farmers in securing land during the conflictive 1970s and 1980s as the agricultural frontier moved westwards from Maranhão, and in key support provided by church-backed STRs in

the resolution of land conflicts. In fact, the founder members of CAT were closely involved in these earlier struggles, either as university-based teachers and researchers or in other capacities such as members of the CPT in Marabá. FATA was set up to represent the interests of small farmers within the CAT programme and, more specifically, to develop new activities in the fields of production, marketing and credit. To this end, the Small Farmer Cooperative of Extractive Producers (COCAT), was established in 1993.

CAT comprises the five rural unions covering the municipalities of Itupiranga, Jacundá, Marabá, São João do Araguaia and São Domingos, an area of 40,000 square kilometres, with some eighty local branch offices (*delegacias*). Nominally, the unions have almost 16,000 members, although the CAT programme itself actively involves about 3,000 small farmer families. A basic principle which underpins the CAT philosophy is that farmers should, following the land conflicts of the past (many of which persist), continue to play an active, participatory role in defining and implementing new development initiatives which attempt to break the current destructive cycle. However, exactly which priorities are identified and the longer-term implications of such choices are matters of some contention within the project.

The agricultural research arm (LASAT)
Exclusive responsibility for undertaking research into current farming practices and for identifying possible innovations to promote more sustainable development options was originally assigned to LASAT. A number of Brazilian government institutions such as the Brazilian Agricultural Research Agency (EMBRAPA) and, the Institute for the Economic and Social Development of Pará (IDESP) have contributed to research efforts, while a close link exists with postgraduate training programmes at the Federal University of Pará. A succession of groups of Master's students from the Nucleus of Higher Amazonian Studies (NAEA) at the university have been involved in agronomic, economic and social research at CAT, producing dissertations on a range of topics, while assisting in the project's own research programme as well. A postgraduate programme (DAZ) has also been set up at the university to train technicians to work with small farmers in Amazonia adopting a farming systems and environmentally sensitive approach.[21]

Notwithstanding any Brazilian collaboration, LASAT's mainstream research activities have been directed by a small group of technicians from France and French Guyana, backed by the Group for Research and Technological Exchange (GRET) and the Office for Scientific Research Overseas (ORSTOM). Since 1989, LASAT has been studying the production cycle of small settler farmers in the region, adopting a Farming Systems Research (FSR) approach.[22] In its research documents, LASAT emphasises the importance of maximising farmer income in the short-run through improvements to existing, relatively well-established farming practices based largely on the cultivation of rice and on cattle rearing. At the same time, LASAT remains, for various reasons which are considered later, highly cautious (even sceptical) regarding the feasibility of agroforestry activities, a priority which has been identified by the FATA. In LASAT's own words, it 'is less concerned with looking for 'miracle' technologies than with the diffusion of existing information' (LASAT, 1992: 26). This contrast in perspective between researchers and rural unions over the appropriate production systems for small farmers has had significant implications for the functioning of CAT, and has perhaps contributed towards the undermining of the project's original unity of purpose.

The Marabá area has this century been subjected to various waves of migrant farmers, each representing different stages of frontier occupation. These range from families which arrived in the 1920s and 1930s to practise extractivism in the 'Brazilnut Polygon', to those who came in the 1960s and 1970s along newly constructed state highways, as well as the official colonists recruited for the *Transamazônica*. The most recent large influx was attracted by major construction projects during the late 1970s and 1980s, including the Tucuruí dam as well as the Carajás iron-ore project and railway (Hall, 1991).

Correspondingly, small-scale farming in the region is far more complex and diverse than suggested by stereotyped images, which often portray peasant cultivators either as universally destructive in rabid pursuit of short-term gain, or driven by unyielding poverty, totally insensitive to longer-term environmental considerations. LASAT's research has confirmed findings reached in many other parts of the world that small farmers make considered calculations about the most appropriate livelihood strategies for the highly variable and situation-specific circumstances in which they find themselves. Choices about production activities and their sustainability over time thus depend on a range of highly variable factors, including the size of holding (which may range from 50 to over 200 hectares), soil quality, rainfall distribution, proximity to urban centres and roads, availability of family labour (conditioned by the stage reached in the household or family cycle) and additional sources of income, as well as the degree of capitalisation from previous activities.

Although individual situations vary considerably, however, LASAT's research shows that there is a typical production cycle followed by most small settlers in this area. After about ten to fifteen years, a technological and economic crisis is generated at the level of the production unit, which needs to be resolved by one means or another. This economic-environmental crisis is brought about by the relative attractiveness of cattle-rearing *vis-à-vis* crop production in the Amazon context. Interpreting research data collected by LASAT and others, four major phases may be broadly distinguished in the production cycle of small settler farmer households: those of arrival, development, consolidation and crisis.

Arrival Typically, as soon as the new settler arrives, a three-hectare plot is cleared for the production of rice and cassava to meet family subsistence needs, supplemented by game and fruits from the still largely intact forested portion of the holding. In addition, timber-extraction rights are sold to logging companies in exchange for the clearing of a lumber trail for farmers' use.

Development After four or five years, a larger area of forest will have been cut down, the family house improved and animal pens for chickens and pigs, etc. built. Any accumulated wealth is invested into cattle, and pasture is sown. Investing in cattle is an economically rational choice for small farmers, at least within existing production patterns. Not only do cattle generate a higher income than annual crops, but prices are far more stable, they are not so affected by climatic vicissitudes and they provide, above all, a secure and geographically mobile capital reserve which complements other forms of wealth creation. This livestock-based strategy is common in other areas of Amazonia such as INCRA colonisation schemes along the Transamazon highway at Altamira, discussed below, as well as in Rondônia (Léna, 1991).[23] The remaining forest produces less and less game to supplement the family diet, while the few isolated brazil-nut trees (*castanheiras*) left standing – their felling is prohibited by law – become sterile and yield no more nuts.

Consolidation A third phase is reached as the area under annual crops is increased to an average of seven hectares in order to finance pasture expansion, which now covers over one-third of the typical fifty-hectare plot. Thus, ten head of cattle on twenty or so hectares of pasture enables a high rate of labour productivity to be generated, with 100–150 days producing an average of $US650 annually. After some fifteen years, cattle comes to play a far more important role in the farming system than annual crops, perennials remaining common but marginal to income-generation. Some cultivators will have kept perhaps 30 per cent of their original forest cover, while in other plots it will have been totally destroyed.

Crisis Where soil, climatic and other conditions such as proximity to urban centres are favourable, the crisis may be averted for a while.[24] Eventually, however, a critical point is reached where there is no more forested land immediately available to replace existing degraded pastures and crop areas, while yields of fodder and subsistence crops drop steadily due to soil exhaustion, and the system falls into a state of disequilibrium. As many researchers have shown (Hecht, 1985; Fearnside, 1990), the fertility of Amazonian pastures declines rapidly, enjoying an average lifespan of eight to fifteen years.

Once this crisis point has been reached, the only options available to the small farmer are either to sell up and move away completely, or buy additional land to reinforce the livestock component. In the latter case, land may be purchased either locally in the case of relatively new frontier zones where it is still available, or further afield if necessary, its price varying widely and determined by a range of factors from soil quality to ease of access and legal status.[25] In either case, growing land concentration and livestock specialisation (*pecuarização*), with accompanying pasture degradation and an inbuilt tendency towards falling yields, inevitably follow. LASAT found in their survey that, as a consequence of this strategy, on average there was a 7 per cent turnover of households in communities over twenty years old.

Thus, evidence from Marabá as well as other parts of Amazonia[26] suggests that peasant farmers, when faced with livelihood strategy choices, are no more inherently disposed to ecologically 'sustainable' practices than larger producers. However, as the present volume hopes to demonstrate, when presented with viable alternatives and appropriate productive conservation strategies, small-scale rural producers will commonly opt for non-destructive methods. Not only is this an economically and technically rational choice in terms of self-interest and preservation of the resource base, but it also often reflects, it is argued here, a deeper sensitivity over the need to preserve natural resources. This awareness is frequently present, but usually suppressed by the daily struggle for existence and the fight for survival.

Despite these pressures, LASAT's own research provides evidence which suggests an unexpected degree of ecological awareness on the part of pioneer settlers in given situations. One example concerns the re-use of cultivated land after the burning of secondary forest, despite the fact that such areas have lower soil fertility and produce inferior rice yields when compared with freshly deforested tracts (the so-called '*capoeira* crisis'). LASAT concluded that this is an economically rational decision on the grounds that the burning of secondary growth, rich in biomass after five years, does serve to replace essential soil nutrients, resulting in comparable levels of agricultural productivity. In addition, it is physically easier work, which can be performed by youngsters, thus absorbing surplus labour in the family production cycle.

Be that as it may, however, the farmers in the CAT project have given as their justification the fact that this practice enables them to 'economise on forest'. Paradoxically, this observation is immediately dismissed by the researchers, otherwise so preoccupied with the expressed 'rationality' of farmers' decision-making, as out of hand and 'not very convincing' (LASAT, 1992: 17). In addition to any immediate agronomic benefits, the practice of secondary forest use, according to the farmers' testimony, also suggests a concern with preserving natural capital not simply for personal future profit, but also with an eye to its wider significance for the local environment and the related sustainability of rural livelihoods generally. Harnessing these individual and collective concerns in order to devise a viable productive conservation strategy for the Marabá region is a major challenge faced by the CAT programme.

Economic projects
Since the CAT programme got under way there have, in addition to

LASAT's research, been two tangible initiatives to strengthen farmers' livelihoods: rice-marketing and agroforestry. Both sets of activities indicate a concern on the part of the project to achieve two complementary aims: firstly, in the short term, to improve the productive base for individuals, while, secondly, in the longer run, to reinforce farmers' more collective perceptions of the need to preserve the remaining forest as a form of investment for the future.

Rice-marketing   Rice is the main subsistence and commercial crop for small settlers in the region. Prices vary considerably over time and geographically, thus placing producers, especially in isolated communities, at a serious disadvantage and subject to the whims of intermediaries. This key problem was soon identified by LASAT, and annual rice-marketing trials were started in 1989 with seven farmers' groups, expanding to over thirty groups by 1992. This involved a good deal of initial cooperation between researchers and farmers' organisations. LASAT was responsible, in collaboration with farmers, for collecting basic data on production levels and market prices, as well as for analysing overall results. FATA took on the job of overseeing implementation of the project. In order to overcome the constraints imposed by the limited availability of working capital through CAT private funding sources, COCAT was set up in 1993 in order to gain access to official credit through special programmes such as the FNO. By 1994, over 500 farmers were marketing their rice through COCAT, at a considerable financial advantage compared with previous arrangements through local traders.

While rice-marketing continues to be popular with farmers in the CAT programme, however, it has come under some criticism. Originally intended as a means of strengthening the cohesiveness of farmers' groups, one evaluation study alleged that participants were interested only in gaining access to credit, processing and storage facilities, and that the workload was borne exclusively by group leaders rather than being shared. In addition, it was observed that this component did nothing actually to diversify production patterns in the region (Castellanet *et al.*, 1994). However, the fact that the rice project has stimulated some group activity and led to the setting up of a cooperative suggests that it may have made a significant contribution in the direction of a more collectively based production strategy. The additional income generated by rice production should in theory lessen pressure on the forest. However, if the surplus is invested into pasture formation and cattle as a form of security for small farmers, it could well produce the opposite effect.

Agroforestry The second major sphere of activity concerns the introduction and dissemination of tree crops to complement short-cycle staples. As the first serious attempt at product diversification within the CAT programme, and running directly counter to LASAT's mainstream agricultural-livestock research priorities, the agroforestry project (PAF) got under way in 1991 following a funding request from FATA to the British ODA.[27] A central demonstration area was set up at CAT headquarters in Marabá and, by 1995, some twenty tree nurseries had been established at community level with almost 300 households participating. Emphasis is being placed on commercially appealing perennial wood, fruit, spice and medicinal crops.[28] Volunteer community extensionists would help spread these new ideas and train settler farmers in tree cultivation techniques, while marketing studies carried out by the project and state authorities were expected to identify outlets for tree crops.

At the same time, socio-economic studies were planned to ascertain the potential for expanding agroforestry activities and to act as a baseline for later evaluation purposes. The aim is that in due course these new crops will boost farmer incomes, while helping to conserve the remaining rainforest. This will be achieved, it is hoped, through a diminution in the need for slash-and-burn practices to sustain livelihoods. In addition, as tree crops become commercially more attractive, it is expected that small farmers will be less dependent upon cattle-raising as an income generator and there will be less pressure to create pasture from existing forested areas.[29]

Execution of the agroforestry sub-component was initially hampered by its poor integration within the CAT programme, including the above-mentioned clash of opinion with LASAT over the direction of research and production activities. By 1996, little actual dissemination from nurseries to the plots of individual farmers had taken place, but this is understandable given the novelty of the agroforestry concept for the vast majority of small settlers in the Marabá region and the relatively substantial investments involved for households in terms of cash, time and labour power in order to establish these new activities.

Extension activities were for a time hampered by an internal dispute over whether community workers should be remunerated to compensate them for the opportunity costs of their work in terms of time away from their plots, or whether their contributions should remain voluntary in order to avoid creating a long-term financial burden for CAT. Additional questions remain to be answered about market potential for agroforestry products, as well as associated problems of transportation, storage and processing. Without assured outlets for their produce, it is unrealistic to expect that small cultivators will risk making major commitments in an untried field.

CAT: towards productive conservation?
Although the CAT programme has been operational for only a few years, and in spite of the inevitable teething problems encountered, there are indications that major progress has been made in the direction of a productive conservation model. The priority attached to burning of secondary as opposed to primary forest suggests a concern for conservation and investment for the future, which, to an extent at least, overrides short-term, profit-maximisation considerations. Forest preservation will receive a boost to the extent that CAT's agroforestry project successfully introduces an economically viable alternative or complement to slash-and-burn farming combined with cattle-rearing, although this income-generating potential on a broad scale has yet to be demonstrated in the context of southern Pará. The traditional importance of fruit trees adjacent to family houses both for domestic consumption purposes as well as a symbol of property rights in land disputes, will facilitate this process.

Yet a number of factors operate which threaten to undermine productive conservation initiatives through CAT. Unlike the Amazonian case-studies mentioned previously, property titles in this instance are solely individual. There is no substantive element of common property except to the extent that individuals perceive the remaining forested areas to be serving both general as well as individual interests. That is, in so far as intact rainforest provides environmental services which operate to the advantage of the whole local population in terms of maintaining climatic stability, preserving soils and resource stocks.

In this respect, part of the challenge facing CAT through its production and its environmental education programmes is to enhance people's awareness of the group benefits, in addition to any potential individual profits to be enjoyed from a more ecologically sustainable model of agricultural production. This strategy will stand a greater chance of success if the project's research arm, LASAT, is able to adopt a more flexible attitude to the introduction of agroforestry as an option for small settlers, supplementing more traditional agro-livestock practices.[30] This will depend on how well research initiatives within CAT can be integrated and a multi-pronged action programme developed.

One of the factors which has allowed CAT to build up such a large base of small farmer support within a relatively short space of time is the strong role played by STRs in land settlement strategies during the 1970s and 1980s. STRs were originally set up in southern Pará by the military regime, essentially as welfare support agencies to assist in the peaceful occupation of Amazonia and to diffuse potential conflicts. This was considered especially important by the authorities in view of counter insurgency activities against Maoist guerrillas during the late 1970s in southern Pará.[31] During the mid-1980s, however, most of the original leaders – nicknamed *pelegos* because of their perceived connivance with the civil and military authorities – had been replaced by new blood, committed to advancing the peasants' struggle for land (Guerra, 1991). Aided by a number of local NGOs such as FASE, CEPASP, MEB and the regional church land commission (CPT) in particular, local unions have been instrumental in defending small farmers in disputes of various kinds by providing legal as well as logistical support.

The founding rural unions within CAT and FATA were at the forefront of these efforts.[32] This has involved a range of activities, from resisting attempts at eviction on the part of local *fazendeiros*, to the occupation of unproductive lands and claims for compensation for those displaced by the Tucuruí reservoir and even the occupation of INCRA offices. Some indication of the local influence wielded by STRs in their campaign for secure access to land may be gauged from the fact that, in 1988, over 200,000 hectares (one-fifth) of the 'Brazilnut Polygon' were expropriated under agrarian reform legislation, largely as a result of these efforts (Hall, 1990, 1991).

However, if rural unions in southern Pará changed from being mere welfare agencies during the 1970s to class-based organisations during the subsequent years of land conflict, the political unity thus forged has not necessarily been sufficient to guarantee widespread adherence to development initiatives discussed here. Of around 16,000 small farmer families in the project area, only 3,000 at the most participate in the CAT programme. While this number will probably grow as the agroforestry and other activities expand, it suggests that the majority of the local population still remains to be convinced of the potential benefits being offered by CAT. At the same time, however, it also indicates the programme's limited resources available to be used to involve all those who might wish to take part.

Yet if a certain degree of reticence is only natural during the formative years of a novel programme such as CAT's, other factors serve to limit people's participation in the scheme. Some of these are physical and social: the geographical dispersal of the population in individual households often separated by several kilometres is an obstacle to communications, while the quality of relationships amongst families varies considerably depending on local circumstances and commonalities or origin. With some exceptions, it is also the case that female participation in both union and agroforestry project activities is extremely limited, reflecting traditional male dominance in production-related activities. This stands in direct contrast to the dynamic and key involvement of women during the land struggle phase of the 1970s (Hébette and Colares, 1990), and may well undermine the building up of collective solidarity for conservation purposes.

However, if local tradition and culture is a part explanation of variable community participation in the CAT programme, other problems are created by the nature of the project itself. For example, FATA insists that all those taking part in the agroforestry sub-project should be union members, thus automatically excluding the majority of the local population, which is non-unionised. While this indicates the unions' desire to lead the latest development phase, in terms of spreading economic benefits and generating a greater environmental sensitivity on the part of small farmers, the rule is highly restrictive and probably generates local resentment against the programme. The choice of research methodology by LASAT, a variant of traditional FSR, has also been seen by some observers as a potential hindrance to the more effective participation of small cultivators and has led to expressions of frustration by FATA that research is not properly serving communities' longer-run needs in terms of reconciling production with preservation. They see such FSR-based research as merely pandering to the profit maximisation goals of some farmers, particularly those wealthier and more capitalised producers who have invested most heavily into cattle and pasture formation.[33]

Programa Agro-Ecológico da *Transamazônica* (PAET)

The Agro-Ecological Programme of the Transamazon highway (PAET) based in Altamira, about 1,000 kilometres west of Marabá, is a direct offshoot of the CAT experience. The programme was formally established in 1993 and, like its sister programme in Marabá, aims to strengthen and diversify peasant farming on and around the *Transamazônica*, while minimising the uncontrolled deforestation typical of small farmer settlement and large-scale cattle-ranching in the region.[34] The programme operates along an 800-kilometre stretch of the highway from Rurópolis, at the junction of the *Transamazônica* and the Santarém–Cuiabá highway, to Repartimento, on Lake Tucuruí.

Following the CAT principle, PAET is a partnership between a group of foreign and Brazilian researchers (the Agro-Economic Laboratory of the Transamazon highway – LAET) and an umbrella organisation representing farmer interests (the Movement for Survival on the Transamazon highway – MPST). Unlike CAT, however, it was decided not to build expensive headquarters as a joint base and training centre, nor establish the kind of institutional ties which exist between LASAT and FATA at Marabá.

This arrangement has had advantages in terms of giving the CAT programme a high profile and strong physical presence, but has been expensive both to construct and maintain, with implications for financial sustainability. Problems have also arisen due to intra-institutional competition between LASAT and FATA over priorities and resources, as discussed above, which the much looser PAET structure seeks to avoid. Rather, PAET involves a system of flexible collaboration between the researchers and farmers' bodies, which have totally separate identities and fund-raising responsibilities, but cooperate in specific activities according to agreed contractual principles. The programme's major priorities were set out at the start following intensive discussions between researchers and farmer representatives (LAET/MPST, 1993; LAET, 1993).

The farmers' movement for survival on the Transamazônica (MPST)

Official settlers along the Transamazon highway were to some degree privileged compared with the majority of 'spontaneous' migrants to the region. Unlike most small farmers involved in the CAT programme, who arrived in eastern Amazonia without state support and had to secure land through private purchase or occupation as squatters (*posseiros*), settlers in PAET's area of influence received 100-hectare plots from INCRA along the main highway and feeder roads as part of the government's directed colonisation programme. As documented by Smith (1982) and others, ambitious plans were laid for absorbing vast contingents of 'surplus' migrant labour from the north-east and centre-south, providing the new frontier zone with carefully planned urban and social infrastructure as well as agricultural production support. During its heyday in the early 1970s as part of the PIN, colonisation of the Transamazon highway received strong political and financial backing from the military government in its strategic plan for developing the region.

However, following the 1974 policy reversal in favour of investment into large-scale, agribusiness enterprises, 'social colonisation' to benefit small cultivators received a severe setback and the *Transamazônica* was virtually abandoned by the federal government. The aptly named MPST sprang from the severe difficulties subsequently experienced by thousands of small farmers and their families, whose illusions about receiving government support were rapidly shattered. Funds for health, education, road maintenance and agricultural credit were drastically cut, while state subsidies were once more redirected overwhelmingly towards *paulista* businessmen and cattle-ranchers.

The first initiatives in response to this situation were organised by church youth groups (*pastorais da joventude*) who set up community shops (*grupos de revenda*). As in the Marabá area, the Catholic church played a key role in the formation of a rural trade-union movement, the first STR being established at Altamira in 1978 (Araújo, 1991). Branches were set up in a number of small towns along the *Transamazônica* (Pacajá, Medicilândia, Uruará, Rurópolis), becoming unions in their own right with the formation of new municipalities in 1988. During the 1970s especially, union activity was curtailed by severe military repression, but by the early 1980s political liberalisation (*abertura*) saw the growth of popular protests nationwide, including along the Transamazon highway. The radical Catholic church was instrumental in helping to strengthen the emerging STR movement at this time. In 1984, a demonstration against the government's policy of neglect closed the highway at Pacal, and the Bishop of Xingú, Dom Erwin Krautler, was arrested. Cooperation among rural unions and other organisations in the region was growing and, the following year, a delegation of some 300 farmers visited Brasilia to demand further government investment into roads, schools and health-care along the highway, as well as reactivation of the sugar refinery at Medicilândia. In these endeavours, they had some success, but only after dramatic confrontations in the capital.[35]

Limited success in obtaining additional resources was followed by a brief economic boom on the highway, as the price of export crops such as cocoa and black pepper leapt and incomes rose, aided by an overvalued currency. This prosperity was relatively short-lived, however, and a period of economic recession and local inactivity ensued. A few sporadic protests took place, such as the occupation in 1988 by farmers of INCRA offices in Rurópolis. In 1987–8, local unions carried out a survey of five municipalities to document their dire situation. Its findings were discussed at a 1989 regional meeting of unionists, church activists, local political leaders and the Xingú dam protest movement. It was decided to adopt a unified regional strategy to lobby for government support and, at this point, the MPST was formally established.

From its small office in Altamira, the MPST is a focal point for a range of community and trade-union organisations, including under its wing some twenty-five local associations, ten rural unions, four farmers' cooperatives, teachers' and health workers' unions, as well as movements of women, youths and blacks along 800 kilometres of the *Transamazônica*, reaching a population of some 10,000. The Annual General Meeting elects a Coordinating Committee, an Executive Committee and organisers for three sectors – agriculture, training and popular movements. The MPST has been instrumental in negotiating directly with government authorities on a number of vital issues, and winning major benefits. In 1990, it commemorated the twentieth anniversary of the *Transamazônica*, with an open letter to the government complaining bitterly about official neglect.[36]

From 1991 to 1993, the MPST successfully lobbied the federal and Pará state governments for special FNO[37] and Special Credit Programme for Agrarian Reform (PROCERA)[38] credit to be made available to small farmers in the region who had previously been denied access, administered through local associations and rural unions.[39] While this is a notable victory, it is also, as will be discussed below, a mixed blessing in terms of enhancing productive conservation initiatives. The MPST has also acquired funds from overseas for various small enterprises, ranging from community fruit- and coffee-processing plants to agroforestry projects. In addition, it is responsible for coordinating funding applications from communities through the Demonstration Projects sub-component of the G7 Pilot Programme to Conserve the Brazilian Rainforest.[40]

Agricultural research on the Transamazônica *(LAET)*
LAET arose from the desire to extend CAT's pioneering work around Marabá. Following initial discussions in Brussels between Brazilian institutions and European funding bodies, a thirty-month project to support LAET formally commenced in mid-1993.[41] A ten-member, multi-disciplinary team was set up in Altamira comprising French and Brazilian agricultural and social scientists.[42] Rather than constituting a closed organisation as such, LAET acts as a coordinating and networking focus for a range of institutions such as the Brazilian Agricultural Research Agency – the Agro-Livestock Research Centre for the Humid Tropics (EMBRAPA–CPATU), the National Cacao Research and Extension Programme (CEPLAC) and the Altamira campus of the Federal University of Pará (UFPa). LAET also participates in the above-mentioned postgraduate training programme for agricultural technicians (DAZ) set up at the Federal University of Pará in Belém, and has forged a close working relationship with the MPST, although the two are totally separate organisations.

LAET's work plan for the initial funding period comprises two distinct components: an analysis of the local farming economy and environment, and provision of support for sustainable family farming along the *Transamazônica*. In subsequent collaboration with the MPST, a number of more specific objectives have been identified: firstly, an analysis of regional agricultural and logging activities, including the design of a new small farmer colonisation model to replace INCRA's standard module; secondly, the introduction of animal traction and small-scale mechanisation; thirdly, support for crop marketing and processing; fourthly, the setting up of a network of 'Rural Family Houses' – essentially basic education and agricultural training institutions for youngsters; and fifthly, participation in the definition of a regional policy for managing natural resources based on agro-ecological zoning and research into agricultural systems (Castellanet et al., 1995). Specific projects are being developed whose relevance is discussed below.

Migration to the *Transamazônica* has taken place in two broad waves. During the first such wave, Altamira was a major centre of government-backed 'social colonisation' from 1971 to 1973, which provided settlers with 100-hectare plots either on the highway itself or on secondary feeder roads (*transversais*). INCRA had hoped to resettle 22,000 families in the PIC Altamira project along an eighty-five kilometre stretch of the highway, within ten kilometres on either side. INCRA's general inability to provide adequate economic and infrastructural support after the early euphoria has been amply documented. The government's relative abandonment of the Transamazon highway as a priority destination for small farmers, coupled with its new enthusiasm for opening up the north-western frontier region in Rondônia (with the POLONOROESTE programme) and Acre through the construction and paving of the BR364 did not, however, lessen the attractiveness of the *Transamazônica* for land-hungry migrants.[43]

Since 1977, a second wave of 'spontaneous' settlers have arrived from the north-east and centre-south of the country, far more than were ever accommodated by INCRA, whose role is now limited almost entirely to granting land titles to existing occupants. These independent farmers have either bought parcels from disillusioned INCRA colonists or, as squatters, occupied less favourable vacant areas along feeder roads at distances of up to fifty kilometres from the main highway. From the early 1990s, there was a rapid increase in the number of small farmers, principally from the north-east, settling on increasingly isolated feeder roads. So pronounced has this process been in some areas that it is being spoken of as a 'new frontier' along the Transamazon highway.[44] Although the services of logging companies are often sought to open up tracks in exchange for lumber-extraction rights, many farmers cut these roads themselves with no outside assistance.

From the mid-1970s, wealthier 'entrepreneur' migrants were

favoured by INCRA with plots of 500 hectares (known as *glebas*), skewing land distribution considerably. Land concentration has also taken place through the market, however, as successful pioneer INCRA colonists have been able to buy up the plots of less prosperous settlers. One study of the Altamira region noted that some small farmers had thus built up their areas to an average 250 hectares, or nearly three times the INCRA module. Others remain landless, obliged to work as sharecroppers (*meeiros*) for colonists while they await the opportunity to become landowners themselves (Castellanet *et al.*, 1995).[45]

A parallel and complementary phenomenon to land concentration on the *Transamazônica* has been a rapid growth in the cattle economy. Following the initial emphasis on short-cycle subsistence crops, official support was given for INCRA colonists to plant perennials such as coffee, black pepper and especially cocoa through CEPLAC's *Procacau* programme from 1986. However, production was badly hit by a combination of crop disease and falling world prices, which left many producers severely indebted. Emulating their wealthier *fazendeiro* neighbours, colonists resorted to cattle-raising, which fitted in well with their subsistence-based farming cycle.[46]

Although herds are heavily concentrated on larger holdings, cattle now form a central part of farming systems on the Transamazon highway smaller than 500 hectares. On average, cattle account for about 40 per cent of settler income, although this proportion varies considerably depending on the category of farmer.[47] Some 30 per cent of income is derived from perennials (cocoa, black pepper and coffee), 11 per cent from short-cycle staples (rice, cassava flour and beans), 9 per cent from small animals and 8 per cent from forest products. Cattle-rearing is the single most profitable activity and the major determinant of economic differentiation. Any surplus earnings from perennials are usually invested into building up animal numbers (da Veiga *et al.*, 1995; Castellanet *et al.*, 1995). FNO-Especial credit has, it was found by the same investigations, encouraged the trend towards livestock specialisation on smallholdings, with some 54 per cent of loans destined for cattle-rearing, and 80 per cent of this sum going to farms of less than 200 hectares.

This credit line is unlikely to encourage the adoption of agroforestry along the *Trasamazônica*. Fewer than 10 per cent of MPST farmers have presented applications to FNO-Especial and the majority of these seem to be interested in the cattle component (Smith *et al.*, 1996). This may be attributed to many factors including lack of farmer organisation, risk aversion due to high interest rates, and a general lack of credibility arising from a lack of transparency in the whole process, a rejection rate of over 80 per cent and long delays in disbursement. No credit lines exist which are specifically targeted at agroforestry, a major policy gap which should be rectified.

These developments on the Transamazon highway – logging in exchange for roads, land concentration and the rapid growth of cattle-ranching – mirror events in other parts of Amazonia such as around Marabá and in Rondônia. Although local circumstances differ somewhat, the growing pace of deforestation on the middle stretch of the *Transamazônica* is an increasingly serious cause for concern. Forest loss is not as far advanced as on eastern sections of the highway within CAT's area of operation, since some 60 per cent of the forested area is still intact.

Like their counterparts in the CAT programme, those involved in the PAET thus face the challenge of trying to contain a growing, if less advanced, agricultural and environmental crisis on and around the Transamazon highway. Yet there is the potential for more sustainable practices to be adopted. Preliminary research findings indicate, for example, that, as in the CAT programme, farmers in the Altamira section of the Transamazon highway are conscious of the environmental consequences inherent in current agro-livestock patterns. In spite of the economic imperative to increase cattle herds felt by small farmers, half of those interviewed were conscious of the potential threat to the family's food security and to the local ecology as a result of uncontrolled pasture formation and forest loss (da Veiga *et al.*, 1995).

The Altamira programme is much younger than CAT and, at the time of writing, it is therefore impossible to evaluate the success of so embryonic an exercise. However, a number of research and development activities have been initiated which are worthy of comment, while, at the same time, attention may be drawn to the problems likely to be faced in their execution. Several studies have been produced as part of LAET's initial participatory research programme, developed in collaboration with the MPST, which provide an initial diagnosis of the region's agricultural economy and social structure while indicating priorities for future research and action.[48] LAET has also been instrumental in setting up a centre for the marketing of smallholders' agricultural produce.

Major lines of enquiry have been identified which closely parallel those highlighted by CAT researchers facing the same challenge; that is, how to strengthen the livelihoods of small farmers while preventing further unnecessary forest loss. Based on the conclusions of a seminar involving farmers and researchers held in August 1993 at the start of the formal PAET programme, as well as on subsequent discussions between LAET and the MPST, these broad areas of action research aims may be identified as follows:[49] firstly, the cultivation of perennial crops such as black pepper, cocoa, cupuaçú and açaí in order to provide small farmers with economic alternative to cattle-raising; secondly, increasing agricultural and livestock yields to limit pressures on the forest, through the use of animal traction and small-scale mechanisation, pasture management, the application of organic fertilizer and sale of dairy products; thirdly, improved management of natural resources by means of initiatives such as increasing the added value of marketed timber as well as ecological zoning at the municipal level; fourthly, sedentarising the family farm population, especially on marginal units located along distant feeder roads, through the improved organisation of producers for training, marketing and credit purposes, rice-processing and other activities; fifthly, building special primary schools ('rural family houses') to cater for the basic educational and vocational training needs of farmers' children, the first of which is has been opened in Medicilândia;[50] and sixthly, the implementation of an urban periphery, market garden model of small farmer colonisation on the outskirts of local towns such as Altamira and Uruará as a more suitable alternative to the standard, 100-hectare INCRA design.[51]

PAET: towards productive conservation?

Small farmers along the Altamira stretch of the Transamazon highway face similar agricultural, economic and environmental challenges to their counterparts around Marabá in their quest for sustainable livelihoods. However, they differ somewhat in terms of their respective settlement histories, their organisational capacity and the institutional framework which has been set up in order to address these problems. While it is far too early to evaluate PAET's success, it is possible to identify particular features which are likely to exert a decisive influence upon eventual outcomes. These relate specifically to: the absence of strong traditions of collective struggle for land around Altamira and its repercussions for grassroots organisation, both economic and political; the weak managerial capacity of the MPST as the umbrella association representing small farmer interests; and the evolving role of LAET in its response to MPST requests for research assistance.

Grassroots organisation At Marabá and in the 'Brazilnut Polygon', as detailed previously, large tracts were occupied by *posseiros* throughout the 1970s and 1980s in a movement which frequently involved violent and often bloody confrontations with larger landowning interests as well as authorities such as INCRA and the police, in what has justifiably become known as Brazil's most violent rural area. Altamira, however, was the centre of a major, government-sponsored Integrated Colonisation Project (PIC) in which 100-hectare plots were allocated to farmers on a carefully selected but highly paternalistic basis.

Subsequently, with the winding down of INCRA's 'social colonisation' programme, newcomers have been able to occupy peacefully the relatively inhospitable areas unfavourably located along feeder roads, distant from the main highway, which remain vacant. Alternatively, capitalised migrants have been able to purchase plots of 100 or 50 hectares from existing colonists anxious to extract a profit and move elsewhere.

Around Altamira, therefore, although settled colonists have developed their own tactics against possible land-grabbing,[52] there has been no organised, grassroots struggle for land, merely the acquisition of plots on the market or as determined by INCRA. What conflicts exist take place between individuals or small groups of colonists on the one hand, and INCRA on the other, over demands for adequate financial and infrastructural support which have been promised but not delivered.

These contrasting backgrounds have, arguably, had a major influence upon respective levels of small farmer organisation in the two regions. Rural unions in southern Pará have been active not just as welfare agencies, but, primarily, as vehicles for the defence of small farmer interests in the battle, both physical and legal, over access to land. In spite of a diminution of overt land conflict in the CAT programme area during the 1990s, as well as the expropriation of large areas and distribution of titles under the PNRA, the rural unions' power and influence has increased steadily around Marabá. For example, the number of local branches has more than doubled, from forty in 1989 to over eighty in 1995.

Union coverage along the middle stretch of the Transamazon highway is, by contrast, far smaller and fragmented. Except for the western portion around Medicilândia which came under the influence of Santarém's progressive STR, there has been little union activity on the ground. This is probably attributable to the lack of a history of land struggle and the paternalistic land distribution model adopted by INCRA, already mentioned, as well as to other factors such as geographical dispersion and socio-economic differentiation. On this last subject, as Hébette (1995) notes, government incentives during the 1980s for the cultivation of perennial crops such as cocoa generated wealth for a few and losses for others, creating inequalities which have probably served to undermine the development of a more collective spirit amongst small farmers. Although there have been mass demonstrations in Altamira, farmers have tended to organise on a very localised basis. About thirty community-based cooperatives and associations have been set up since 1991, specifically in order to qualify for FNO credit, as well as to obtain from other sources such as overseas NGOs.

Another factor identified by some analysts as seriously undermining attempts at collective farmer mobilisation along the highway, whether through rural unions or independent associations, is the activity of the church, both Catholic and Adventist. While progressive church activists have played a vital role in organising community action and protest, and continue to do so, others follow a paternalistic line which is non-confrontational and based on a 'discourse of love' (Alves, 1993, 1994b). In contrast to the teachings of Liberation Theology and the Freirian emphasis on self-determination, these priests and nuns stand accused of 'delivering' projects to entirely passive communities in exchange for their personal loyalty. Schemes involving the donation of rice-hullers and plots of land, for example, are funded by external resources obtained through the church apparatus with no effort on the part of beneficiaries, perpetuating the kind of welfarist, dependency syndrome encouraged by INCRA in its settlement procedures.[53] The proliferation of Pentecostal sects in Amazonia, as in the rest of Brazil, has also served to undermine collective action (Araújo, 1991). Their emphasis on individualism and asceticism and their condemnation of political activity, especially by women, as inherently sinful, stands in direct contrast with the doctrines of radical Catholic activists.

The fragility and potential dangers inherent in these kinds of organisational responses have already been manifested in several ways, notably the fact that the myriad of small economic projects which started with the aid of FNO and foreign funds during 1992–5 have been characterised by a very high failure rate. Community schemes such as rice-hullers and coffee-processing plants, as well as the use of lorries, tractors and motorcycles, have produced few tangible benefits, rapidly falling into disrepair or failing to meet their objectives. This has been attributed to maladministration, poor project design and feasibility criteria, and a general lack of accountability.[54] While these problems cannot be attributed directly to the lack of rural union organisation per se, the fragmented nature of association activities makes coordinated planning and implementation highly problematic. Most community associations in the region were set up overnight purely as a vehicle for obtaining credit, and lack any basic socio-political foundations.

MPST leadership and management   In the absence of a strong union movement, the MPST has taken on the role of coordinating development action by small farmers along this 800-kilometre stretch of the *Transamazônica*. Clearly, the movement has played a key role in negotiating benefits for farmers such as special FNO credit. However, its ability to oversee a programme comprising a range of interventions aimed at achieving diversification and sustainability is severely constrained by its limited resources and managerial capacity. With only a small technical staff and minimal funding, courtesy of foreign donors, the MPST cannot even begin to do justice to the growing demands for extension support placed upon it by communities. The movement does not have the human or financial resources to maintain adequate contacts at the grassroots level. In order to overcome problems of poor project planning and implementation, the movement must explore ways of increasing the level of support it is able to give to farmers' groups, either directly or in association with government agencies, local agencies and other NGOs. The initiative taken by the municipality of Uruará is one example of such action.[55]

These administrative difficulties are perhaps also symptomatic of a more fundamental problem concerning the broader role of the MPST. The movement has been highly self-critical of its own perceived failure to define its developmental role more clearly. A major debate, for example, concerns the extent to which the MPST should be a mere service-provider to small farmers' associations, filling the shoes of absent state agencies, and how far the movement should be more politically active, aggressively lobbying the authorities for policy changes in favour of small settlers, while aiming for a more integrated strategy.[56] According to one view (Hébette, 1994), if the MPST was once able to represent a broad range of local interests during the early struggles to bring state resources to the Altamira region, it should now nail its colours firmly to the mast, declare its class interest and concentrate exclusively on assisting small farmers.

Role of LAET The aim of LAET is to set up a participatory research programme, 'in which producers are involved from the moment that research objectives are defined right through to the feedback of results, analysis of their validity and their significance for small farmers' (Castellanet *et al.*, 1994: 2). Conceived within the spirit of FPR, the LAET approach eschews classical FSR, which is strongly criticised for over-emphasising the importance of technical packages while treating contextual factors such as land, credit, etc. as given, and considering farmers as essentially passive objects, unable to determine their own futures.

LAET considers that the adoption of an FPR methodology enables farmers to exercise greater decision-making power, so that 'these organised actors may influence the social and economic circumstances which guide technological choice' (Castellanet, n.d.: 2). In order to facilitate such a participatory approach, it is therefore seen as crucial to establish an equal 'partnership' between researchers and farmers from the outset, so that the process is as democratic as possible. A programme of basic research to determine the major characteristics of the rural economy and society along the *Transamazônica* will be followed by specific applied research projects in response to farmers' needs, articulated through the MPST.

The nature of the MPST as a pre-existing umbrella organisation for local farmers' associations, unions and cooperatives is seen as favouring such a participatory methodology. If the effectiveness of the MPST has been compromised to some degree by the fragmented, paternalistic nature of the colonisation process around Altamira as well as by subsequent management problems, it has one distinct advantage over its counterpart (FATA) in Marabá. By the time that LAET was set up in 1993, the MPST was already well established in its own right, with its own priorities and evolving programme of action. Although problems of poor organisation and of dependency exist at the grassroots level within the programme, as already discussed, the MPST itself has been able to retain its integrity and negotiate independently with LAET over an appropriate research agenda for the *Transamazônica*.

Within CAT, this independence has been compromised by the inclusion of both farmers' and researchers' organisations within a single administrative framework through the CAT centre. This has led to a sometimes uneasy relationship between LASAT and FATA over the determination of research priorities and allocation of resources. In order to help avoid a repetition of such in-fighting and reduce the risk of dependence within the companion programme at Altamira, it was decided to strengthen the administrative and financial autonomy of the research team and the farmers' organisation, a feature which is contractually recognised.[57]

While the LAET–MPST institutional arrangement within the Altamira programme goes a long way towards avoiding problems encountered within CAT, it is not clear how 'equal' a partnership can really be established in practice. As the founding father of both CAT and PAET has himself freely admitted, there is an inevitable class relationship between poor farmers and urbanised, educated technicians. Although the tendency, at least on the part of some researchers, is to pretend that this clash of perspectives does not exist, the challenge is to create 'a community of interests within a partnership which acknowledges this heterogeneity of interests' (Hébette, 1996: 48).

Such conflicts, latent or otherwise, may be due to obvious differences in socio-economic status or researchers' command over project resources, both human and financial. They seem in fact to be recognised implicitly if not openly by the parties involved, and renders researcher-farmer relationships something of a power struggle to gain control over inputs and action. In Altamira, this is reflected most obviously in the subtle tension which has existed between LAET and the MPST, virtually since the inception of the PAET programme, over which research projects should be prioritised. As might be expected, the MPST is anxious to identify economic projects with a quick return to address farmers' pressing problems. LAET researchers naturally adopt a more cautious approach and are keen that action should be guided by careful research in order to minimise the risk of subsequent project failure.

Productive conservation on the Transamazon highway

At first glance, the plight of small farmers along the Transamazon highway is significantly different from that of the fishing communities and rubber-tappers. On the *Transamazônica* the design of new productive conservation strategies is, in the final analysis, the concern of particular property-holders, whether titled landowners or *posseiros*. There are no overt common property issues to be resolved in the sense that it is necessary to reconcile the individual and collective use of natural resources via the formulation of a formal management plan, as in the case of Mamirauá and the extractive reserves. However, key features of the Transamazon highway situation suggest that individual solutions will only be feasible if conceived and executed within a more collective framework of action.

To a greater or lesser extent, both CAT and PAET face the same basic problem: how to avert a growing production crisis brought about by the rapid spread of cattle-ranching and pasture formation. This process of *pecuarização* is gradually increasing levels and rates of forest loss, undermining environmental services provided by the rainforest and threatening the long-term sustainability of settlers' livelihoods, as soils become permanently degraded. While individual farmers may have as their top priority the desire to boost incomes through diversification and CPRs are not formally under discussion, it is also recognised by many participants that a more integrated approach is required which is able to reconcile personal and group aims and responsibilities. Recognition of the need for an integrated approach is also evident, of course, in the setting up of umbrella organisations for farmers within the two programmes, FATA and the MPST, to articulate not only people's individual or community-level needs but also their more common concerns relating to natural resource-use.

Although in their infancy, both CAT based in Marabá and PAET in Altamira can be loosely considered new productive conservation movements whose members have certain common interests and a degree of collective identity around land, production and conservation issues. They were both formed specifically for the purpose of dealing with serious problems facing small cultivators. Yet there is not necessarily a direct correlation between radical or combative origins and the subsequent capacity to successfully mobilise for productive conservation. Although FATA has its roots in the violent land struggles of the 1970s and 1980s in southern Pará, many of which were collectively organised by peasant farmers, the movement nowadays is less than unified and somewhat compromised by intra-institutional complications within the CAT structure. The MPST, on the other hand, is a more recent phenomenon, born of farmers' conflicts with INCRA and the federal government. Yet while it remains a relatively fragmented movement of community associations, cooperatives and new rural unions, the MPST retains its independence from LAET researchers and is perhaps in a stronger negotiating position in terms of being able to prioritise an appropriate research agenda.

Both programmes are characterised by extremely varied levels of involvement on the part of the mass membership. Not only are APRs still limited but DPRs vary considerably for several reasons. Members closer to the centres of decision-making tend, not surprisingly, to be favoured by greater contacts with project research and extension staff. The structure of relationships within rural families invariably means that males play the most important decision-making roles in relation to production for the market and in political activities. However, this situation is beginning to change with the greater involvement of women in union activities. Growing economic differentiation will also probably serve to undermine collective action.

The solidarity which, at least superficially, characterised those early group struggles against hostile forces, be they land-grabbers or government authorities such as INCRA, has been difficult to sustain in more peaceful times. In the 'sustainable development' phase of small farmer settlement along the Transamazon highway as exemplified by CAT and PAET, the challenge of eliciting collective support for a common productive conservation agenda is proving a daunting one. These two innovative programmes will undoubtedly continue in their attempts to overcome these obstacles, with farmers acquiring an increasingly proactive role in decision-making, negotiating with research, support and funding bodies. Research in eastern Amazonia suggests that diversified production strategies such as those being proposed for the Marabá and Altamira areas are more likely to be successful in older frontier zones, which are better integrated into the local expanding urban economy and where extension support from dedicated NGO and church organisations for addressing farmers' needs is forthcoming.[58] Farmer support from committed organisations is certainly present in these *Transamazônica* programmes, while urban markets are in the process of formation. Although they have taken only the first steps towards the definition of new small settler strategies of productive conservation, the Marabá and Altamira initiatives form part of a pioneering wave of diversified land-use experiences in Amazonia which include the sustainable management of natural resources alongside more conventional agro-livestock practices.

Notes

1 Sawyer notes that the large, unregistered informal sector in both rural and urban areas is a product of the opening of the highway network and expansion of communications, as well as the continued dependence upon informal credit arrangements. 'The urban network of the frontier makes pioneer agriculture feasible for economic and social reasons, by providing productive and social infrastructure. Where it is vigorous, the agricultural frontier is strongest' (1989: 14). Reinforcing this observation, Schwartzman (1990) found that a quarter of households in Rio Branco, state capital of Acre, gained over half their income from rural activities such as rubber tapping and agriculture.

2 For example, in a 1987 study of over 800 farmers on the official Machadinho colonisation project in Rondônia, 60% of respondents had worked in urban areas before migrating, half of them in cities with over 100,000 population (Gama Torres, 1991).

3 According to figures issued by the now-extinct Ministry of Reform and Agrarian Development (MIRAD), between the military takeover of 1964 and 1986, some 1,500 people died in Brazilian land conflicts. One-third of this total occurred during 1975–85 alone, and one-half of these deaths took place in Amazonia (Hall, 1991; Fajardo, 1988)

4 In only 27 of these 1,017 cases – which involved the deaths of small farmers, rural union activists, radical priests and nuns as well as lay-workers – were the perpetrators brought to trial, 17 being imprisoned

and 10 acquitted. As noted by one report, 'The life of a small settler in the Parrot's Beak is worth as much as a good meal in a São Paulo restaurant' ('Matadores de Aluguel', *Isto É* 19 May, 1993).
5 For a more detailed account of land conflicts in the Carajás region during this period, see Hall (1991), Asselin (1982) and Wagner (1994).
6 See Hébette (1988) and Hébette and Colares (1990) for details of organised peasant land occupations in eastern Amazonia during the 1980s.
7 Wagner provides a detailed account of recent land conflicts and related issues in Eastern Amazonia. In his view, the Brazilian state is not only omissive in its control of rural violence but connives in perpetuating a notorious lack of accountability for the perpetrators, so that 'massacres become the norm for resolving antagonisms' (1994: 327).

As if to prove his point, major violent incidents and the depressingly familiar lack of accountability on the part of perpetrators continue unabated, despite the advent of formal democracy in Brazil in 1985. In April 1996, for example, nineteen rural workers were killed by police during a protest on the Belém–Marabá highway at Eldorado do Carajás. See chapter two for further details.
8 Fearnside (1990: 10–11) distinguishes between traditional 'shifting cultivation' and pioneer farmer 'slash-and-burn' farming. While the former is viable in areas of low population density and tied to other sustainable *caboclo* and indigenous practices, the latter is becoming increasingly serious as a cause of Amazonian deforestation. Slash-and-burn pioneer farmers adopt only brief cropping and fallow periods, with a view to maximising short-term cash gains and/or associated with speculative motives for planting pasture for resale of the land and quick capitalisation.

Official policy encourages such practices by, for example, accepting pasture as proof of productive land-use for various purposes, such as: (i) land-titling by INCRA, (ii) eligibility for receipt of official agricultural credit, and (iii) exemption from expropriation under Brazil's land reform law (Hall, 1990).
9 Notable examples include the Peruvian Amuesha and Bora groups, the Huastec in Mexico, the Napo Quichua of Equador, Mayans in Central America and the Kayapó of Brazil (Posey, 1985, 1989a; Gradwohl and Greenberg, 1988; Eden, 1990; Anderson, 1990b).
10 These practices are more common than is generally appreciated, but they have remained largely undocumented, although recent research is shedding more light on this field. Anderson (1990b), for example, has investigated the 'tolerant' forest-management system developed by riverine *coboclo* communities in the 25,000-square-kilometre floodplain of the River Amazon at Combú Island near the city of Belém. This

system, which has evolved over generations, permits the extraction and sale of a range of forest products such as fruits, vegetables, fibres, latex and medicinals, while conserving natural resources.

11 'Agroforestry' is defined here as the combination of a perennial crop with at least one other crop, annual or perennial (Smith *et al.*, 1996).

12 Tomé-Açu was established in 1924 by Japanese–Brazilian farmers from southern Brazil. Starting off as subsistence farmers, they have developed Tomé-Açu into a sustained yield agroforestry system, growing over fifty-five different crops. Its 280 smallholders each cultivate plots of between twenty and eighty hectares. Careful land management enables the production of fast-growing annual crops (cotton, rice and beans) intercropped with perennial vines (black pepper and passion fruit) as well as tree crops (cocoa, oil palm and rubber). The cooperative, CAMTA, has been able to provide technical assistance and marketing support for the sale of produce on national and international markets. The success of Tomé-Açu is attributed to the farming skills of its Japanese-descended population and to the strong supporting financial and administrative links with southern cooperatives through CAMTA. For further details, see Barrow (1990), Gradwohl and Greenberg (1988), Eden (1990), Subler and Uhl (1990).

13 RECA is situated on the BR364 highway at Nova Califórnia, on the border between Acre and Rondônia. The community is made up of INCRA colonists from the southern states of Santa Catarina, Paraná and Minas Gerais, who were resettled from Rondônia in 1984 on 50-hectare plots on an ex-rubber estate. With church backing, a strong community association successfully lobbied the Acre state government for electricity supplies, health and education infrastructure.

Since 1988, slash-and-burn farming has been gradually replaced by mixed short-cycle and annual fruit tree crops (brazil nuts, *pupunha* and *cupuaçu*), credit and extension advice being provided to over 200 participating farmers cultivating a total of 400 hectares; these are divided into sixteen work/discussion groups, each with a representative on the project council. A *cupuaçu* processing plant also been set up. The project has received substantial foreign funding from church organisations such as CEBEMO, while technical assistance has been provided by official Brazilian agencies such as EMBRAPA, the official agricultural research agency, and PESACRE, a local NGO.

Current problems being addressed by the project include the high cost of implementation (at several thousand dollars per family), difficulties of securing outlets for processed *cupuaçu* in a market which is rapidly becoming saturated, and over-dependence on foreign donations.

ASPRUVE, located nearby at Vila Extrema, has suffered from similar problems and seen its active membership reduced from 100 to a few dozen. COAPEX, a breakaway project from ASPRUVE, has 120 members and manages to sell processed brazil nuts at competitive prices and experiments with a variety of cropping patterns, leaving farmers to choose their own agroforesty combinations.

(This account is based on the author's field visits during 1993–6; Lopes, 1993; and Smith *et al.*, 1996)

14 Like RECA, the community of Granada comprises smallholder settlers from southern Brazil, who were moved northwards from Rondônia following the failure of INCRA colonisation schemes, and resettled on an ex-rubber estate. The 100 farmers involved set up an association in 1991 and decided to diversify production, combining staple crops such as rice, beans and cassava with agroforestry. A tree nursery distributes seedlings to association members for bananas, coffee, cashew, guava, *cupuaçu*, mangos and pineapple. Technical assistance is given by PESACRE, a local NGO, as well as SINPASA, the state-level union federation for small farmers.

15 In an area of rapid deforestation, four communities of small settlers along the River Capim have set up a communal nursery to plant fruit trees in areas which have been cleared by slash-and-burn farming. Each farmer chooses an annual crops such as oranges, limes, black pepper, *cupuaçu* and *acerola*, whose sale provides an income to complement staple crops such as cassava (Lyra, 1993).

16 Walker and Homma *et al.*, 1993.

17 Anderson (1990a), Smith *et al.* (1996), Dubois (1996).

18 Field research carried out in 1990 of this longer settled frontier zone, with 69 properties covering over 2,300 hectares, revealed a highly diversified intensive and extensive production system. This has been gradually developed since the mid-1970s after the settlers had first adopted the traditional slash-and-burn model. Some 70% of production is now marketed with perennial crops (black pepper, rubber, cashew, cocoa and oranges, etc.) providing 42% of net profits, vegetables on raised beds provide 25%, annual crops (rice, beans and cassava) 7% and ranching 27%.

The total value of production in 1990 was just under $US430,000, providing and average annual profit per family of $US2,413 or $US93 per ha p.a., which compares very favourably alongside the $US4.11 per ha p.a. obtained from the extensive ranching common over much of eastern Amazonia. The authors conclude that 'the diversified agricultural approach at Uraim produces more food and greater gross and net returns, while also generating more jobs and taxes than an area of equal dimensions dedicated to ranching' (Toniolo and Uhl, 1995: 968; 1996).

19 In Rio Branco, a pioneering experiment is under way in which selected

rural migrants from the urban informal sector are being offered plots of deforested land on the outskirts of the city. Some 500 hectares is being set aside for 200 families, which will produce staples, fruits and vegetables in agroforestry systems, as well as processed products, to supply Rio Banco's rapidly expanding market (Rio Branco, n.d.).

20 The headquarters of CAT is an impressive complex of offices, meeting rooms and associated facilities, designed by architects from the Federal University of Pará. CAT has received technical assistance from a range of institutions such as the Federal University of Pará (UFPa), the Pará Faculty of Agricultural Sciences (FCAP), official Brazilian research (EMBRAPA) and extension (EMATER) agencies, the Pará Institute for Economic and Social Development (IDESP) and the National Institute for Amazonian Research (INPA) as well as the Group for Research and Technological Exchange (GRET), the International Agricultural Research Centre for Development (CIRAD) and the Office for Scientific Research Overseas (ORSTOM) (France). Financial aid has been granted by the Federal University and Brazilian research funding bodies such as FINEP. Bilateral aid has been provided by the ODA (UK) and the European Commission, as well the Ford Foundation, Inter-American Foundation (USA) and Christain Aid (UK).

21 The programme in Amazonian Family Farming and Agro-Environmental Development (DAZ) involves intensive coursework at the University in Belém, together with extensive fieldwork experience in the CAT area of operation.

22 In Brazil, this is known as 'Pesquisa, Formação, Desenvolvimento', or PFD. ('Research, Training, Development').

23 Lena notes that, in the case of INCRA colonists on the Ouro Preto resettlement scheme in the western state of Rondônia, cattle provided a form of security while the first harvests from perennial crops such as cocoa were awaited (Lena, 1991: 298–9).

24 Such as the 'Pau Seco', area of dairy cattle production near Marabá cited by LASAT (1992: 23).

25 LASAT (1992) found that the price of virgin land per hectare in the Marabá region varied from $US5 to $US7, while land with pasture and other 'improvements' ranged from $US40 to $US140. The value of a 50-hectare tract could be increased from $US250 to between $US1,000 and $US2,000 simply by virtue of being occupied, while with pasture the price rose substantially to between $US2,000 and $US5,000.

26 See Thiele (1990) on Bolivian agroforestry experience, for example.

27 The ODA provided support totalling over £1 million from 1991–4 (subsequently extended) for technical assistance, training material and equipment. It followed the successful ODA-funded experience with agroforestry at the BTAM/CIAT project in Santa Cruz, Bolivia.

28 Some thirty crops are being considered, ranging from avocados (*Persea americana* Mill.), acerola (*Malpighia glaba* L.), bacuri (*Platonia insignis* Mart.) and cupuacú (*Theobroma grandiflorum*) to brazil nut (*Bertholletia excelsa* H.B.K.), mahogany (*Swietenia macrophylla* King.) and black pepper (*Piper nigrum* L.).
29 However, pasture formation is also encouraged by other factors such as land speculation and as proof of 'productive' land-use for land-titling purposes. These are likely to remain important incentives to deforest until the legal, fiscal and macro-economic situation changes in Brazil.
30 This is indeed a declared aim within the project's workplans for the future, which include integrating perennial tree crops into existing production systems (LASAT, 1994). This aspect receives relatively little emphasis, however, compared with agriculture and cattle-raising.
31 For a first-hand account of the *guerrilla do Araguaia*, see Portela (1979). From 1972, some ninety PC do B members were active in the region of Xamboiá in the Bico do Papagaio, mobilising 3,200 members of the armed forced in a military campaign which by 1974 had wiped out the movement as well as many of the guerrillas themselves.
32 These were set up as follows: São João do Araguaia 1974, Itupiranga 1979, Jacundá 1980 and Marabá 1980.
33 Author's conversations with FATA staff.
34 In its own words, PAET aims to 'Contribute to the development of sustainable family farming in the long term while better managing natural resources through a programme of research-training-participatory development on the Transamazon highway …' (Castellanet *et al.*, 1995).
35 In one of the most enthusiastically recounted anecdotes of this event, demonstrators cornered Jader Barbalho, then governor of Pará state, in his car at the presidential Palácio da Alvorada in Brasília. As the story is told, he escaped only by making a promise (subsequently broken) to arrange a meeting for the delegation with President Sarney, and then fled to Belém. The sugar refinery was later reopened as a cooperative, while the federal government provided funding for social and transport infrastructure (Hamelin, 1991).
36 The *Carta da Transamazônica* declared that the government's policy of 'land without men for men without land' had been 'no more than a pipe-dream for thousands of farmers from all over the country … the government should make good its mistakes to create the conditions for economic and social development … respecting the environment and making rational use of the forests and rivers … and put an end to the situation of abandonment by the government in which we have been left for the past twenty years' (MPST, 1990).
37 The Fundo Constitucional de Financiamento do Norte (FNO) became

available in 1992 through BASA for an agroforestry package which includes ten head of cattle and a mix of perennial crops which varies according to local conditions, but is usually drawn from *cupuaçú*, oranges, coconut, peach palm *(pupunha)* and robusta coffee.

38 PROCERA forms part of the agrarian reform programme (PNRA) and is targeted at small colonists on INCRA settlements (Hall, 1990).

39 The 1988 Brazilian Constitution (chapter 6, section VI, article 159, para. c) sets aside 3% of tax revenues for establishing regional development funds or 'Fundos Constitucionais' for the north, north-east and centre-west (Brazil, 1988). However, in the face of bureaucratic complications which effectively denied small farmers access to these funds, the state Federation of Agricultural Workers in Pará, FETAGRI, organised a number of demonstrations ('*Gritos do Campo*' and '*Gritos da Amazônia*') during 1991–6 to have the regulations changed, in which the MPST played a key part.

Negotiations with BASA resulted in small farmer organisations being made eligible for subsidised credit from the FNO, which was distributed to 325 farmers on the Transamazon highway in 1992 through the MPST. In 1993 a further 600 farmers received assistance from the 'FNO Especial', as it became known, benefitting some 3,000 settlers by 1995 (*O Liberal*, 14 May 1993; MPST, 1995b).

40 See chapter two for further details.

41 In April 1991, a meeting was held in Brussels involving Brazilian and European groups interested in expanding support for family farming in Amazonia based on production-conservation principles similar to those envisaged in the CAT programme. Funding was obtained from the EU (DG-1) and France (GRET, ORSTOM) as well as commitments on the Brazilian side from EMBRAPA (CPATU) and the Federal University of Pará (MPST/PAET, 1993).

42 This initially comprised five agronomists, an economist, sociologist, geographer and biologist.

43 For further details on the settlement of Rondônia and Acre, see Martine (1990) and Bakx (1990). On the history of the Transamazon highway, see Smith (1982).

44 Alves (1994a) found that in the municipality of Uruará, near Altamira, feeder roads had increased from 630 kilometres in 1989 to almost 1,000 kilometres in 1993. This phenomenon is also documented by Hamelin (1991).

45 According to the study carried out by Castellanet *et al.* (1995), sharecroppers account for 23% of the labour force receiving on average, in exchange for their services, 39% of cocoa production, 14% of black pepper production and 30–50% of staple food crops such as rice.

46 For example, rice and corn can be rotated with pasture to recuperate

land from weed invasion, while the straw is useful for animal fodder. Manure is applied to perennial crops, whose residues make good animal feed. Furthermore, as mentioned already, cattle are a mobile asset which act as a useful capital reserve and maintains its economic value well.

47 Studies by Castellanet et al. (1995) distinguished between seven categories of settler. Cattle provide 60% of income for the longest settled, wealthier farmers who have acquired larger than average plots of 500 ha. *(glebistas)* and enjoy an average annual income of $US9,000 from the sale of meat and dairy products. At the other end of the scale, recently arrived *posseiros* derived less than 1% of their income from cattle.

48 See, for example: Castellanet et al. (1994, 1995), Simões (1995), Alves (1993, 1994b) and MPST/LAET (1995b).

49 Based on MPST/LAET (1993), Castellanet et al. (1995).

50 The 'Casa Familiar Rural' concept is based on educational innovations carried out in Europe, the developing world and southern Brazil. It aims to combine basic primary education with training in agricultural skills to replace conventional schooling, which is either unavailable or seen as inappropriate to the needs of local children (MPST/LAET, 1995b).

51 The idea is that intensively cultivated, 10-hectare plots would form a green belt around local towns, at once providing employment for hundreds of landless families, while boosting supplies of basic foods, fruit and vegetables for the rapidly expanding urban population. Adequate farming systems and cultivation techniques would replace destructive, slash-and-burn techniques commonly used in the countryside. These projects would be linked to INCRA and municipal secretariats of agriculture. This model has been proposed for the resettlement of some 350 INCRA colonists settled in error on the Araras II indigenous reserve, as an alternative to their being relocated on isolated feeder roads, where their chances of success are limited (Discussions with LAET staff, 1995; Uruará, 1994).

This is comparable to the peri-urban agroforestry project currently being implemented by the municipality of Rio Branco (see above).

52 For example, Alves (1994b) notes that an extended family will often occupy several contiguous plots in order to defend themselves against fragmentation at the hands of land speculators or even violent attacks by land-grabbers. This grouping often forms a local power centre, providing the local teacher, CEB leader or association head.

53 One such case-study concerns the community of Anapú and its apparent domination by the Catholic church, whose local members are seen as having created a personal fiefdom on the basis of externally funded projects, encouraging servile dependence on the part of the local com-

munity, benefiting those loyal to the church and excluding those who dare to question its authority (Alves, 1993).
54 This conclusion was reached by some thirty community representatives from the MPST's area of operation who met in Altamira in March 1995 to evaluate the success of mini-projects.
55 In Uruará, a number of state, municipal and other local organisations have carried out joint discussions and analysis of possible development priorities for this portion of the Transamazon highway, including the MPST and LAET, with a view to coordinating future actions (Hamelin, 1991; Uruará, 1994).
56 These issues were debated at length during the fourth annual general meeting of the MPST, held in Altamira in January 1995, involving representatives from forty-five local organisations from thirteen municipalities (MPST, 1995b).
57 The contract states: 'In view of their common long-term objective to promote sustainable development in the region and the complementarity of their main activities, the MPST and LAET agree to work together in a three-year agreement, renewable by mutual consent, to define a common working methodology in the areas of agro-livestock, agroforestry, marketing and processing of agricultural produce, the management of natural resources and preservation of the environment. ... LAET will prepare an annual research proposal to be presented to the Movement. The Movement will prepare its own programme of technical activities and requests for research. Based on consideration of these two proposals, a joint programme will be prepared ... LAET will not participate directly in the search for funding for the Movement' (MPST/LAET, 1993).
58 The success of Uraim in this regard is attributed in large measure to the proximity of Paragominas, a town of over 40,000 inhabitants which has prospered, ironically, as a result of the logging industry. Not only is there a ready market for rural produce, but the value of agricultural land has risen steadily, allowing unsuccessful farmers to sell their plots to farmers and urban-based entrepreneurs who have taken up commercial agriculture. The strong influence of NGOs and grassroots religious groups at Uraim is also highlighted as a key factor in the project's success, although no details are given of the precise inputs provided by these agents (Toniolo and Uhl, 1995).

6
Amazonia: towards productive conservation

For centuries the Amazon Basin remained an isolated and sparsely populated hinterland of largely exotic interest to outsiders. In the wake of the nineteenth-century 'rubber boom', the region became an abandoned frontier whose economic fortunes were limited by the small and volatile nature of markets for exported forest products. The 'rediscovery' of Amazonia by the military regime during the 1970s was based on the belief that this huge chunk of territory could be used to serve simultaneously a number of economic, strategic and socio-political purposes to serve national development. Natural resources could be legitimately exploited with scant regard for the ecological or human costs. The regional population affected by this process, especially the poor, was assumed to have little or no direct influence.

Passive acceptance of these tactics by the majority was the implicit assumption not just of government planners but of development theorists. It is not always recognised just how strongly conventional theories of frontier expansion, of whichever ideological persuasion, seemed to confirm the inevitability of such a top-down, predatory development model for Amazonia. Whether seen from the perspective of economic modernisation and geopolitical integration, growing state institutional control or neo-Marxist capital subsumption, the endeavours of individuals and resource-user groups are invariably assumed to be totally controlled, directly or indirectly, by large-scale forces beyond their ability to influence. Governments and the owners of capital, it is argued, dictate the policy agenda and any initiatives which might be undertaken. These reductionist theories assume an exclusive, determining role for structural and contextual factors, denying any substantial power to grassroots groups.

During the 1960s and 1970s, Brazilian policy-makers and military strategists shared a vision of Amazonia as offering major opportunities for furthering national progress. As the Brazilian economic 'miracle' got under way influenced by the Sorbonne group of the Higher War College (ESG), modernisationist principles were deemed highly appropriate for rural as well as urban Amazonia. New technologies would have to replace so-called 'primitive' and 'backward' methods of the Amazon based on extractivism and other indigenous methods, whose persistence was seen as antithetical to mainstream economic development. As the state of knowledge about regional potential improved, Amazonia came to be seen as 'a vast resource domain yet to be plundered' (Nugent, 1993a: 14). The sheer scale of government support during the 1970s and 1980s for a variety of environmentally destructive activities including cattle-ranching, land speculation, logging and mining, is testimony to the strength of the modernisationist plan. However, this view was clearly tempered by strategic and other political priorities which led to economically and environmentally disastrous decisions being taken.

The outright failure of cattle-ranching to spearhead Amazonia's economic 'take-off', despite billions of dollars in government subsidies, is perhaps the best-known and clearest example of such expediency. As discussed in chapter two, strategic concerns have reinforced the apparent economic rationale behind the drive to occupy Amazonia. Nationalistic preoccupations surrounding international designs on the region's resource base had long been expressed and periodically resurrected. Counter-insurgency operations of the 1970s have been followed by preoccupations with enhancing border security via Calha Norte and strengthening regional surveillance mechanisms with the SIVAM project.

Amazonian integration has been strongly predicated on a belief in the power of the state to direct regional development to serve national goals. In the Weberian, institutional-incorporation mould, this view holds that central government has the power and relative autonomy from class-determined interests to be able to influence the course of development towards goals set by official planners. Public participation is considered an unnecessary prerequisite for progressive change, at best obstructive and at worst potentially subversive. Its convenient assumptions of a common rationality amongst planners and politicians, especially if power can be wrested from the periphery and concentrated at the centre, supposedly place control in the hands of technocrats. Local populations at the grassroots are thus assumed to have little influence over the course of policy formulation or implementation.

Similar conclusions are reached by neo-Marxist writers in the 'logic of capital' tradition, for whom rural development patterns and state policies are determined by external forces. Agrarian crisis and ensuing environmental problems are seen as the result of dependent and uneven capitalist expansion in 'peripheral' regions, causing poverty and proletarianisation. Such dependency analyses have been applied to Amazonia in relation to the Carajás Programme, for example.[1] In a similar vein, Amazon frontier incorporation theories see small farmer settlement as a state-backed strategy underpinned by national and foreign interests for the gradual expansion of capital to outlying areas and their integration into the mainstream national economy (Velho, 1972, 1976; Foweraker, 1981). The state, reflecting capitalist interests, is viewed as adopting policies which close the frontier to peasants, reserve land for commercial and speculative enterprises and create a 'reserve army' of cheap estate labour.[2]

Kept constantly on the move through rural violence and lack of state support, the peasantry, it is argued, is politically weakened and denied long-term, stable access to land or natural resources. Landownership becomes heavily concentrated, while so-called 'pre-capitalist' or 'petty commodity' forms of production such as subsistence farming and extractivism are largely replaced by large-scale, capitalised units. Explicitly or implicitly, the rural population is considered a largely passive social force, victims of a harsh state machine controlled by capitalist interests, powerless to take the initiative to promote alternative development strategies which might better serve the people's interests. In both modernisationist and neo-Marxist discourse, the *caboclo* peasant population of Amazonia has been marginalised, relegated to the status of an 'invisible' majority (Nugent 1993b).

As outlined in the opening chapter of this volume, the present work rejects the deterministic notion that Amazonia's population of small settlers is bound to be the passive victim of overwhelming forces exercised by the state machine and allied capitalist interests. Adopting an action-oriented approach, it has been suggested that, while structural factors impose clear limits on the freedom of choice which small producers may exercise, they are nevertheless learning to become masters of their own destiny. To varying degrees, they have shown that it is possible to overcome obstacles which only a few years ago would have been considered virtually 'insurmountable.

Perhaps the clearest and most widespread demonstration of such decisive action in support of people's livelihoods has been the struggle to gain access to land through the occupation of under-utilised estates, with all the violent conflict that this process has entailed. This has occurred either through sporadic, locally based initiatives, or via region-wide, organised movements such as the MST in southern Brazil and, latterly, in Amazonia itself.[3] Much land redistribution under the agrarian reform programme is in fact merely the ratification and legalisation of areas already appropriated *de facto* by means of direct peasant action.[4]

The rise of productive conservation

Conventional development strategies in Amazonia have, since the 1960s, resulted in widespread and indiscriminate erosion of the region's natural resources. Policies of biological conservation implemented from the 1970s and 1980s in the form of parks and reserves have been variably effective in setting aside protected areas, but, even when successful, provide only a partial solution to the problem of environmental degradation. Brazil's generally unfavourable policy context for sustainable Amazon development is clearly a fundamental issue, and is taken up below. Be that as it may, however, another limiting factor both in the execution of an effective conservation policy, as well as in small farmer development generally, has been the lack of grassroots organisations in Amazonia capable of defending the interests of groups conventionally ignored by the machinery of government.

The present study highlights a phenomenon which has begun to emerge, broadly speaking, since the early 1980s with the onset of political liberalisation in Brazil. Although the individual characteristics of such initiatives vary considerably, they can all be said to share one basic common feature: people's need to undertake collective action for the defence and sustainable management of key natural resources which form a major basis of their livelihoods. In this sense, the issues at stake are clearly not those of 'green' environmental concern as such, but of survival. While *caboclo* and indigenous groups in Amazonia have for centuries devised their own forms of natural resource regulation, utilising forest products while avoiding wanton destruction of the resource base, the phenomenon of productive conservation is itself somewhat distinctive.

This refers to new forms of environmental and resource control which are being adopted as a response to growing pressures on forest dwellers' livelihoods. Although productive conservation frequently builds upon traditional methods (such as rubber tapping, small-scale farming and traditional fishing techniques, for example), new forms of technology, organisation and policy support are also required in today's more complex Amazonia, where natural resources have come under commercial and demographic pressure. In order to help explain the emergence of productive conservation as a phenomenon of growing significance in Amazonia, three relevant conceptual strands were brought together.

Firstly, local mobilisation around productive conservation strategies is consistent, it was suggested, with theories of new social movements. Groups with little or no history of joint action have banded together, united at least temporarily by common livelihood concerns and the presence of external threats to their natural resource base. This was linked closely to a second set of issues centred on the challenge of governing common-pool resources. A large proportion of Amazonia's rural population utilises resources which are, to varying degrees, under some form of collective governance. Many closed access resource systems exist in the region which have long been effectively managed by local communities. In the case-studies examined here, the issue of joint management is crucial for the fisherpeople of Mamirauá and of growing relevance for extractive reserve populations, but of rather less importance for small farmers on the Transamazon highway.

The propensity of such groups to cooperate in the task of resource management can be explained, it was suggested, by a modified form of resource-mobilisation theory, which justifies such group action based on a combination of instrumental self-interest on the part of individuals, together with the evolution of collective identity in which personal and group perceptions become intertwined. The key challenge faced by today's productive conservation movements is how to reconcile the short-term needs of households and the inherent danger of resource-over exploitation with the long-term interests of the community to conserve resources, thus averting a possible 'tragedy of the commons'.

Thirdly, concepts of community participation were used to help identify ways in which groups organise to formulate and execute plans for systematic resource management. By disaggregating forms of community action according to key dimensions (objectives, scope, strength and timing), it was possible to identify specific and vital forms of people's involvement in such initiatives. Generally speaking, successful productive conservation will be highly dependent on a diverse range of participatory interventions on the part of local groups, gradually moving from passive forms of involvement to proactive and decisive action, in negotiation and collaboration with outside agencies of government and civic society. A number of lessons have emerged from an examination of productive conservation exercises in contrasting Amazonian sub-ecosystems.

The first and perhaps most obvious of these is that standardised, blueprint-type solutions for dealing with resource depletion problems will simply not work. Amazonia's diversity of topography, resource endowments, demographic and socio-political history signifies that environmental and resource-management strategies must be tailored to meet the specific requirements of each situation. Even within superficially similar environments, it is necessary to be aware of subtle local and regional differences. What is appropriate for the Chico Mendes extractive reserve in southern Acre may not, for example, be suitable in the more isolated and historically distinct Juruá reserve in the northern part of the state. Likewise, a strategy implemented at Mamirauá in the upper reaches of the Amazon will need rethinking for replication along the middle reaches of the river, where aquatic systems are different and fish stocks more vulnerable to exploitation by commercial vessels. Similarly, areas with an existing tradition of defending and controlling CPRs will invariably find it easier to adopt a collectively managed environmental plan than recent settlers faced with the need to undertake action in defence of their livelihoods.

A second major conclusion of the present analysis is that, within this diversity of situations requiring locale-specific solutions, one of the most important prerequisites for success is the presence of a vigorous local movement able to reconcile individual household and broader community interests, and capable of balancing the immediate use of local natural resources with the need for longer-term conservation. It has long been recognised that an appropriate institutional framework is essential for the effective governance of local assets, especially where common-pool resources are concerned (Ostrom, 1990; Ostrom et al., 1993). The need for appropriate organisational arrangements to ensure access to and control over natural resources, common pool or otherwise, has been expressed in the notion of 'environmental entitlements' (Mearns, 1995).

It is argued in the present volume that local organisation is the major institutional key to success. Although there is a high degree of interdependence amongst all the organisations involved in productive conservation activities, local agency is perhaps the single most vital ingredient. The kinds of community-based action illustrated by the case-studies examined above form the major component of the institutional structure required for helping to buttress environmental security. Such mobilisation helps to ensure that users not only have access to, but that they are also able to exercise a degree of effective control over this resource base. In this way, they are in a position to offer a better guarantee that resource entitlements may be perpetuated for both present and future generations.

Grassroots socio-environmental movements have often been highlighted in the literature as crucial players in strategies for defending natural resources and livelihoods. Much hyperbole has surrounded their supposed attributes in alleviating poverty while reducing environmental degradation. Yet there has been little systematic analysis of the precise ways in which such collective action may contribute to the attainment of environmentally sound development. The common tendency amongst some western environmentalists to romanticise grassroots efforts in the developing world as a panacea for ecological degradation has surely not been helpful. It has led to an exaggerated, quasi-populist belief in the inherent capacity of such collective action by small-scale producers to bring about positive change, and has often masked the severe constraints under which these movements operate, leading to an uncritical appreciation of their roles on the part of planners and policymakers.

Local action for resource governance

Case-studies of three Amazonian productive conservation experiences in this volume shed light on some of these issues, and may, it is hoped, lead to a clearer picture being drawn of the possible role of local community action in reconciling the economic use of natural resources with their conservation for present and future generations. Such movements perform distinctive roles during particular phases of this process, and the case-studies discussed in this volume each highlight their own singular features in this respect. Although the point has been made that every productive conservation experience is a unique product of its own circumstances and needs, it is nonetheless possible to draw out key characteristics which, in different measures, are common to all three and which are likely to be encountered in similar projects elsewhere. Thus, a number of vital resource governance functions may identified which local movements are instrumental in performing.

Local control

A first and obvious prerequisite for any viable integrated development-conservation initiative is that the local population should have secure access to basic natural resources. Given the growing competition over rights to land and water in Amazonia, people's mere presence in an area is clearly not itself sufficient to guarantee such access. In addition to any perceived traditional territorial or resource-use rights which groups might have, they must become actively involved in legitimising that claim against competing demands from outside interests. Only when such claims have the force of collective action to back them up can a legitimate command be established over livelihood resources. Groups with no such defensive strategy will invariably be decimated by overpowering forces, as has so often been the case in Amazonia with indigenous and peasant populations.

All three case-studies examined in the preceding chapters demonstrate the fundamental importance of grassroots action for securing and legitimising basic claims to and command over natural resources. The best known and most dramatic of these is, of course, the rubber tappers of southern Acre. Their strategy of using stand-offs or *empates* to prevent vast areas of rubber stands being taken over and deforested for setting up cattle ranches and for commercial logging was a milestone, which has raised the global profile of socio-environmental movements, while serving as an example to other threatened groups of what collective action may achieve.

Similar tactics were employed by the fisherpeople of Mamirauá, who used aquatic *empates* to exclude large commercial vessels which were threatening fish stocks with predatorial extraction techniques for the maximisation of short-term profit at the expense of community livelihoods. On the Transamazon highway around Marabá in southern Pará, a large proportion of small settlers have only managed to stake their claims after long drawn-out battles with traditional estate-owners and incoming cattle-ranchers, involving many casualties on both sides. Even after more than two decades of struggle over land in the region, these conflicts continue.

Once a local movement has established effective command over natural resources for the local population, the immediate problem of self-defence is solved, but there remains the challenge of systematically managing the resource base in a sustainable fashion. This requires that an institutional framework be set up for the longer-term governance of the environment in order to ensure that productive use of the resource base for economic purposes is reconciled with its conservation. Community movements play a vital role in this process of governance, although they are only one component in a much larger association of participants. Nevertheless, they form a particularly crucial element, since it is often the case that only local populations possess certain attributes necessary to make governance viable. These, which might be termed 'governance functions', testify to a wide scope of participatory roles exercised by communities. They range across a broad spectrum, from the ability of grassroots movements to articulate local needs and harness indigenous knowledge to their more recent involvement in active planning and even policy-making.

Following initial victories over claims to natural resources, it is necessary to consolidate local control, making sure that a monitoring system is instituted which permanently excludes potentially destructive commercial groups. In view of the increasing pressures to which many ecosystems in Amazonia are now being subjected, most productive conservation projects require an infrastructural set-up which enables permanent vigilance to be maintained and authorities notified when infractions are committed. This varies from the floating guardposts situated at Mamirauá's principal lake entrances, to the appointment of community environmental monitors on extractive reserves. Such vigilance is highly dependent on the local population's own efforts, since no environmental control agency (IBAMA in this case) has the human or financial resources to police effectively the vast areas involved. In a very real and practical sense, therefore, the inhabitants of the forests are its best guardians. Yet the construction, maintenance and application of such systems is also contingent upon support from external bodies such as state agencies and aid donors.

Needs articulation
A second governance role performed by grassroots movements is articulation of local interests and the feeding back of these demands into the environmental planning process. Conventionally, official planning in Brazil has not involved the consultation of impacted groups except where the application of political pressure has obliged authorities to engage in dialogue with communities about their perceptions of appropriate solutions to particular problems, as in the case of the power sector.[5] This process has commonly been facilitated by NGOs, which frequently act as a communications channel between community associations on the one hand and, on the other, outside government agencies and funding bodies. It is essential that effective participatory structures be established which permit the effective articulation of local needs in the first instance, as well as on-going decision-making and project management in the longer term. This is a challenge which all three of the case-studies examined here are currently facing.

Research and information
A further stage in setting up an appropriate institutional framework for resource management is that of research and information-gathering of various kinds. This constitutes a third and absolutely vital governance function in which local communities play an indispensable role. Although many groups of forest-dwellers such as extractivists and fisherpeople have evolved means of earning a livelihood while conserving their resource base, this equilibrium has been undermined by demographic, as well as commercial and speculative pressures. Productive conservation therefore requires new or modified, location-specific strategies tailored to the needs of sub-ecosystems and their populations as they are subjected to these changing influences: permanent or temporary population migrations from rural to urban and between rural areas, as well as the arrival of cattle-ranching, commercial logging and large-scale fishing. Accurate information is needed about current patterns of local resource-

use and how they should be modified to establish viable productive conservation initiatives, the socio-economic and political organisation of communities, and the social characteristics and needs of local groups and markets for forest products, amongst others.

The 'discovery' of grassroots activism around socio-environmental issues has tended to obscure the fact that traditional peoples have for centuries been systematically and consciously shaping their environments for livelihood-conservation purposes, unassisted by outsiders.[6] This accumulated 'indigenous knowledge' is only now beginning to receive serious consideration from development planners and policy-makers and to be more systematically incorporated into multi-institutional strategies of productive conservation. The critical value of harnessing traditional or indigenous knowledge in designing sustainable interventions has come to be widely recognised (Conroy and Litvinoff, 1988; UNCED, 1992; RAFI, 1994). An understanding of how fragile ecosystems function and of acceptable limits to resource extraction, of their 'carrying capacity', is thus absolutely essential. Social scientists are also contributing towards the design of organisational structures and production systems which will strengthen 'socio-cultural fit' within local circumstances (Cernea, 1991a).

There are, however, inherent dangers in using indigenous knowledge to serve a development agenda which may be imposed largely by outsiders. Commonly, a populist approach is adopted, based on bringing professionals and local people closer together, blending and reconciling indigenous knowledge with formal Western science. The dangers of crude knowledge 'extraction' by outsiders to serve a predetermined plan are clearly evident (Thompson, 1996). An alternative, 'political economy' view would recognise the socially constructed and conflictive nature of knowledge in given situations. It would thus seek to negotiate common ground between research scientists and local groups for carrying forward sustainable and productive development initiatives, avoiding either blueprint or unduly presumptuous populist processes which, despite the rhetoric of participation, do not 'empower' communities at all, but merely seek their acquiescence. In situations where local people are not organised in a manner which enables them to negotiate with outsiders or utilise their knowledge in the planning process, it is incumbent upon social scientists to assist grassroots organisations in becoming stronger and more autonomous (Cernea, 1996).

All three experiences examined in this volume have attempted to tap into local knowledge systems for planning through processes of dialogue and exchange between project technicians and community organisations at various levels. At Mamirauá, for example, a detailed research programme has been undertaken by natural scientists into key aspects of water-based and terrestrial resource systems. An understanding of fish and aquatic mammal populations and their movements will directly inform decisions by project scientists and local user populations on the final environmental management plan; for example, the quantities of fish that can be taken from which locations at what times of the year in order to avoid depletion of stocks, which would threaten the long-term viability of the strategy.

In Brazil's four federal extractive reserves supported by the G7 Pilot Programme, the traditional knowledge of rubber tappers is being employed to improved production technologies and to devise appropriate environmental monitoring and control techniques. On the Transamazon highway, sociologists and agronomists have established two pioneering research programmes on local agro-livestock and agroforestry usage around Marabá and Altamira. In close cooperation with local farmers' groups, new approaches and production mixes are being examined with a view to strengthening people's livelihoods through enhancing the sustainablility and productive capacity of farming systems. None of these projects would be viable without key information inputs by local resource-user groups. In all three cases, the pressures to engage in populist-type, indigenous knowledge extraction and persuasion are ever-present. To an extent, this is inevitable, since the projects documented represent an interface between two different if not actually mutually exclusive development agendas: that of local groups striving to earn a livelihood by making economic use of resources, and that of outside policy-makers and practitioners with their conservationist priorities geared towards broader environmental debates. Negotiation of a mutually acceptable compromise arrangement is thus critical.

Cost-sharing

A fourth governance function fulfilled by local resource-user groups in the cases examined is that of cost-sharing. As mentioned in chapter one, cost-sharing is often dismissed as a manipulative tool imposed by external authorities anxious to promote development on the cheap. While there may often be some mileage in this criticism, it is frequently a valuable means of mobilising extra key resources while eliciting people's commitment to the project and reducing the risks of paternalism. Direct cash contributions towards projects are not usually feasible, given the huge gap between the relative poverty of households and the huge costs of maintaining project infrastructures, which have to be met by the state and foreign donors.

However, some types of cost can only be effectively assumed by local communities. For example, there is the need to devote time and effort to police resources and occasionally mobilise to defend against outside (or internal) abusers. Had the fishing communities of Mamirauá and rubber tappers of southern Acre not taken on these roles, their territorial integrity would today be seriously undermined and doubt cast over the possibility of their developing long-term productive conservation plans.

The long-standing land struggles of small settlers along the Transamazon highway and elsewhere in the region also bear testimony to massive social and psychological costs incurred by families and communities, reflected in evictions, deprivation and, not infrequently, death at the hands of hired gunmen and police. Such battles have, quite literally, formed the foundation of current attempts to develop sustainable strategies in many parts of Amazonia. Without secure land tenure as a starting point, initiatives such as those analysed above would not be viable. Small producers would be reluctant to invest their time and resources into developing new, sustainable activities whose returns only become evident in the longer term, and would instead continue to rely overwhelmingly on more predatory practices such as slash-and-burn farming. These massive and frequently hidden costs are generally not acknowledged by planners, although in fact they represent a huge sacrifice by small cultivators in their bid to strengthen livelihoods.

Strategic alliances

The above four governance functions concern resources and skills emanating principally from user groups themselves, in terms of self-defence and monitoring, the systematic expression of local needs, supply of traditional knowledge and sharing of project costs. However, it would be pointless to pretend that communities can, on their own, make productive conservation a viable strategy for Amazonia.

There has been a tendency in some quarters to romanticise and exaggerate the inherent potential of forest populations to manage their affairs sustainably and unassisted. However successful traditional communities might have been in achieving this degree of equilibrium and independence in the past, such pastoral idealism is increasingly untenable as pressure on natural resources mount.

One of the notable features of the productive conservation experiences analysed here is that they all depend for their very existence, let alone their future success, on establishing strategic alliances with a number of organisations. In differing combinations, rubber tappers, fisher people and small farmers have all required the support of outside agencies to capitalise upon and complement their own contributions to productive conservation strategies. This ability to form key alliances with important support groups constitutes a fifth governance role performed by local organisations.

Conventional resource-conservation policies in Amazonia have tended, as observed in chapter two, to place undue emphasis on the policing role of the state and the exclusion of local populations from areas such as national forests and parks. The backlash response from the grassroots as well as from critical NGOs has often been to decry the role of central government and proclaim guardianship of the forests as the unique domain of its traditional *caboclo* and indigenous inhabitants. Yet is it clear that active cooperation amongst all 'stakeholders' or interested parties involved is necessary for viable productive conservation plans to be devised and executed. Each participant has distinctive contributions. The skills, knowledge and other resources provided by local communities are a necessary but not a sufficient precondition for sustainable options to be realised.

State agencies must supply technical services, and logistical and financial support. At the same time, a suitable legislative framework must be created to legitimise these new territorial and administrative arrangements to cater for this approach to environmental management, which involves ceding protected areas to the care and productive use of local populations. In terms of technical assistance, all three experiences under consideration have benefited from significant state involvement from a variety of agencies for agricultural research (EMBRAPA), extension (EMATER) and environmental control (IBAMA), as well as in the health and education fields. At both Mamirauá and in the case of extractive reserves, maintenance costs have been partly covered by government.

The first substantial new piece of environmental legislation which recognised the rights of forest populations to exploit natural resources within designated protected areas was that in 1990 which gave rise to the first four federal extractive reserves. Statutory provision for Amazonia's inland fishing communities received an impetus with the declaration in 1996 of Mamirauá as a 'Sustainable Development Reserve' under Amazonas state law. Draft legislation currently (1996) being considered by the Brazilian Congress concerns the reformulation of policy for the country's National System of Nature Conservation Units (SNUC). This proposes setting up new guidelines for Brazil's 165 protected areas, which would provide for the formal incorporation of local populations and other agencies into their management, thus helping to defuse potential resource conflicts, improve their administration and promote socio-economic justice. A particularly interesting aspect is the introduction of a new category of conservation unit, the Ecological-Cultural Reserve, which would integrate traditional populations practising sustainable forms of resource-use into their management and protection. This would cater for the development-conservation needs of many groups which fall outside the present federal legislative framework, such as Mamirauá.[7]

If communities and central government have major roles to play in the design and implementation of new sustainable approaches in Amazonia, the participation of NGOs is no less important. Local NGOs perform a number of key functions. At the local level, they may directly assist communities to organise for the purposes of self-defence and for articulating people's views more effectively. This can be especially valuable in situations where there is little tradition of collective organisation. In the cases examined here, most rubber-producing areas outside southern Acre as well as along the middle stretches of the Transamazon highway, neither of which have experienced prolonged land struggles, would fall squarely into this category. The IEA, for example, was instrumental during the 1980s in helping *seringueiros* to organise at national level through the CNS, and then to lobby successfully for policy and legislative change. At Marabá and Altamira on the *Transamazônica*, CAT and LAET respectively have provided technical and infrastructural support of various kinds in support of local farmers' movements to diversify production along more sustainable lines. The SCM has also supplied major inputs to the joint research and resource-management strategy undertaken with local communities. As in the case of the IEA and the rubber tappers, the SCM has been actively lobbying for changes in the policy and legal environment to support productive conservation.

Although state institutions and NGOs both play key roles in assisting local resource-users to implement productive conservation undertakings, relatively little attention has so far been paid to the potential contribution of the business sector. Yet, for these projects, constructive links with private enterprise are crucial to their economic viability. The 'products' of productive conservation must be processed and marketed in order to generate an income flow to sustain livelihoods as well as contribute towards project running costs. Extractive goods such as latex and brazil nuts, cultivated NTFPs, arguably timber itself in measured quantities, as well as fish, must all be sold for a realistic profit. In Amazonia, given the rapid expansion of communications and human settlement, the notion of isolated, self-contained groups producing to meet household subsistence-needs largely independently of commercial markets is an increasingly rare phenomenon.

The private business sector in southern Brazil has remained cautious about venturing into Amazonian product development due to the embryonic nature of national and overseas markets and the consequently high levels of perceived risk. This situation is beginning to change as *sulista* entrepreneurs are becoming interested in the region not for the government subsidies and speculative advantages available, but for incipient commercial opportunities there. These include such initiatives as the purchase of high-quality latex from rubber tappers' associations, production of *couro vegetal* to make clothing and bags, the use of brazil nuts in confectionary, and the growing sale of tropical fruits for the manufactures of juices and ice-cream. Although these are in some sense pioneering efforts on Brazilian and international markets, they indicate what is possible through effective organisation. What is fairly evident is that, in the majority of productive conservation experiences, the commercial potential of these and other forest products will have to be systematically tapped through contractual arrangements with private firms if the projects in question are to become remotely viable in economic terms.

While grassroots organisations, state agencies and NGOs together meet most of the organisational prerequisites for running productive conservation projects, funding remains a major challenge. In the long run, enough commercial profit may be generated to provide a sound economic basis. However, capital investment and running costs over the first few years can be substantial, running literally into millions of dollars. It is almost inevitable, therefore, that, at least during the initial phase, foreign support will be necessary to cover set-up and initial running costs. Foreign aid forms a critical element in this strategic alliance, whether through official or international NGO channels. Such help invariably gives rise to accusations of dependency and manipulation to serve the global environmental and more specific commercial interests of overseas donors, rather than those of Amazonian producers.[8]

Be that as it may, however, aid support is indispensable and has been actively sought by both the Brazilian state and NGO sector. The key issue is not so much whether aid is given, but for what purpose and with what consequences. All three programmes considered in this volume have so far depended heavily on a combination of technical assistance and capital aid from a range of bilateral, multilateral and NGO sources. One of the major challenges they face is how to minimise reliance on external funding in future and find alternative sources to ensure financial sustainability.

People as providers of solutions

The single most notable and overriding characteristic of all three experiences analysed here is the transformation of resource-users from passive victims to active providers of solutions. As such, this governance function is both a culmination and an extension of the above attributes. Through the medium of productive conservation movements, local populations have been able to throw off the mantle of helpless objects, securing development benefits in the face of strong opposition from entrenched interests in the larger-scale commercial production and speculative sectors, which have so far enjoyed a relatively free rein to use and abuse Amazonia's resource base. The struggles of rubber tappers, small farmers, dam displacees and indigenous groups in Brazil and Latin America generally have changed this situation quite dramatically, reversing their image from that of inevitable victims and unwitting destroyers of the environment to that of potential saviours.

Perhaps unsurprisingly, this new image is often at odds with the capacity of local movements to fulfil the high conservation-development expectations which have been created. In the search for quick solutions to Amazonia's social-ecological problems, outside observers have often been guilty of romanticising the environmental sensitivities of local resource-users and of overestimating their inherent capacity and willingness to manage resources sustainably.[9] Yet, although the pendulum may in some respects have swung too far in the direction of unrealistic optimism, this change of perception has certainly permitted a major re-evaluation of several key issues relating to the diverse origins of ecological destruction and preservation, as well as the range of potential solutions open to consideration. Above all, it has slowly dawned upon official policy-makers that local populations are vital agents in the conservation of natural resource stocks in Amazonia, and that strenuous efforts must be made to harness their collaboration in systematically promoting more sustainable development practices.

The stereotypical modernisationist views prevalent during the 1950s and 1960s, which, for example, saw peasants as inherently submissive and stoical bearers of their fate, has given way to a far more complex picture. Whether expressed through noncompliance via 'everyday forms of peasant resistance'[10] or through more collective manifestations, opposition to oppressive forces on the part of small cultivators is recognised not as an aberration, but as a manifestation of legitimate political action for the defence of livelihood interests. While peasant groups have always been involved in forms of religious and political mobilisation for local or broader revolutionary causes, the 1980s have seen a major surge in protest movements centred around socio-environmental issues, not just in Brazil but all over the developing world.

The three major examples considered in this book have illustrated different ways in which such group action has itself contributed towards this process. Grassroots movements undoubtedly need the financial, technical and political support of other organisations in order to realise their aims. Yet the direct participation of producer groups is an essential prerequisite without which productive conservation efforts would not be viable. In the three examples studied here, the active participation of resource-user groups at different stages of project-planning and execution has been absolutely critical to the successes achieved so far. As detailed in the preceding chapters, this involvement ranges from the provision of vital local knowledge, skills and labour to participation in important decision-

Towards productive conservation

making processes at project and even policy levels.

What could be called 'passive' (but no less important) contributions revolve, as we have seen, around the provision of vital local knowledge, skills and labour, all of which are essential and cannot be provided by outsiders. Yet, more aggressive, proactive forms of people's involvement have always been important and continue to be so. In one sense, small producers in Amazonia have for a long time, with varying degrees of success, been active defenders of their lands and livelihood resources. The history of Amerindian resistance to territorial appropriation and of the explosion of land conflicts since the 1970s in Amazonia bear witness to a process of continuing struggle. Active participation in productive conservation projects has added a new dimension to people's attempts to exercise greater control over their own destinies. Local groups in Amazonia have always manipulated their immediate natural environments in a conscious manner in order to achieve sustainability.[11]

The difference, however, is that now local organisations are being formally incorporated into structured resource-management and production plans. These new arrangements have become necessary as terrestrial and aquatic ecosystem-based livelihoods are increasingly threatened by outside commercial pressures and traditional controls are no longer adequate to guarantee resource entitlements for local people. In a very real sense, therefore, they have been obliged to reconquer their environments, to reassert their rights of access to natural resources upon which they depend. Only by adopting a forceful role in the process of resource management is this possible. Grassroots organisations cannot rely entirely on third parties to guarantee such rights, whether the state, NGOs or international donors. At the end of the day, it is a politically negotiated process in which local groups must become an effective countervailing power, able to engage in dialogue with outside support agencies from a position of strength.

The first and perhaps most critical proactive role performed by people's organisations is to secure territorial integrity for resource system users. This has been clearly manifested in all three projects examined in this volume. Since the 1980s, both rubber tappers in Acre and fishing communities along the River Amazon have used the *empate* to ward off predatory outside groups (cattle-ranchers, logging and commercial fishing companies) whose principal objective has been to maximise short-term profit, thus jeopardising resource stocks and local people's livelihoods. On the Transamazon highway around Marabá, small settlers were obliged to engage in protracted land struggles against individual and corporate landed interests in order to secure plots and develop their own farming systems.

Beyond this initial phase, local groups have been actively involved in many other ways essential for the projects to function. On extractive reserves, this has taken the form of local monitoring and control of incursions by outsiders, the formation of local associations, design of reserve utilisation plans and setting up of management infrastructures. At Mamirauá, communities have played a major role in continued vigilance against commercial vessels, as well as in zoning the ecological station for fishing and conservation purposes. Along the *Transamazônica*, farmers have, through their associations, become closely involved in dialogue with extensionists and researchers to determine the most appropriate forms of agriculture and agroforestry which will meet the needs of people yet minimise deforestation. In addition, they have been actively lobbying state authorities for access to resources such as subsidised credit, normally channelled towards more politically powerful landowners.

If there has been growing participation of resource-user groups in self-defence and project-planning activities, another mark of their more proactive position in the implementation of productive conservation strategies lies in their influence on policy-making. Through their strategic alliances with outside groups such as domestic and international NGOs, as well as influential bilateral and multilateral donors, local groups have had what could be called a *socio-political multiplier effect*. Largely ineffectual on their own, community-based movements working and lobbying together with other agencies have started to have a major influence on the reformulation of Amazon development policy in the interests of small producers. In the cases studied here, environmental policy change has not been initiated by small groups within the state machine, as is usually the case (Keck, 1994), but by networks and alliances exerting pressure on government, often with the collaboration of progressive-minded state managers.

The most notable example of this was 1990 federal legislation to set up extractive reserves. This came about as the result of a combination of lobbying by the rubber tappers through the CNS, as well as international pressure for reform following the death of Chico

Mendes in a situation of accelerating deforestation and heightened global concern over the environment during the run-up to the UNCED. The alliance between rubber tappers and international environmentalists was particularly successful in achieving its aims because it managed to accumulate support at a number of progressively higher levels, each with its own sympathetic audience. 'Beginning as a local struggle by a traditional extractivist population over land use rights, it became part of a broader movement for social justice and finally part of a global environmental struggle' (Keck, 1995b: 410). This combination of domestic and international circumstances generated such pressure on the Brazilian government as well as on key donors such as the World Bank, that indifference was no longer an option. While it has to be admitted that such a favourable conjuncture for policy reform is rare, similar combinations of factors have led to substantial changes in the design and implementation of major development schemes.[12]

In the absence of an inland fisheries policy for Brazil, the success of Mamirauá in protecting Amazonian várzeas from overexploitation has also showed the need for an appropriate 'aquatic reserve' category which would legalise the economic use of natural resources within a wetlands conservation unit. Although fisherpeople have not enjoyed the same high international profile as rubber tappers, they have nonetheless been quietly working to change existing legislation. The consequent reclassification of Mamirauá as a Sustainable Development Reserve by the Amazonas state government, which for the first time legally permits both economic activity and preservation, is a major advance. Eventual reformulation of Brazil's National System of Conservation Units to regulate human use and occupation, as already noted, should also help to create a more realistic policy framework for Amazonian inland fisheries generally.

As far as small farmers are concerned, the policy impacts of their productive conservation work along the Transamazon highway have been slower to materialise. Minor victories have been won in terms of gaining access to resources such as technical assistance and, in particular, subsidised credit, which were previously inaccessible to the majority of small cultivators due to political and bureaucratic obstacles. In a more general sense, continuing 'invasions' of idle properties by landless rural workers, especially in southern Pará, has reinforced pressure on the government to maintain a land reform programme of sorts, distributing purchased property to defuse pockets of tension. There has been a long history of such attrition, which continues due to the growing political strength of the MST.[13] Such concessions notwithstanding, however, the struggle by grassroots organisations and development activists continues to exert pressure on official agrarian development policy-makers towards better serving the interests of small farmers.

The rocky road ahead

It has been argued here that grassroots movements have played a pivotal role in the design and execution of productive conservation strategies adapted to a variety of Amazonian sub-ecosystems. The participation of local resource-users has, it is suggested, been a precondition for their progress to date and potential longer-term viability. Three case-studies have highlighted major areas in which collective activities have been pivotal: self-defence and environmental monitoring, needs articulation, provision of vital resources, proactive involvement in planning and implementation, formation of strategic alliances with outside partners and pressure for policy reform. Without the distinctive environmental governance functions performed by local communities to complement other external inputs, it is highly unlikely that the economic use of natural resources and their preservation for the benefit of future generations could be reconciled.

Yet although it is possible to identify emerging patterns of cooperation between local and outside institutions as part of a new, joint approach to environmental management in Amazonia, it is evident that many factors will frustrate attempts to promote its wider replication. Some of the major hindrances at project or programme level in terms of physical obstacles, social fragmentation, political factionalism and household livelihood strategies have been discussed in relation to the individual case-studies and will not be repeated here. It is worth, however, drawing attention to some of the broader or more contextual constraints over which project participants have little or no control.

However successful productive conservation projects might be, they are likely to come under growing pressure. As the case-studies analysed in this volume have shown, threats from commercial and speculative enterprises such as logging and ranching will loom large for the foreseeable future. Yet internal migration by small farmers within Amazonia from old to new frontiers is also likely to put growing pressure on reserves and other conservation areas (Osório de Almeida and Campari, 1995; Richards, 1996). Thus, policies are needed to create agriculturally sustainable frontiers which encourage farmers to cultivate already settled and deforested areas rather than engage in the familiar vicious circle of migratory slash-and-burn farming. As the cases examined here demonstrate, decentralised forms of locally relevant infrastructural and institutional support based on new configurations of governmental and non-governmental agencies offer hope that these aims are achievable.

Locally designed and implemented strategies would, for example, promote agro-ecological zoning to guide land use, as has started to take place in Rondônia under PLANAFLORO. Systematic knowledge of more appropriate forms of technology such as agroforestry is gradually being accumulated and documented. However, further research as well as extension, marketing and credit services would have to be provided in order to apply such technologies efficiently.[14] More effective fiscal policies to tax agricultural and speculative income, to penalise deforestation and to encourage more ecologically friendly practices have also been suggested, although implementation of such policies in the Brazilian context has always been highly problematic.[15]

To take one key issue, agricultural credit in Brazil has traditionally been monopolised by large landowners and corporate enterprises, while small farmers have benefited relatively little.[16] Paradoxically, however, where targeted small producer credit programmes have existed in Brazil, they have been highly cost-effective. Such has been the case of FNO loans in Amazonia (discussed above in chapter five) and the PROCERA scheme for land reform beneficiaries (Hall, 1990; FAO/PNUD, 1992).[17] In a context where billions of dollars of state subsidies in fiscal incentives and cheap credit have been channelled towards financing the destruction of the Amazon rainforest, mainly for the speculative and commercial gain of a few, there is a strong case to be made for a redirection of such support to smaller-scale activities which offer greater economic, social and environmental returns. A step in this direction was taken by Brazilian banks, which signed an agreement, or 'Green Protocol', in 1995 to promote sustainable development through the use of economic incentives.[18] The earmarking of FNO credit through the PRODEX scheme specifically for extractive reserve populations is another case in point.[19]

Yet such support for small producers and extractivists must be measured and cautious in order not to provoke undue pressure on natural resources. Experience along the Transamazon highway with sometimes politically inspired farmer credit programmes has pointed to the dangers of over-investment in cattle and pasture formation. In Peru, favourable land and credit policies for small farmers during the 1980s following the agrarian reform encouraged migration into fragile environments in western Amazonia and the subsequent degradation of open-access natural resources, obliging local communities to mobilise in defence of their livelihoods, in a similar fashion to the cases discussed here.[20] Programmes of small producer support must therefore be carefully tailored to meet the needs of local populations within a purposeful management strategy.

State-sponsored action in Brazil should also include research into new marketing opportunities and the provision of appropriate infrastructure. Instability of land tenure and indefinition of property rights, whether collective or individual, will continue to frustrate attempts at devising more stable, sedentary productive conservation systems. The potentially huge economic yield of non-timber forest products compared with lumbering has been highlighted by research, but public policy has failed to recognise the potential of agroforestry for Amazonia.[21] More affirmative action in these areas might help provide the basic security which would persuade many itinerant small producers to adopt more sustainable methods. Lack of effective land-use planning further encourages the adoption of environmentally inappropriate production systems. The strengthening of ecological zoning, monitoring and control procedures would therefore help to address this problem.

The general lack of government investment into the kinds of productive conservation activities for small farmers discussed in this volume has been a major handicap. Yet the need for economic support and incentives for the sustainable use of natural resources is now widely recognised, finding expression in the Convention on Biodiversity.[22] Although Brazilian counterpart funding under the G7 Pilot Programme has gone some way towards rectifying this imbalance, a greater channelling of resources in this direction is essential. This would reduce the long-term dependence on foreign aid, which is presently very high in the environmental management sphere but is clearly not sustainable in the long term. Although continued use of overseas assistance is tempting under conditions of austerity, the great danger is that when foreign funding is eventually phased out, these initiatives will collapse due to under-prioritisation by federal and state governments.

Other contextual obstacles are less easily controllable through direct government action, at least in the short term. Broader processes of habitat destruction may well undermine local efforts at promoting sustainability. For example, deforestation fuelled by land speculation in response to macro-economic influences may enhance market pressures on small farmers, threatening their attempts at switching from migratory to a more sedentary production and capitalisation system. Increased commercial logging as a consequence of market gaps resulting from diminishing supplies of south-east Asian timber could threaten the integrity of extractive reserves or the delicate ecological balance in wetlands such as Mamirauá. Temporary or even permanent migration of rural populations to urban areas, which research has shown to be an increasingly important household livelihood strategy in Amazonia, could easily sabotage productive conservation initiatives which are reliant on local people's constant presence to oversee and manage natural resources.

Attempts to promote a participatory rather than top-down approach to the management of natural resources in the developing world, whether building upon customary practices or introducing totally new procedures, have been under way for some time. Africa, for example, has witnessed a variety of attempts at the community management of wildlife, involving greater or lesser degrees of community initiative (IIED, 1994; Barrett and Arcese, 1995). Many examples may be cited from the developing world of parks and other multiple-use protected areas where communities have played a major role in conservation through their active participation in defending the environment and in local resource management.[23] The growing volume of literature in this field tends to agree on one fundamental point: the limited impact and outright impracticality of top-down resource-conservation policies and the need actively to engage local populations in the formulation and implementation of environmental management strategies for them to have any reasonable chance of success.

In Brazil such an approach has been slow to materialise. Since the

1970s environmental policy for Amazonia has been based largely on setting aside protected areas such as national parks and forests, in which the presence of people has been seen as incompatible with resource conservation. This approach has been complemented, especially through IBAMA during the 1990s, by monitoring and control policies of extremely limited effectiveness. Although peasant and indigenous groups have in many instances evolved their own customary resource-management practices, these have, conventionally, been ignored by policy-makers.

The onus to devise more appropriate and effective resource-management strategies has, in effect, been placed upon those user groups whose livelihoods have been directly threatened by environmental degradation on various fronts. They have been left with little choice but proactively to defend their territory from predatory exploitation, collaborating with other interested organisations to devise and carry out location-specific productive conservation plans. This can be said to constitute a new paradigm of environmental management as far as Brazilian Amazonia is concerned. How far the experiences recounted in this volume can be replicated elsewhere in the region remains to be seen. Although attention was focused on three particular examples from contrasting situations, many small-scale experiences exist across Amazonia which combine similar principles, even if their scale is perhaps more modest. These comprise a variety of community projects, supported by a combination of domestic and overseas funds, which are attempting to diversify production and provide community services in an attempt to strengthen well-being and livelihoods, while minimising destruction of their respective ecosystems.

Clearly, grassroots mobilisation will provide no magical cure for environmental degradation in Amazonia. It is, nonetheless, often a necessary if not a sufficient precondition for reconciling the economic use of natural resources with their conservation for the benefit of present and future generations. Attempts at environmental management which ignore the needs and wishes of the resident population are bound to fail. This message has finally been taken on board and is reflected in the significant reformulation of development guidelines for Amazonia (Brazil, 1995a). Although couched in rather ambiguous and sometimes contradictory terms, incorporating a strong modernisation bias, for the first time in the history of the region, macro-policy directives officially acknowledge the importance of incorporating communities into the process of environmental management and setting of development priorities.[24] Moves are under way to update Brazil's legislative framework for conservation units, providing for the active involvement of local populations in their economic use and preservation, reflecting a new official pragmatism.[25] Alongside official policy innovation, NGO-sponsored conservation-development initiatives in Amazonia, such as the Jau National Park, are reinforcing this message.[26] In July 1996, the federal government announced new measures in an 'Amazon Package' to limit Amazonian deforestation. which, if effectively implemented, will help reinforce the move towards more sustainable forms of land use in the region.[27]

The official policy rethink for Brazilian Amazonia has undoubtedly been influenced in no uncertain manner by the advent of the Rainforest Pilot Programme, which, despite its strong support for conventional agro-economic zoning, environmental monitoring and control, has, through several of its components, emphasised the parallel importance of productive conservation activities as a sustainable strategy for the region.[28] These innovative 'pilot' experiences will, it is hoped, stimulate national debates and bring the issue of community participation and local resource management in Amazonia more firmly onto the planning agenda.

Since the mid-1980s in Brazil there has been a steady evolution in the analysis of and response to environmental problems. This has led to a greater appreciation of their complexity and of the need for multi-faceted solutions involving all interested parties. In Amazonia, this process has been spearheaded by the setting up of productive conservation initiatives which have combined the forces of grassroots organisations, NGOs, progressive state agencies, the private sector and international donors.

The cases analysed in this volume have shown that, despite the many inherent problems, local communities have a decisive role to play in the sustainable management of local resources. It has also been demonstrated that grassroots action may act as a catalyst for broader policy innovation. While certainly no panacea for the challenge of introducing more sustainable development practices to Amazonia, productive conservation is a new paradigm which offers a major avenue for strengthening people's livelihoods while minimising destruction of natural resources. If the opportunity to support such progress is wasted, the cost for Amazonia and its people will be incalculable.

Notes

1 See Hall, 1991 (chapter six).
2 Cardoso and Muller (1977), Becker (1982), Branford and Glock (1985) and Lisansky (1990).
3 While active mainly in southern Brazil, the MST has in recent years become increasingly involved in organising land occupations in the Amazon. An MST-backed *invasão* of the Fazendas Tres Voltas and Palmares in the Parauapebas region of southern Pará took place in May 1996, for example. The MST also organised the occupation of the nearby Fazenda Macaxeira at Curionópolis in southern Pará, on which nineteen peasant farmers were massacred by military police in April of that year (various reports in the *Folha de São Paulo*).
4 This phenomenon is discussed at greater length in chapter two. For additional information, see Hall (1990) and Romeiro *et al.* (1994).
5 For a discussion of the role of grassroots organisations and other agencies in the design of resettlement policy for hydropower schemes in Brazil, see Hall (1994).
6 For further details of traditional rainforest environmental management strategies, see Anderson (1990b), Eden (1990) and Place (1993).
7 Fernando Gabeira, Federal Deputy for the Green Party, introduced the draft bill to Congress in 1992. Framed largely within the existing structure of 'direct use' (sustainably managed areas, such as national forests and extractive reserves) and 'indirect use' (fully protected areas, such as national parks and ecological stations) units, it aims to lay down guidelines for integrating resident as well as adjacent populations in their management. In addition to state agencies, NGOs and the private sector would be involved in the process.

The bill was originally criticised for not including new legal categories which would take fuller account of the need to reconcile protection and rational resource-use, but it has been modified to include new categories such as the 'Ecological-Cultural Reserve' (Article 20) and the 'Integrated Ecological Reserve', the latter designed for areas with diversified ecosystems and management requirements (Gabeira, 1996).

Due to the long legislative and bureaucratic process, the proposed law was expected to take a decade before entering the statute books (Capobianco, 1996). Another problem concerns the lack of complementary measures necessary to implement the conservation units once they are legally decreed. Under current legislation, the Executive must enforce these measures within five years or the unit is declared null and void. Most execution problems relate to legalisation of land transfers from other government organisations such as INCRA and the states, divestiture of land rights from private owners within units and resettlement of squatters. In 1994, some twenty-one conservation units faced extinction due to such problems. It was estimated that it would cost over $R440 million to pay for costs of land divestiture in existing units, and take over 400 years at current rates of expenditure (Barbanti, 1994).

8 Nugent, for example, questions the feasibility of attempting to reconcile environmental conservation with profitable production, what he calls the 'sustainability thesis'. This is driven, he maintains, by western concerns over Amazonia's contribution to the global environmental crisis as well as business profit motives, those 'who view Amazonia as an admirable resource domain rather than a place occupied by people with a history' (1993a: 4).

9 Keck (1995b: 41) forcibly makes the point that the stereotypical view of forest peoples as saviours of the environment rather than its destroyers, 'is often hard to reconcile with the messier realities of real communities'.

10 See, for example, Scott (1986).

11 'Sustainability' is used here as defined in chapter one. See Anderson (1990b) and Posey (1985) for examples of long-standing natural resource management by Amazonian peoples.

12 For example, the reformulation of POLONOROESTE and PLANAFLORO, the Itaparica dam and resettlement project, and the cancellation of hydropower development on the River Xingú and in southern Brazil (see chapter two).

13 An example of this was the Eldorado do Carajás incident in southern Pará, in April 1996, in which nineteen landless peasant squatters were shot dead by police, after which many of those who had not fled were resettled elsewhere. On the history of land conflicts in southern Pará, see Hall (1991). See chapter two for further details of the Eldorado do Carajás incident.

14 For a recent technical discussion of agroforestry techniques for Amazonia, see Dubois *et al.* (1996).

15 For a more detailed discussion of the role of fiscal policy in encouraging more sustainable agricultural, ranching and logging practices, see Osório de Almeida and Campari (1995, chapter six) and Almeida and Uhl (n.d.).

16 Based on World Bank figures, Goodman (1986) estimates that in the late 1970s only 20–5% of rural producers had access to credit. This is typically concentrated in the south, within the export crop sector (coffee, soybean, sugar, wheat) and on large farm units. The small, semi-subsistence farm sector is almost totally excluded except for 'special' programmes such as the FNO and PROCERA.

17 An evaluation of the economic performance in selected agrarian reform settlement projects throughout Brazil concluded that 'Government

loans through PROCERA had a positive effect in alleviating the problem of decapitalisation in some regions', thus contributing towards the improved incomes of beneficiaries (FAO/PNUD, 1992: 13).
18. In May 1995, a group of national and regional banks (BNDES, Banco do Brasil, BASA, BNB and the Caixa Econômica Federal) signed the Protocolo Verde in accordance with directives under the National Environmental Policy, instituted in 1981. This envisages a transition towards greater reliance on economic incentives through the banking sector to 'favour the financing of projects that are less aggressive to the environment and present characteristics of sustainability' (Brazil, 1995b: 33).
19. See chapter three for further details of PRODEX.
20. The Tamishyacu-Tahuayo Communal Forest Reserve was set up by the regional government in 1991, covering 322,500 hectares of rainforest (Coomes, 1995).
21. In their seminal article, Peters, Gentry and Mendelsohn (1985), based on research carried out near Iquitos in Peru, demonstrated the substantially higher net revenues which may accrue from the exploitation of minor forest products when compared with timber extraction, which is also ecologically damaging. The ability to realise this potential, however, depends upon the provision of adequate infrastructure to facilitate extractivism and agroforestry and on the adequate management of resources.
22. Articles six and eleven.
23. See, for example: Pimbert and Pretty (1996), IUCN (1995), Kemf (1993), Mearns (1995), Colchester (1992, 1994), Perkin and Stocking (1994), Broad (1994), Friedmann and Rangan (1993), Ghai and Vivian (1992).
24. The text questions mainstream development policies which have in the past channelled benefits to a limited number of producers, and calls for 'the adoption of diversified forms of development relevant to the natural and cultural plurality of Amazonia', stressing the need to encourage 'community planning and management' (Brazil, 1995a: 17, 25).
25. See chapter two for further details on the SNUC proposals.
26. The Jaú National Park in Amazonas state, the largest such park in Brazil and the second largest in South America, was set up in 1981 with NGO support. Covering an area of 22,270 square kilometres, the project aims to protect the region from turtle hunters and animal traffickers, a management plan is being devised involving the 1,000 local inhabitants, with the assistance of the Brazilian NGO Fundação Vitória Amazônica (FVA) and the WWF. See Cornell (1996).
27. The 'pacote amazônico', passed by executive decree and provisional law, which do not require Congressional approval, comprised a number of measures designed to protect natural resources in the Amazon. These

included: (i) a two-year moratorium on new logging permits for mahogany and virola, two of the most valuable species; (ii) a deforestation ban on properties where existing clearings are mismanaged or under-utilised; (iii) an increase from 50 to 80% of designated forest reserve on properties originally covered by forest; as well as (iv) preferential credit and tax incentives to encourage the productive use of degraded pastures.

28 Kohlhepp (1995: 25) emphasises this when, in his discussion of the Pilot Programme, he observes: 'The execution of sustainable development projects will be impossible without a great effort to recover traditional local knowledge accumulated by indigenous and *caboclo* groups.' The most important components of the Pilot Programme from this point of view are the extractive reserves and the demonstration projects' support for community and NGO initiatives, as well as some directed research projects.

References

ACTIONAID, ICVA and EUROSTEP (1993), *The Reality of Aid: An Independent Review of International Aid*, ACTIONAID, London.
Abel, C. and C. Lewis, eds. (1993), *Welfare, Poverty and Development in Latin America*, Macmillan, London.
Adams, P. (1991), *Odious Debts: Loose Lending, Corruption and the Third World's Environmental Legacy*, Earthscan, London.
Adams, P. and L. Solomon (1985), *In the Name of Progress: The Underside of Foreign Aid*, Earthscan, London.
Adams, W. (1990), *Green Development: Environment and Sustainability in the Third World*, Routledge, London.
Afsah, S. (1992), *Extractive Reserves: Economic-Environmental Issues and Marketing Strategies for Non-Timber Forest Products*, ENVAP, World Bank, Washington DC. (draft).
Alencar, E. F. (1993), Memórias de Mamirauá, *mimeo.*, Belém.
Alexander, S. (1996), Colombia's Pacific Plan: Indigenous and Afro-Colombian Communities Challenge the Developers, in Collinson, ed., 74–81.
Allegretti, M. (1990), Extractive Reserves: An Alternative for Reconciling Development and Environmental Conservation in Amazonia, in Anderson, ed., 252–64.
Allegretti, M. (1994a), Reservas Extrativistas: Parâmetros para uma Política de Desenvolvimento Sustentável na Amazônia, in Arnt, ed., 17–47.
Allegretti, M. (1994b), Policies for the Use of Renewable Natural Resources: the Amazonian Region and Extractive Activities, in Clüsener-Godt and Sachs, eds., 14–33.
Allegretti, M. (1995), Extracting Activities in the Amazon, in Clüsener-Godt and Sachs, eds., 157–74.
Almeida, J. R. de, ed. (1993), *Planejamento Ambiental*, Thex Editora, Rio de Janeiro.
Almeida, M. W. B. de and M. A. Menezes (1994), Acre – Reserva Extra-

tivista do Alto Juruá, in Arnt, ed., 164–225.
Almeida, O. T., ed. (1996), *A Evolução da Frontera Amazônica: Oportunidades para um Desenvolvimento Sustentável*, IMAZON, Belém.
Almeida, O. T. and C. Uhl (1995), Developing a Quantitative Framework for Sustainable Resource-Use Planning in the Brazilian Amazon, *World Development*, 23 (10), 1745–64.
Almeida, O. T. and C. Uhl (n.d.), O Imposto Territorial Rural Como Instrumento para Incentivar Usos Produtivos e Sustentáveis do Solo na Amazônia Oriental, *mimeo.*, IMAZON, Belém.
Alves, J. (1993), Um Estudo Preliminar da Dinâmica Social na Região de Anapú, *mimeo.*, LAET, Altamira.
Alves, J. (1994a), A Organização da Sociedade na Transamazônica, *mimeo.*, LAET, Altamira.
Alves, J. (1994b), Apresentação da Cidade de Uruará, *mimeo.*, LAET, Altamira.
Amnesty International (1988), *Brazil: Authorized Violence in Rural Areas*, London.
Anderson, A. (1990a), Extraction and Forest Management by Rural Inhabitants in the Amazon Estuary, in Anderson, ed., 65–85.
Anderson, A., ed. (1990b), *Alternatives to Deforestation: Steps Towards Sustainable Use of the Amazon Rain Forest*, Columbia University Press, New York.
Anderson, A. (1992), Land-use Strategies for Successful Extractive Economies, in FOE, 213–23.
Anderson, A., P. May, and J. Balick (1991), *The Subsidy From Nature: Palm Forests, Peasantry and Development on an Amazon Frontier*, Columbia University Press, New York.
Aragón, L., ed. (1994), *What Future for the Amazon Region?* Proceedings of the International Symposium, 48th International Congress of Americanists, Institute of Latin American Studies, Stockholm University, Stockholm, July.
Araújo, R. (1991), Campo Religioso e Trajetórias Sociais na Transamazônica, in Léna and Engrácia de Oliveira, eds., 125–43.
Arnt, R., ed. (1994), *O Destino da Floresta: Reservas Extrativistas e Desenvolvimento Sustentável na Amazônia*, Relume Dumará, Rio de Janeiro.
Asselin, V. (1982), *Grilagem. Corrupção e Violência em Terras do Carajás*, Vozes/CPT, Petrópolis.
Ayres, D. L., E. F.Moura, M. A. Macedo and M. Souza (1995), A Reprodução Social de Grupos Domésticos em Comunidades de Mamirauá: uma análise preliminar, *mimeo.*
Ayres, J. M. (1993), *As Matas de Várzea do Mamirauá*, CNPq, Brasilia.
Bakx, K. (1990), The Shanty Town, Final Stage of Rural Development?, in Goodman and Hall, eds., 49–69.

Bamberger, M. (1988), *The Role of Community Participation in Development Planning and Project Management*, Economic Development Institute, World Bank, Washington DC.

Barbanti, O. (1994), Brazilian Approaches to Conservation Units, *mimeo*.

Barraclough, S. and K. Ghimire (1995), *Forests and Livelihoods: The Social Dynamics of Deforestation in Developing Countries*, UNRISD, Geneva.

Barrett, C. and P. Arcese (1995), Are Integrated Conservation-Development Projects (ICDPs) Sustainable? On the Conservation of Large Mammals in Sub-Saharan Africa, *World Development*, 23 (7), 1073–84.

Barrow, C. (1990), Environmentally Appropriate, Sustainable Small-farm Strategies for Amazonia, in Goodman and Hall, eds., 360–82.

Barthem, R. (1995), Development of Commercial Fisheries in the Amazon Basin and Consequences for Fish Stocks and Subsistence Farming, in Clüsener-Godt and Sachs, eds., 175–204.

Bates, R., ed. (1988), *Toward a Political Economy of Development: A Rational Choice Perspective*, University of California Press, Berkeley, Los Angeles and London.

Becker, B. (1982), *Geopolítica da Amazônia*, Zahar, Rio de Janeiro.

Becker, B. (1987), The Frontier at the End of the Twentieth Century – Eight Propositions for a Debate on Brazilian Amazonia, in Muegge and Stohr et al., eds., *International Economic Restructuring and the Regional Community*, Avebury, Aldershot.

Becker, B. (1992), Desafiando Mitos: Amazônia, Uma Selva Urbanizada, *Documentos Básicos*, Conference on Sustainable Development in the Humid Tropics, Manaus.

Becker, B. and P. Egler (1992), *Brazil: A New Regional Power in the World Economy*, Cambridge University Press, Cambridge.

Benedicto, N. (1995), Couro Vegetal: Um Novo e Refinado Ciclo da Borracha, in *Icaro-Revista de Bordo VARIG*, 132.

Berger, P. (1977), *Pyramids of Sacrifice*, Penguin, Harmondsworth.

Berkes, F., ed. (1989), *Common Property Resources: Ecology and Community-Based Sustainable Development*, Belhaven, London.

Berkes, F. (1995), Community-Based Management and Co-Management as Tools for Empowerment, in Singh and Titi, eds., 138–46.

Bhatnagar, B. and A. Williams (1992), *Participatory Development and the World Bank: Potential Directions for Change*, World Bank Discussion Paper 183, World Bank, Washington DC.

Binswanger, H. (1991), Brazilian Policies that Encourage Deforestation in the Amazon, *World Development*, 19 (7), July, 821–9.

Bonner, J. (1994), Battle for Brazilian Mahogany, *New Scientist*, 22 October.

Bourne, R. (1978), *Assault on the Amazon*, Gollancz, London.

Bradford, C., ed. (1994), *Redefining the State in Latin America*, OECD, Paris.

References

Branford, S. and O.Glock (1985), *The Last Frontier: Fighting Over Land in the Amazon*, Zed Press, London.

Brazil (1985), *Plano Nacional de Reforma Agrária-PNRA*, MIRAD/INCRA, Brasília.

Brazil (1988), *Constituição da República Federativa do Brasil 1988*, Editora Tecnoprint, Brasília.

Brazil (1994), *Projeto Unidades de Conservação de Uso Direto: Subprojeto Reservas Extrativistas*, Programa Piloto para Proteção das Florestas Tropicais do Brasil, Governo do Brasíl/ IBRD/ EEC, Brasília.

Brazil (1995a), *Política Nacional Integrada para a Amazônia Legal*, MMA/CONAMAZ, Brasília.

Brazil (1995b), *Protocolo Verde, 1995*, Brasília.

Brazil (1996), Proposta Conceitual e Metodológico para os Projetos de Assentamento Extrativistas, *mimeo.*, Ministério Extraordinário de Colonização e Reforma Agrária/INCRA, Brasília, June.

Brazil (n.d., a), *SIPAM – Sistema de Proteção da Amazônia*, SAE, Brasília.

Brazil (n.d., b), SIVAM – *Sistema de Vigilância da Amazônia*, Ministério da Aeronáutica/SAE, Brasília.

Bromley, D. and M. Cernea (1989), *The Management of Common Property Natural Resources: Some Conceptual and Operational Fallacies*, World Bank Discussion Paper 57, World Bank, Washington DC.

Broad, R. (1994), The Poor and the Environment: Friends or Foes? *World Development*, 22 (6), 811–22.

Browder, J. (1992), Extractive Reserves and the Future of the Amazon's Rainforest: Some Cautionary Observations, in FOE, 224–35.

Burkey, S. (1993), *People First: A Guide to Self-Reliant, Participatory Rural Development*, Zed Books, London.

CAEX/CNPT/IBAMA (1993), Projeto Implantação de Uma Usina de Beneficiamento de Borracha Natural, *mimeo.*, Brasília, November.

Capobianco, J. P. (1996), *Projeto de Lei sobre Conservação Avança Pouco, Parabólicas*, 18, May.

CAPOIB (1996), Documento do CAPOIB – Conselho de Articulação dos Povos e Organizações Indígenas do Brasil – Entregue aos Representantes do Banco Mundial, Brasília, 6 February.

Cardoso, F. H. and G. Muller (1977), *Amazônia: Expansão do Capitalismo*, Editora Brasilense, São Paulo.

Carrier, J. (1987), *Marine Tenure and Conservation in Papua New Guinea*, in McCay and Acheson, eds., 142–67.

Carroll, T. (1992), *Intermediary NGOs: The Supporting Link in Grassroots Development*, Kumarian Press, West Hartford.

Castañeda, J. (1994), *Utopia Unarmed*, Vintage Books, New York.

Castellanet, C. (n.d.), Observações Sobre o Programa LAET em Altamira, *mimeo.*, LAET, Altamira.

Castellanet, C., J. Alves and B. David (1994), A Participação das Organizações de Produtores na Pesquisa Agro-Ecológica, *mimeo.*, LAET, Altamira.

Castellanet, C., A. Simões and P. C. Filho (1995), Diagnóstico Preliminar da Agricultura Familiar na Transamazônica: Pistas para Pesquisa-Desenvolvimento, *mimeo.*, LAET, Altamira.

Cernea, M. (1988), *Nongovernmental Organizations and Local Development*, World Bank Discussion Paper 40, World Bank, Washington DC.

Cernea, M. (1991a) Knowledge from Social Science for Development Policies and Projects, in Cernea, ed., 1–41.

Cernea, M., ed. (1991b), *Putting People First: Sociological Variables in Rural Development*, World Bank/Oxford University Press, Oxford.

Cernea, M. (1996), Social Organization and Development Anthropology: The 1995 Malinowski Award Lecture, *Environmentally Sustainable Development Studies and Monographs Series No.6*, World Bank, Washington DC.

Cernea, M. and S. Guggenheim, eds., *Anthropological Approaches to Resettlement*, Westview, Boulder, Co.

Chambers, R. (1983), *Rural Development: Putting the Last First*, Longman, London.

Chambers, R. (1992), Rural Appraisal: Rapid, Relaxed and Participatory, Institute of Development Studies, University of Sussex, Discussion Paper 311, October.

Chambers, R. (1993), *Challenging the Professions: Frontiers for Rural Development*, Intermediate Technology Publications, London.

Chambers, R. (1995), The Primacy of the Personal, in Edwards and Hulme, eds., 207–17.

Chambers, R., A. Pacey, and L. Thrupp, eds. (1990), *Farmer First: Farmer Innovation and Agricultural Research*, Intermediate Technology Publications, London.

Clark, J. (1991), *Democratizing Development: The Role of Voluntary Organizations*, Earthscan, London.

Cleary, D. (1991), *The Brazilian Rainforest: Politics, Finance, Mining and the Environment*, Economist Special Report No. 2100, Economist Intelligence Unit, London.

Cleary, D. (1993a), Environmental Issues in Brazil. Domestic Policies and International Ramifications, in *Brazil: The Struggle for Modernisation*, Institute of Latin American Studies, University of London, 56–9.

Cleary, D. (1993b), After the Frontier: Problems with Political Economy in the Modern Brazilian Amazon, *Journal of Latin American Studies*, 25, 331–49.

Clüsener-Godt, M. and I. Sachs, eds. (1994), *Extractivism in the Brazilian Amazon: Perspectives on Regional Development*, MAB Digest 18, UNESCO, Paris.

References

Clüsener-Godt, M. and I. Sachs, eds. (1995), *Brazilian Perspectives on Sustainable Development of the Amazon Region*, UNESCO, Paris.

CNS (1992), *III Encontro Nacional dos Seringueiros*, Conselho Nacional dos Seringueiros.

CNS (n.d.), *Diretrizes para um Programa de Reservas Extrativistas na Amazônia*, Conselho Nacional dos Seringueiros, Rio Branco.

CNS/FUNTAC/CIDA (1992), *Relatório do Levantamento Sócio Econômico da Reserva Chico Mendes e Projetos de Assentamentos Extrativistas da Região do Acre Purus*, Rio Branco.

Cohen, J. (1985), Strategy or Identity: New Theoretical Paradigms and Contemporary Social Movements, *Social Research*, 52 (4), Winter, 663–716.

Colby, M. (1990), *Environmental Management and Development: The Evolution of Paradigms*, World Bank Discussion Paper 80, World Bank, Washington DC.

Colchester, M. (1992), *Sustaining the Forests: The Community-Based Approach in South and South-East Asia*, Discussion Paper No. 35, UNRISD, Geneva.

Colchester, M. (1994), *Salvaging Nature: Indigenous Peoples, Protected Areas and Biodiversity Conservation*, UNRISD/World Rainforest Movement/WWF, UNRISD, Geneva.

Collins, J. (1986), Smallholder Settlement of Tropical South America: The Social Causes of Ecological Destruction, *Human Organization*, 45 (1), 1–10.

Collinson, H., ed. (1996), *Green Guerrillas: Environmental Conflicts and Initiatives in Latin America and the Caribbean*, Latin America Bureau, London.

Conroy, C. and M. Litvinoff, eds. (1988), *The Greening of Aid: Sustainable Livelihoods in Practice*, Earthscan, London.

Coomes, O. (1995), A Century of Rain Forest Use in Western Amazonia: Lessons for Extraction-Based Conservation of Tropical Forest Resources, *Forest and Conservation History*, 39, July, 108–20.

Cornell, B. (1996), Residents Conserve Brazil's Largest National Park, *mimeo.*, WWF.

Davis, S. (1977), *Victims of the Miracle*, Cambridge University Press, Cambridge.

Dawes, R. (1973), The Commons Dilemma Game: An N-Person Mixed-Motive Game With a Dominating Strategy for Defection, *ORI Research Bulletin*, 13, 1–12.

Dean, W. (1987), *Brazil and the Struggle for Rubber: A Study in Environmental History*, Cambridge University Press, Cambridge.

Derickx, J. and J. Trasferetti (1993), *Juruá. O Rio Que Chora*, Vozes, Petrópolis.

Diegues, A. C., ed. (1994), *Deforestation and Livelihoods in the Brazilian*

Amazon, UNRISD/NAPAUB, São Paulo.
Dória, P., S. Buarque, V. Carelli and J. Sautchuk (1978), *A Guerrilha do Araguaia*, Alfa-Omega, São Paulo.
Drabek, A., ed. (1987), Development Alternatives: The Challenge for NGOs, Special Issue of *World Development*, Autumn.
Dubois, J., M. Vianna and A. Anderson (1996), *Manual Agroflorestal para a Amazônia*, REBRAF/Ford Foundation, Rio de Janeiro.
The Ecologist (1992), Whose Common Future? 22 (4), July/August.
The Ecologist (1995), Overfishing. Causes and Consequences, 25 (2/3), March–April, May–June.
The Economist (1991), In the Forest, 7 December.
The Economist (1994), Foreign Aid: The Kindness of Strangers, 7 May, 21–6.
Eden, M. (1990), *Ecology and Land Management in Amazonia*, Belhaven, London.
Eden, M., D. McGregor and N. Vieira (1990), Pasture Development on Cleared Forest Land in Northern Amazonia, *The Geographical Journal*, 156 (3), November, 283–96.
Edwards, M. and D. Hulme, eds. (1992), *Making a Difference: NGOS and Development in a Changing World*, Earthscan, London.
Edwards, M. and D. Hulme, eds. (1995), *Non-Governmental Organisations – Performance and Accountability: Beyond the Magic Bullet*, Earthscan, London.
Entine, J. (1995), When Rainforest Ice Cream Melts: The Messy Reality of 'Socially Responsible Business', *mimeo*.
Escobar, A. and S. Alvarez, eds. (1992), *The Making of Social Movements in Latin America: Identity, Strategy and Democracy*, Westview, Boulder, Co.
Etzioni, A. (1993), *The Spirit of Community: The Reinvention of American Society*, Simon and Schuster, New York.
Fairlie, S., M. Hagler and B. O'Riordan (1995), The Politics of Overfishing, *The Ecologist*, 25 (2/3), March/April, May/June, 46–73.
Fajardo, E. (1988), *Em Julgamento: A Violência do Campo*, Vozes/FASE, Rio de Janeiro.
FAO/PNUD (1992), *Principais Indicadores Sócio-Econômicos dos Assentamentos de Reforma Agrária*, FAO/Ministry of Agriculture, Brasília.
Farrington, J. and A. Bebbington (1993), *Reluctant Partners? Non-Governmental Organizations, the State and Sustainable Agricultural Development*, Routledge, London.
Faulhaber, P. (1987), *O Navio Encantado. Etnia e Alianças em Tefé*, Museu Paraense Emílio Goeldi, Belém.
Fearnside, P. (1990), Environmental Destruction in the Brazilian Amazon, in Goodman and Hall, eds., 179–225.
Fearnside, P. (1993), Deforestation in Brazilian Amazonia: The Effect of

Population and Land Tenure, *Ambio*, 22 (8), December, 537–45.
Fernandes, R. (1994), *Private but Public: The Third Sector in Latin America*, Civicus and Network Cultures, Washington DC.
FOE (1992), *The Rainforest Harvest*, Friends of the Earth, London.
Foresta, R. (1991), *Amazon Conservation in the Age of Development: The Limits of Providence*, University of Florida Press, Gainseville.
Foweraker, J. (1981), *The Struggle for Land*, Cambridge University Press, Cambridge.
Foweraker, J. (1995), *Theorizing Social Movements*, Pluto Press, London.
Fox, J. and D. Brown, eds. (1997), *The Stuggle for Accountability: The World Bank, NGOs and Grassroots Movements*, MIT Press, Cambridge, Mass.
Franco, M. P. (1996), O Couro que Dá em Árvore, *Parabólicas*, 18, May.
Freire, P. (1975), *Pedagogia do Oprimido*, Paz e Terra, Rio de Janeiro.
Friedmann, J. (1992), *Empowerment: The Politics of Alternative Development*, Blackwell, Cambridge.
Friedmann, J. and H. Rangan, eds. (1993), *In Defense of Livelihood: Comparative Studies on Environmental Action*, Kumarian/UNRISD, West Hartford, Connecticut.
Gabeira, F. (1996), Draft bill presented to the Brazilian Congress for Projeto de Lei 2829/92 instituting the National System of Conservation Units (SNUC), *mimeo.*, Brasília.
Gama Torres, H. (1991), Migração e o Migrante de Origem Urbana na Amazônia, in Léna and Engrácia de Oliveira, eds., 291–303.
Gasques, J. and C. Yokomizo (1986), Resultados de 20 Anos de Incentivos Fiscais na Agropecuária na Amazônia, *XIV Encontro Nacional de Economia*, ANPEC 2, 47–84.
Ghai, D. and J. Vivian, eds. (1992), *Grassroots Environmental Action: People's Participation in Sustainable Development*, Routledge, London.
Glance, M. and B. Huberman (1994), The Dynamics of Social Dilemmas, *Scientific American*, 270 (3), March, 58–63.
Gomes, M. and L. Felippe (1994), Tutela Jurídica sobre as Reservas Extrativistas, in Arnt, ed., 73–89.
Goodman, D. (1986), Agricultural Modernisation, Market Segmentation and Rural Social Structures in Brazil, *mimeo.*, Department of Economics, University College London.
Goodman, D. and A. Hall, eds. (1990), *The Future of Amazonia: Destruction or Sustainable Development?* Macmillan, London.
Goulding, M. (1981), *Man and Fisheries on an Amazon River*, W. Junk, The Hague.
Goulding, M. (1983), Amazonian Fisheries, in Moran, ed., 189–210.
Goulding, M. (1990), *Amazon: The Flooded Forest*, Sterling, New York.
Goulding, M., N. Smith and D. Mahar (1996), *Floods of Fortune: Ecology*

and Economy Along the Amazon, Columbia University Press, New York.

Gradwohl, J. and R. Greenberg, eds. (1988), *Saving the Tropical Forests*, Earthscan, London.

Gran, G. (1983), *Development By People: Citizen Construction of a Just World*, Praeger, New York.

Gross, A. (1989), *Fight for the Forest: Chico Mendes in His Own Words*, Latin America Bureau, London.

Gross, A. (1990), Amazonia in the Nineties: Sustainable Development or Another Decade of Destruction?, *Third World Quarterly*, 12 (3–4), 1–24.

Gross, D. (1975), Protein Capture and Cultural Development in the Amazon Basin, *American Anthropologist*, 77, 526–549.

Guerra, G. A. D. (1991), *A Identidade do Posseiro: Elementos de Caracterização Social Trabalhados pelo Movimento Sindical do Sudeste do Pará*, MSc dissertation, NAEA/PLADES, Federal University of Pará, Belém.

Guimarães, R. (1991), *The Ecopolitics of Development in the Third World: Politics and the Environment in Brazil*, Lynne Rienner Publishers, Boulder and London.

Hall, A. (1978), *Drought and Irrigation in North-East Brazil*, Cambridge University Press, Cambridge.

Hall, A. (1986), Community Participation and Rural Development, in Midgley, *et al.*, 87–104.

Hall, A. (1990), Land Tenure and Land Reform in Brazil, in Prosterman, *et al.*, eds., 205–32.

Hall, A. (1991), *Developing Amazonia: Deforestation and Social Conflict in Brazil's Carajás Programme*, Manchester University Press, Manchester. (Original edition 1989)

Hall, A. (1992), From Victims to Victors: NGOs and the Politics of Empowerment at Itaparica, in Edwards and Hulme, eds., 148–58.

Hall, A. (1993a), Non-Governmental Organizations and Development in Brazil Under Dictatorship and Democracy, in Abel and Lewis, eds., 421–37.

Hall, A. (1993b), Making People Matter: Development and the Environment in Brazilian Amazonia, *International Journal of Contemporary Sociology*, 30 (1), 63–80. Also published as *Occasional Paper* No.4, Institute of Latin Americam Studies, University of London.

Hall, A. (1994), Grassroots Action for Resettlement Planning: Brazil and Beyond, *World Development*, 22 (12), December, 1793–1809.

Hall, A. (1995), Towards New Actions in Social Policies for Sustainable Development, *mimeo*.. Paper presented at the UNDP meeting on 'Sustainable Human Development: Actions for New Generation Policies', Buenos Aires, December.

Hall, A. (1996), Did Chico Mendes Die in Vain? Brazilian Rubber Tappers in the 1990s, in Collinson, ed., 93–102.

Hall, A. and J. Midgley, eds. (1988), *Development Policies: Sociological Perspectives*, Manchester University Press, Manchester.

Hamelin, P. (1991), O Fracasso Anunciado, in Léna and Engrácia de Oliveira, eds., 161–76.

Hancock, G. (1991), *Lords of Poverty*, Mandarin, London.

Hardin, G. (1968), The Tragedy of the Commons, *Science*, 162 (13), December, 1243–8.

Hartshorn, G. (1990), Natural Forest Management by the Yanesha Forestry Cooperative in Peruvian Amazonia, in Anderson, ed., 128–38.

Heady, C., J. McGregor and A. Winnett (1994), *Poverty and Sustainability in the Management of Inland Capture Fisheries in South and Southeast Asia*, End of Project Report for the ODA, Centre of Development Studies, University of Bath.

Hébette, J. (1988), A luta sindical em resposta às agressões dos grandes projetos na Amazônia, *mimeo.*, Núcleo de Altos Estudios Amazônicos, Universidade Federal do Pará, Belém, Pará. Paper presented to the 46th International Congress of Americanists, Amsterdam.

Hébette, J. ed. (1991), *O Cerco Está Se Fechando*, Vozes, Petrópolis.

Hébette, J. (1994), O Movimento pela Sobrevivência na Transamazônica. Passado e Futuro, Glórias e Desafios, *mimeo.*, Altamira.

Hébette, J. (1995), Relações Pesquisadores-Agricultores. Diálogo? Parceria? Aliança? Uma Análise Estrutural, *mimeo.*, Belém.

Hébette, J. (1996), Relações Pesquisadores-Agricultores. Diálogo? Parceria? Aliança? Uma Análise Estrutural, *Agricultura Familiar: Pesquisa, Formação e Desenvolvimento*, Núcleo de Estudos Integrados Sobre Agricultura Familiar, Universidade Federal do Pará.

Hébette, J. and J. A. Colares (1990), Small-farmer Protest in the Greater Carajás Programme, in Goodman and Hall, eds., 288–305.

Hecht, S. (1985), Environment, Development and Politics: Capital Accumulation in the Livestock Sector in Eastern Amazonia, *World Development*, 13 (6), June, 663–84.

Hecht, S. (1989), The Sacred Cow in the Green Hell, *The Ecologist*, 19 (6), November/December, 229–34.

Hecht, S. (1994), Decentralization, Women's Labor and Development in Extractive Reserves, *mimeo*.

Hemming, J., ed. (1985), *Change in the Amazon Basin, Vol.I: Man's Impact on Forests and Rivers*, Manchester University Press, Manchester.

Heneberg, H. ed. (1995), *Investigaciones Alemanas de Geografía en América Latina*, Regional Conference of Latin America and Caribbean Countries, International Geographical Union, Tübingen.

Hildeyard, N. (1989), Adios Amazonia? A Report from the Altamira Gathering, *The Ecologist*, 19 (2), March–April, 53–62.

Hiraoka, M. (1995), Aquatic and Land Fauna Management Among the

Floodplain Ribereños of the Peruvian Amazon, in Nishizawa and Uitto, eds., 201–25.

Homma, A. (1993), *Extrativismo Vegetal na Amazônia: limites e oportunidades*, EMBRAPA-SPI, Brasília.

Homma, A. (1994), Plant Extractivism in the Amazon: Limitations and Possibilities, in Clüsener-Godt and Sachs, eds., 34–57.

Human Rights Watch (1991), *Rural Violence in Brazil*, Americas Watch, New York

IEA (1991), *Seminário Alternativas Econômicas para as Reservas Extrativistas*, Rio Branco, Acre.

IEA (1993a), *Manual de Plantas Amazônicas*, Curitiba.

IEA (1993b), *Laboratório Ambiental. Comunicação e meio ambiente: desafios para o desenvolvimento*, Macapá.

IIED (1994), *Whose Eden? An Overview of Community Approaches to Wildlife Management*, International Institute for the Environment and Development, London.

INCRA (1986), *Estatísticas Cadastrais Rurais (Dados Preliminares)*, MIRAD/INCRA, Brasília.

Informativo IEA (various issues).

Isto É (various issues)

IUCN (1995), *Indigenous Conservation in the Modern World*, IUCN/ Earthscan, London,

Keck, M. (1994), Sustainable Development and Environmental Politics in Latin America, in Bradford, ed., 91–105.

Keck, M. (1995a), Parks, People and Power: The Shifting Terrain of Environmentalism, *NACLA Report on the Americas*, 28 (5), March/April, 36–41.

Keck, M. (1995b), Social Equity and Environmental Politics in Brazil: Lessons from the Rubber Tappers of Acre, *Comparative Politics*, July, 409–24.

Keck, M. (1997), Planafloro in Rondonia: The Limits of Leverage, in Fox and Brown, eds.

Kemf, E., ed. (1993), *Indigenous Peoples and Protected Areas: The Law of Mother Earth*, Earthscan, London.

Kimerling, J. (1996), Oil, Lawlessness and Indigenous Struggles in Ecuador's Oriente, in Collinson, ed., 61–73.

Kohlhepp, G. (1995), El Programa Piloto Internacional Para La Amazonia: Un Modelo de Desarrollo Regional Sostenible, in Heineberg, ed., 9–30.

Kohlhepp, G. and A. Schrader, eds. (1987), *Homem e Natureza na Amazônia*, ADLAF/Forschungsschwerpunkt Lateinamerika, Geographisches Institut, Universität Tübingen.

Korten, D. (1987), Third Generation NGO Strategies: A Key to People-Centered Development, in Drabek, ed., 145–59.

Kottak, P. (1991), When People Don't Come First: Some Sociological Lessons from Completed Projects, in Cernea, ed., 431–64.
Kurien, J. (1992), Ruining the Commons and Responses of the Commoners: Coastal Overfishing and Fishworkers' Actions in Kerala State, India, in Ghai and Vivian, eds., 221–58.
Kurien, J. (1993), Ruining the Commons: Overfishing and Fishworkers' Actions in South India, *The Ecologist*, 23 (1), January–February, 5–11.
Kurien, J. (1995), Joint Action Against Joint Ventures: Resistance to Multinationals in Indian Waters, *The Ecologist*, 25 (2/3), March–April, May–June, 115–19.
LAET (1993), Programa Agro-Ecológico da Transamazônica, *mimeo.*, Altamira, September.
LAET/MPST (1993), Relatório do Seminário 'Pesquisa Agro-Ambiental na Região da Transamazônica', *mimeo.*, Altamira, August.
LAB (1982), *Brazil: State and Struggle*, Latin American Bureau, London.
LASAT (1992), Elementos de análise do funcionamento dos estabelecimentos familiares da região de Marabá & Pesquisa-Formação-Desenvolvimento no programa CAT, *mimeo.*, CAT, Marabá.
LASAT (1994), *Programa Trienal de Pesquisa 1994–96*, CAT, Marabá.
Lélé, S. (1991), Sustainable Development: A Critical Review, *World Development*, 19 (6), June, 607–21.
Léna, P. (1991), Estratégias Camponesas de Capitalização no PIC Ouro Preto, in Hébette, ed., 288–318.
Léna, P. and A. Engrácia de Oliveira, eds. (1991), *Amazônia: A Fronteira Agrícola 20 Anos Depois*, SCT/CNPq, Belém.
Lescure, J. P., L. Emperaire, F. Pinton and O. Renault-Lescure (1992), Non-Timber Forest Products and Extractive Activities in the Middle Rio Negro Region, Brazil, in Plotkin and Farmolare, eds., 151–7.
Lescure, J. P., F. Pinton and L. Emperaire (1994), People and Forest Products in Central Amazonia: The Multidisciplinary Approach of Extractivism, in Clüsener-Godt and Sachs, eds., 58–88.
Lisansky, J. (1990), *Migrants to Amazonia: Spontaneous Colonization in the Brazilian Frontier*, Westview, Boulder, Co.
Long, N. (1988), Sociological perspectives on agrarian development and State intervention, in Hall and Midgley, eds., 108–33.
Long, N. and A. Long, eds. (1992), *Battlefields of Knowledge*, Routledge, London.
Lopes, S. (1993), Associação dos Agrosilvicultores do Projeto Reflorestamento Econômico Consorciado e Adensado (Reca), in IEA, 1993b, 34–5.
Lyra, P. (1993), Projeto Piloto de Manejo Sustentado de Madeira e Projeto Agroflorestal Comunitário, em Paragominas, do WWF, in IEA, 1993b, 37–8.
Mahar, D. (1989), *Government Policies and Deforestation in Brazil's*

Amazon Region, World Bank, Washington DC.

Mamirauá (1996), *Estação Ecológica Mamirauá: Plano de Manejo (versão resumida)*, Sociedade Civil Mamirauá, Tefé.

Margulis, S., ed. (1990), *Meio Ambiente: Aspectos Técnicos e Econômicos*, IPEA/PNUD, Rio de Janeiro.

Marsden, D. and P. Oakley, eds. (1990), *Evaluating Social Development Projects*, Oxfam, Oxford.

Martine, G. (1990), Rondônia and the Fate of Small Farmers, in Goodman and Hall, eds., 23–48.

Matheson, C. (1996), Fruit Farming in the Brazilian Amazon: A Sustainable Alternative, in Collinson, ed., 103–7.

May, P. (1992), Babassu Palm Product Markets, in Plotkin and Farmolare, eds., 143–50.

May, P. (1993), Ecological Economics for Equitable Development: A Strategy for Brazil, *mimeo.*, Rio de Janeiro.

May, P. and E. Reis (1993), The User Stucture in Brazil's Tropical Rain Forest, *mimeo.*, Kiel Working Paper 565, Kiel Institute of World Economics.

McCay, B. and J. Acheson, eds. (1987), *The Question of the Commons: The Culture and Ecology of Communal Resources*, University of Arizona Press, Tucson.

McDonald, N. (1991), *Brazil: A Mask Called Progress*, Oxfam, Oxford.

McGoodwin, J. (1990), *Crisis in the World's Fisheries*, Stanford University Press, California.

McGrath, D. (1993), Varzeiros, Geleiros e o Manejo dos Recursos Naturais na Várzea do Baixo Amazonas, *Cadernos do NAEA*, 11, November, 91–125.

McGrath, D., F. de Castro, C. Futemma, B. de Amaral and J. de Calabria (1993), Fisheries and the Evolution of Resource Management on the Lower Amazon Floodplain, *Human Ecology*, 21 (2), 167–95.

McLaren, P. and C. Lankshear, eds. (1994), *Politics of Liberation: Paths from Freire*, Routledge, London and New York.

Mearns, R. (1995), Environmental Entitlements: An Outline Framework for Analysis, and a Mongolian Case Study, Working Papers, 15, February, Institute of Development Studies, University of Sussex.

Meggers, B. (1954), Environmental Limitation on the Development of Culture, *American Anthropologist*, 56, 801–24.

Melby, J. (1942), Rubber River: An Account of the Rise and Collapse of the Amazon Boom, *Hispanic American Historical Review*, 23, 452–69.

Melucci, A. (1989), *Nomads of the Present: Social Movements and Individual Needs in Contemporary Society*, Temple University Press, Philadelphia.

Menezes, M. A. (1994), As Reservas Extrativistas como Alternativas ao

Desmatamento na Amazônia, in Arnt, ed., 49–72.
Midgley, J. (1986), Community Participation: History, Concepts and Controversies, in Midgley *et al.*, 13–44.
Midgley, J. (1995), *Social Development: The Developmental Perspective in Social Welfare*, Sage, London.
Midgley, J., A. Hall, M. Hardiman, and D. Narine (1986), *Community Participation, Social Development and the State*, Methuen, London.
Millikan, B. (1994), The Agricultural Frontier and Deforestation in Rondônia, in Diegues, ed., 70–107.
Monbiot, G. (1992), *Mahogany Extraction from Indian Reserves in Brazil*, Friends of the Earth, London.
Moore, M. (1990), The Rational Choice Paradigm and the Allocation of Agricultural Development Resources, *Development and Change*, 21, 225–46.
Moran, E. ed. (1983), *The Dilemma of Amazonian Development*, Westview, Boulder, Colorado.
Moran, E. (1993), *Through Amazonian Eyes: The Ecology of Amazonian Populations*, University of Iowa Press, Iowa City.
Moser, C. (1993), *Gender Planning and Development: Theory, Practice and Training*, Routledge, London.
Mougeot, L. (1987), O Reservatório da usina hidrelétrica de Tucuruí, Pará, Brasil: uma avaliação do programa de reassentamento populacional (1976–85), in Kohlhepp and Schrader, eds., 387–404.
Mougeot, L. (1990), Future Hydroelectric Developments in Brazilian Amazonia: Towards Comprehensive Population Resettlement, in Goodman and Hall, eds., 90–129.
Mouzelis, N. (1990), *Post Marxist Alternatives: The Construction of Social Orders*, Macmillan, London.
MPST (1990), Carta da Transamazônica, *mimeo.*, 1990.
MPST (1995a), Historico, *mimeo.*, Altamira.
MPST (1995b), Relatório. IV Assembléia Geral do MPST, *mimeo.*, Altamira, January.
MPST/LAET (1993), Convénio Entre o Movimento pela Sobrevivência na Transamazônica (MPST) e o Laboratório Agro-Ecológico da Transamazônica (LAET), *mimeo.*, 31 August.
MPST/LAET (1995a), Proposta Para Uma Política de Desenvolvimento Sustentável na Região da Transamazônica: A Contribuição do Programa Agro-Ecológico da Transamazônica – PAET, *mimeo.*, Altamira, March.
MPST/LAET (1995b), Casa Familiar Rural – C.F.R., *mimeo.*, Altamira.
Murrieta, J. and R. Rueda, eds. (1995), *Reservas Extrativistas*, CNPT/IUCN, UK and Switzerland.
Myers, N. (1984), *The Primary Source: Tropical Forests and Our Future*, W. Norton, New York and London.

Nishizawa, T. and J. Uitto, eds. (1995), *The Fragile Tropics of Latin America: Sustainable Management of Changing Environments*, United Nations University Press, Tokyo.

Nitsch, M. (1994), 'Zoneamento' in Brazil: Problem or Solution for Man and Nature in the Amazon?, *mimeo*. Paper presented at the 46th International Congress of Americanists, Stockholm, July.

Nogueira-Neto, P. (1992), *Ecological Stations: A Saga of Ecology and Environmental Policy*, Empresa das Artes, São Paulo.

Nugent, S. (1993a), From 'Green Hell' to 'Green' Hell: Amazonia and the Sustainability Thesis, Occasional Paper No.57, Amazonian Paper No.3, Institute of Latin American Studies, University of Glasgow.

Nugent, S. (1993b), *Amazonian Caboclo Society: An Essay on Invisibility and Peasant Economy*, Berg, Providence, R.I.

Nugent, S. (1996), Amazonian Indians and Peasants: Coping in the Age of Development, in Collinson, ed., 84–92.

Oakley, P. and D. Marsden (1984), *Approaches to Participation in Rural Development*, International Labour Office, Geneva.

ODA (1995), *A Guide to Social Analysis for Projects in Developing Countries*, HMSO, London.

OECD (1995), *Development Cooperation: Development Assistance Committee 1994 Report*, Organisation for Economic Cooperation and Development, Geneva.

Okali, C., J. Sumberg and J. Farrington (1994), *Farmer Participatory Research: Rhetoric and Reality*, Intermediate Technology Publications, London.

Oliveira, L. and B. Millikan (1994), Open letter to the World Bank, 14 June.

Oliveira Filho, J. P. de (1990), Frontier Security and the New Indigenism: Nature and Origins of the Calha Norte Project, in Goodman and Hall, eds., 155–76.

Olson, M. (1965), *The Logic of Collective Action. Public Goods and the Theory of Groups*, Harvard University Press, Cambridge, Mass.

Osório de Almeida, A. L. and J. Campari (1995), *Sustainable Settlement in the Brazilian Amazon*, Oxford University Press, New York.

Ostrom, E. (1990), *Governing the Commons: The Evolution of Institutions for Collective Action*, Cambridge Unversity Press, Cambridge.

Ostrom, E., L. Schroeder and S. Wynne (1993), *Institutional Incentives and Sustainable Development*, Westview, Boulder, Co.

Park, C. (1992), *Tropical Rainforests*, Routledge, London and New York.

Parrotta, J. and M. Kanashiro, eds. (1995), *Management and Rehabilitation of Degraded Lands and Secondary Forests in Amazonia*, International Institute of Tropical Forestry, United States Department of Agriculture Forest Service, Rio Piedras, Puerto Rico.

Paul, S. (1987), *Community Participation in Development Projects: The World Bank Experience*, World Bank, Washington DC.

Pearse, A. and M. Stiefel (1979), Inquiry Into Participation: A Research Proposal, *mimeo.*, UNRISD, Geneva.

Peixoto, R. (1991), Ação Cultural e Concepção Política Entre a Igreja Católica e os Camponeses (Um Estudo da Região de Marabá), in Léna and Engrácia de Oliveira, eds., 145–60.

Perkin, S. and M. Stocking (1994), The Ngorongo Conservation Area, Tanzania: A Model of Multiple Land-Use? *mimeo*. Paper presented at the Second MAA Conference on Culture and Development, 30 May–3 June, Arusha, Tanzania.

Peters, C., A. Gentry and R. Mendelsohn (1985), Valuation of an Amazonian rainforest, *Nature*, 329, 29 June, 655–56.

Pezzoli, K. (1993), The Struggle of Seringueiros: Environmental Action in the Amazon, in Friedmann and Rangan, eds., 106–26.

Pimbert, M. and J. Pretty (1996), *Parks, People and Professionals: Putting 'Participation' Into Protected Area Management*, Discussion Paper No. 57, UNRISD, Geneva.

Place, S., ed. (1993), *Tropical Rainforests: Latin American Nature and Society in Transition*, Scholarly Resources, Inc., Wilmington, DE.

Plotkin, M. and L. Farmolare (1992), *Sustainable Harvest and Marketing of Rain Forest Products*, Island Press, Washington DC.

Popkin, S. (1979), *The Rational Peasant*, University of California Press, Berkeley.

Portela, F. (1979), *Guerra de Guerrilhas no Brasil*, Global, Rio de Janeiro.

Posey, D. (1985), Native and Indigenous Guidelines for New Amazonian Development Strategies: Understanding Biological Diversity through Ethnoecology, in Hemming, ed., 156–81.

Posey, D. (1989a), Alternatives to Forest Destruction: Lessons from the Mêbêngôkre Indians, *The Ecologist*, 19 (6), November–December, 241–4.

Posey, D. (1989b), From Warclubs to Words, *NACLA Report on the Americas*, 22 (1), May, 13–18.

Polshek, P. (1993), Projeto Mamirauá: an Integrated Conservation Initiative, *TCD Newsletter*, Tropical Conservation and Development Program, Centre for Latin American Studies, University of Florida, Gainesville.

Pompermayer, M. (1984), Strategies of Private Capital in the Brazilian Amazon, in Schmink and Wood, eds., 419–38.

Pratt. B. and J. Boyden (1985), *The Field Directors' Handbook: An Oxfam Manual for Development Workers*, Oxford University Press, Oxford.

Prosterman, R., M. Temple and T. Hanstad, eds. (1990), *Agrarian Reform and Grassroots Development: Ten Case Studies*, Lynne Rienner, Boulder and London.

RAFI (1994), *Conserving Indigenous Knowledge: Integrating Two Systems of Innovation*, Rural Advancement Foundation International and UNDP, New York.

Rahman, M. (1993), *People's Self-Development: Perspectives on Participatory Action Research*, Zed Books, London.

Ramos, A. (1996), Governo Reinveste no Calha Norte 'Social', *Parabólicas*, 3 (16), March.

Redclift, M. (1987), *Sustainable Development: Exploring the Contradictions*, Methuen, London.

Redwood, J. (1993), *World Bank Approaches to the Environment in Brazil: A Review of Selected Projects*, Operations Evaluation Department, World Bank, Washington DC.

Reis, A. C. F. (1982), *A Amazônia e a Cobiça Internacional*, Civilização Brasileira, Rio de Janeiro.

Revkin, A. (1990), *The Burning Season: The Murder of Chico Mendes and the Fight for the Amazon Rain Forest*, Collins, London.

Rich, B. (1994), *Mortgaging the Earth: The World Bank, Environmental Impoverishment and the Crisis of Development*, Earthscan, London.

Richards, P. (1996), Stabilising the Amazon Frontier: Technology, Institutions and Policies, *Natural Resource Perspectives*, 10, July.

Rio Branco (n.d.), Polo Municipal de Produção Agroflorestal, *mimeo*. Secretaria de Agricultura e Abastecimento, Prefeitura de Rio Branco.

Rodrigues, E. (1991), *Mapeamento das Relações Sócio-Econômicas das Reservas Extrativistas do Cachoeira e São Luis do Remanso*, FUNTAC, Rio Branco.

Romeiro, A., C. Guanziroli, M. Palmeira and S. Leite, eds. (1994), *Reforma Agrária: Produção, Emprego e Renda*, Vozes, Rio de Janeiro.

Rondinelli, D. (1983), *Development Projects as Policy Experiments*, Methuen, London.

Ros Filho, L. C. (1994), *Políticas Públicas e Meio Ambiente*, Instituto de Estudos Amazônicos e Ambientais, Brasília.

Runge, C. (1986), Common Property and Collective Action in Economic Development, *World Development*, 14 (5), 623–35.

Sabatier, P. (1993), Introduction, in Ostrom, *et al.*, xix–xxi.

SAE/IBGE (1993), *Diagnóstico Ambiental da Amazônia Legal*, FIBGE, Rio de Janeiro.

Sawyer, D. (1989), Urbanisation on the Brazilian Frontier, *mimeo*.

Sawyer, D. (1992), Population Growth and Migration in the Amazon, in Schneider, Annex 1, 1–19.

Scharf, R. (1996), Madeireiras Asiáticas já Dominam um Sergipe, *Parabólicas*, 20, July.

Schmink. M. and C. Wood, eds. (1978), *Frontier Expansion in Amazonia*, University of Florida Press, Gainsevillle, Florida.

Schmink, M. and C. Wood (1992), *Contested Frontiers in Amazonia*, Columbia University Press, New York.

Schneider, B. (1988), *The Barefoot Revolution*, IT Publications, London.

Schneider, R. (1992), *Brazil: An Analysis of Environmental Problems in the Amazon*, Report No.9104-BR, World Bank, Washington DC.

Schwartzman, S. (1990), Marketing of Extractive Products in the Brazilian Amazon, *mimeo.*, Environmental Defence Fund, Washington, DC.

Schwartzman, S. (1994), Mercados para Produtos Extrativistas na Amazonia Brasileira, in Arnt, ed., 247–57.

Schwartzman, S., A. V. Araújo and P. Pankarurú (1996), The Legal Battle Over Indigenous Land Rights, *NACLA Report on the Americas*, 29 (5), March/April, 36–42.

Scoones, I. and J. Thompson (1994), *Beyond Farmer First: Rural People's Knowledge, Agricultural Research and Extension Practice*, Intermediate Technology Publications, London.

Scott, A. (1990), *Ideology and the New Social Movements*, Unwyn Hyman, London.

Scott, J. (1986), Everyday Forms of Peasant Resistance, *Journal of Peasant Studies*, 13 (2), January, 5–35.

Serra, M. T. (1993), Resettlement Planning in the Brazilian Power Sector: Recent Changes in Approach, in Cernea and Guggenheim, 63–85.

Shankland, A. (1993), Brazil's BR-364 Highway: A Road to Nowhere? *The Ecologist*, 23 (4), July–August, 141–7.

Silberling, L. and M. P. Franco (1995), Couro Vegetal da Amazônia, S.A.: Adaptando Un Produto Artesanal para o Mercado Internacional, *mimeo.*, Rio de Janeiro.

Silva, M. (1996), Linha de Crédito para o Extrativismo, *Discurso preferido no Plenário do Senado Federal, pela Senadora Marina Silva, em 18 de março de 1996*, Senado Federal, Brasília.

da Silva-Forsberg, M. and P. Fearnside (1995), Agricultural Management of Caboclos on the Xingu River: A Starting Point for Sustaining Populations in Degraded Areas in the Brazilian Amazon, in Parrotta and Kanashiro, eds., 90–5.

Simões, A. (1995), O Processo de Construção da Pesquisa-Desenvolvimento Participativa: A Experiência no Acompanhamento da Introdução da Mecanização na Transamazônica, *mimeo.*, LAET, Altamira.

Singh, N. and V. Titi (1995), Empowerment for Sustainable Development: An Overview, in Singh and Titi, eds., 6–28.

Singh, N. and V. Titi, eds. (1995), *Empowerment: Towards Sustainable Development*, Zed, London.

Smith, N. (1982), *Rainforest Corridors: The Transamazon Colonization Scheme*, University of California Press, Berkeley.

Smith, N., J. Dubois, D. Current and E. Lutz (1996), Agroforestry Experiences in the Brazilian Amazon: Lessons Learned and Implications for Agricultural Development and Biodiversity Conservation (preliminary version), *mimeo.*, G7 Pilot Programme To Conserve the Brazilian Rainforest, Brasília.

Souza Martins, J. (1975), *Capitalismo e Tradicionalismo: Estudos Sobre as Condições da Sociedade Agrária no Brasil*, São Paulo.

Sternberg, H. O'Reilly (1995), Waters and Wetlands of Brazilian Amazonia: An Uncertain Future, in Nishizawa and Uitto, eds., 113–79.

Stiefel, M. and M. Wolfe (1994), *A Voice for the Excluded: Popular Participation and Development*, Zed, London.

Stocks, A. (1987), Resource Management in an Amazon *Varzea* Lake Ecosystem: The Cocamilla Case, in McCay and Acheson, eds., 108–20.

Streeten, P., S. Burki, M. Ul Haq, N. Hicks and F. Stewart (1981), *First Things First: Meeting Basic Needs in Developing Countries*, Oxford University Press, Oxford.

Subler, S. and C. Uhl (1990), Japanese Agroforestry in Amazonia: A Case Study of Tomé-Açu, Brazil, in Anderson, ed., 152–66.

Sugden, R. (1984), Reciprocity: The Supply of Public Goods through Voluntary Contributions, *Economic Journal*, 94, 772–87.

Sutton, A. (1994), *Slavery in Brazil*, Anti-Slavery International, London.

Switkes, G. (1994), Ecuador: The People vs. Texaco, *NACLA Report on the Americas*, 28 (2), September/October, 6–10.

Tavares, R. (1995), Land and Democracy: Reconsidering the Agrarian Question, *NACLA Report on the Americas*, 28 (6), May/June, 23–9.

Thiele, G. (1990), Are Peasant Farming Systems in the Amazon Sustainable? Institute of Development Studies, Discussion Paper 282, December.

Thompson, J. (1996), Moving the Indigenous Knowledge Debate Forward, *Development Policy Review*, 14 (1), March, 105–12.

Toniolo, A. and C. Uhl (1995), Economic and Ecological Perspectives on Agriculture in the Eastern Amazon, *World Development*, 23 (6), 959–73.

Toniolo, A. and C. Uhl (1996), Perspectivas Econômicas e Ecológicas da Agricultura na Amazônia Oriental, in Almeida, ed., 67–96.

Touraine, A. (1988), *The Return of the Actor: Social Theory in Post-Industrial Society*, University of Minnesota Press, Minneapolis.

Trebat, T. (1983), *Brazil's State-Owned Enterprises: A Case-Study of the State as Entrepreneur*, Cambridge University Press, Cambridge.

Turner, J. (1967), Barriers and Channels for Housing Development in Modernizing Countries, *Journal of the American Institute of Planners*, 33, 167–81.

UNCED (1992), *Agenda 21: Programme of Action for Sustainable Development*, United Nations, New York.

UNDP (1993), *Human Development Report 1993*, Oxford University Press, Oxford.

Uruará (1994), Primeira Conferência Municipal Uruarense Sobre Projetos Econômicos Alternativos, *mimeo.*, Uruará, March.
Vasquez, M. P., C. Padoch and J. C. Inuma (1995), Identifying and Understanding Agricultural and Forest Management Systems and Techniques Practised in Mamirauá, *mimeo.*, Mamirauá, 1995.
da Veiga, J. B., J. F. Tourrand and D. Quanz (1995), *A Pecuária na Fronteira Agrícola da Amazônia: O Caso do Município de Uruará-PA na Transamazônica*, EMBRAPA-CPATU, Belém.
Veja (various issues)
Velho, O. (1972), *Frentes de Expansão e Estrutura Agrária*, Rio de Janeiro.
Velho, O. (1976), *Capitalismo Autoritário e Campesinato*, São Paulo.
Veríssimo, A., P. Barreto, R. Tarifa and C. Uhl (1995), Extraction of a High-Value Natural Resource in Amazonia: the Case of Mahogany, *Forest Ecology and Management*, 72, 39–60.
Viola, E. (1993), The Brazilian Environmental Movement Facing the Challenge of Institutionalisation and Sustainable Development, 1987–1992, *mimeo.*, CEDLA, Amsterdam.
von Behr, M. (1995), Reservas Extrativistas do Ciríaco, Mata Grande e Extremo Norte do Tocantins, in Murrieta and Rueda, eds., 105–15.
Wagner, A. (1990), The State and Land Conflicts in Amazonia, 1964–88, in Goodman and Hall, eds., 226–44.
Wagner, A. (1991), O Intransitivo da Transição: O Estado, os Conflitos Agrários e a Violência na Amazônia (1965–1989), in Léna and Engrácia de Oliveira, eds., 259–90.
Wagner, A. (1994), *Carajás: A Guerra dos Mapas*, Falangola, Belém.
Walker, R. and A. Homma. (1993), Sustainable Farm Management in the Amazon Piedmont, *mimeo.*, Congresso Brasileiro de Economia e Sociologia Rural, Ilhéus, Bahia.
Wappenhans, W. (1992), Effective Implementation: The Key to Development Impact, *mimeo.*, World Bank, Washington DC.
Wawzyniak, J. (1994), Rondônia – Reserva Extrativista do Rio Ouro Preto, in Arnt, ed., 151–63.
WCED (1987), *Our Common Future*, Oxford University Press, Oxford.
Whitsell, E. (1994), Future Grasroots Reserves in the Amazon Basin: Alternative Landscapes of Conservation, in Aragón, ed., 99–109.
Wilson, J. and A. Alicbusan-Schwab (1991), Development Policies and Health: Famers, Goldminers and Slums in the Brazilian Amazon, *mimeo.*, Policy and Research Division, Divisional Working Paper No. 1991-18, World Bank, Washington DC.
Wood, C. and M. Schmink (1978), Blaming the Victim: Small Farmer Production in an Amazon Colonisation Project, *Studies in Third World Societies*, 7, February, 77–93.

World Bank (1975), *Housing: Sector Policy Paper*, World Bank, Washington DC.

World Bank (1990), *World Development Report 1990*, World Bank, Washington DC.

World Bank (1992), *Cooperation Between The World Bank and NGOs: 1991 Progress Report*, International Economic Relations Division, External Affairs Dept., World Bank, Washington DC.

World Bank (1994), *Resettlement and Development: The Bankwide Review of Projects Involving Involuntary Resettlement 1986–93*, Environment Department, World Bank, Washington DC.

World Bank (1995), *Pilot Program to Protect the Brazilian Rain Forest: Report on the Second Meeting of the Participants*, Belém, July.

World Bank (1996a), *Rain Forest Pilot Program Update*, 4 (1), January.

World Bank (1996b), Report to the International Advisory Group on Progress of the Pilot Program to Conserve the Brazilian Rain Forest, *mimeo.*, Brasília, February.

World Bank (1996c), World Bank and NGOs Hopeful on Future of Amazonian Project, *Press Release*, Brasília.

Index

Note: 'n' after a page reference indicates the number of a note on that page.

Agroforestry
  concept 206n.11
  projects in Amazonia 175–6,
    185, 206n.12–19, 211n.51,
    212n.58, *Plates 10–13*
Allegretti, Mary 92, 98, 126n.13,
  129n.37
Amazonia
  deforestation, causes of 49–51
    cattle ranching 49–50, *Plate 1*
    commercial logging 50–1, 67,
      80n.13–16, 87n.56, *Plate 3*
    small scale farming 49, *Plate 2*
  deforestation, data on 45–6,
    79n.3
  environmental policy
    conservationism in 1980s
      53–5
    frontier economics
      perspective 52
    G7 Pilot Programme *see* Pilot
      Programme to Conserve the
      Brazilian Rainforest
    joint resource management
      68–78
    National Integrated Policy for
      66
    Nossa Natureza 55–6,
      79n.11, 81n.24
    Operation Amazonia 56,
      82n.27
    regulation and protection
      55–68
  land conflicts 172–4, 204n.3–7,
    205n.7
    in the 'Parrot's Beak' 77–8,
      173
  land distribution 51–2, 79n.6
  land values in 50, 80n.12
  'Legal' and 'Classic' 79n.1
  militarisation of 63–5, 85n.50,
    n.52
  modernisation and integration
    of 46
  tax incentives 50, 79n.11
  urbanisation 69–70, 87n.61
'Amazon package' 239, 242n.27
Ayres, Dr Márcio 146

Banco da Amazônia S.A. (BASA)
  49
Biosphere reserves 53, 81n.20
Brandão Cavalcanti, Henrique 61
Brundtland Commission 62

Calha Norte project 57, 82n.28–29
Carta da *Transamazônica* 209n.36
Centro Agrombiental do Tocantins
    (CAT) 176 *passim*
  economic projects 183–6
  support for 180, 208n.20
Chico Mendes 56, 98, 101–2,
    126n.12, Plate 4
church
  Liberation Theology 71
  role at Mamirauá 144–5
collective choice *see* social
    movements; productive
    conservation movements
Collor de Mello, Fernando 58
Comissão Executiva do Plano de
    Lavoura Cacaueira
    (CEPLAC) 192, 194
common pool resources *see*
    common property resources
  definition of 11–12
  and extractive reserves 105, 115
  and fishing 136–8
  and small farmers 202
community participation
  concepts and dimensions 24, 26
    (Table 1.1)
  on extractive reserves 108–15
  grassroots action 219
  at Mamirauá 154
  objectives of
    capacity-building 28
    cost sharing 26–7
    empowerment 28–30
    project effectiveness 27–8
    project efficiency 27
  obstacles to 39–41
  scope of
    coverage 30–2
    strategic alliances 32–6
    strength 36–7
    timing 37–8
  on the Transamazon highway
    196–204
  and United Nations 21–2
Conselho Nacional da Amazônia
    Legal (CONAMAZ) 61
Conselho Nacional do Meio
    Ambiente (CONAMA) 54,
    59, 63
Conselho de Segurança Nacional
    (CSN) 63
conservation units 83n.33,
    84n.39
Cooperativa Agroextrativista de
    Xapurí (CAEX) 116–18,
    124, 132n.47
Coutinho Jorge, Fernando 61

development pole theory 48

empate see rubber tappers, stand-
    offs
Empresa Brasileira de Pesquisa
    Agropecuária (EMBRAPA)
    179, 192
Escola Superior de Guerra (ESG)
    48, 214
extractive reserves
  concept 98–100, 128n.23
  details of 101 (Table 3.1), 104
    (Table 3.2)
  distribution of 103 (Fig. 3.1)
  legislation 102
  management of 107
  procedures for setting up 105–6
  sustainability 115
extractivism
  practice 125n.4, 130n.38, 39
  theories 91–2

farming cycle 181–3
fishing
  conflicts 138–9, 167n.9
  crisis in Amazonia 134–6
  as a source of livelihood 135

Index

forestry code 53
Fundação Agrária do Tocantins-Araguaia (FATA) 178–9, 188
Fundação Nacional do Indio (FUNAI) 75–6
Fundo Constitucional de Financiamento do Norte (FNO) 192, 194–5, 209n.37, 210n.39, 235

G7 Pilot Programme *see* Pilot Programme to Conserve the Brazilian Rainforest
Goldemberg, José 61
Group de Recherche et d'Echanges Technologiques (GRET) 180
grassroots action *see* community participation
Grupo Executivo do Baixo Amazonas (GEBAM) 63
Grupo Executivo das Terras do Araguaia-Tocantins (GETAT) 63
guerrilla war 49, 63, 187, 209n.31

Hardin, Garret 12, 42n.2
Hébette, Jean 198

Iara project 139–40
indians
    and Decree 1775, 75–6
    and the environment 175
    grassroots action by 74, 88n.70, n.71
    institutional incorporation theory 214
Instituto Brasileiro de Desenvolvimento Florestal (IBDF) 52, 82n.26
Instituto Brasileiro do Meio Ambiente e dos Recursos Renováveis (IBAMA) 56–9, 68, 82n.27, 84n.39
Instituto Nacional de Colonização e Reforma Agrária (INCRA) 49, 172, 191, 193–4, 197
International Union for the Conservation of Nature (IUCN) 53
Island Biogeography Theory 53, 81n.21
Itaparica 44n.14

Krause, Gustavo 61

Laboratório Agro-Econômico da Transamazônica (LAET) 189, 192–6
Laboratório Sócio-Econômico do Tocantins (LASAT) 179–81, 188
land conflicts *see* Amazonia, land conflicts
land reform 77–8, 89n.75
LANDSAT 64
local action *see* community participation
logic of capital 215
Lutzenberger, José 59–61, 85n.43

Mamirauá project 140
    church involvement in 144–5
    community participation in 154
    funding of 146
    location of 141 (Fig. 4.1)
    management structure 147–53
    phase II 164–5, 169n.34
    vigilance 157–8, *Plates* 7–8
    zoning 160
Ministério do Meio Ambiente, dos Recursos Hídricos e da Amazônia Legal (MMA) 61

Movimento dos Trabalhadores
  Rurais Sem Terra (MST)
  77–8, 240n.3
  and Eldorado do Carajás
    massacre 78, 89n.75
Movimento pela Sobrevivência na
  Transamazônica (MPST)
  190–2, 199–200

national zoning commission 59,
  84n.36
non-governmental organisations
  (NGOs) 71–4
Núcleo de Áltos Estudos
  Amazônicos (NAEA) 179

Olson, M. 12, 16, 42–3n.3
Office de la Recherche Scientifique
  Outre Mer (ORSTOM) 180
Ostrom, Elinor 14–17
Overseas Development
  Administration (ODA) 146,
  185, 208n.20, n.27

Perri, Flávio 61
Pilot Programme to Conserve the
  Brazilian Rainforest 66,
  86n.54
  and extractive reserves 106–7,
  116, 123, 224, 236–7
Pinheiro, Wilson 98, 126n.12
Plano Agropecuário e Florestal de
  Rondônia (PLANAFLORO)
  57–8, 83n.31, 32, 111, 235
Plano de Desenvolvimento
  Integrado do Noroeste do
  Brasil (POLONOROESTE)
  57, 99
Plano de Integração Nacional
  (PIN) 47
Plano Nacional do Meio Ambiente
  (PNMA) 59, 84n.37
Pleistocene Refuge Theory 53,
  81n.21
post modernism 2
prisoner's dilemma game 12, 42n.3
productive conservation 216
  on extractive reserves 115–25,
    236
  and group identity 9–10
  and natural resources 8–9
  and resource mobilisation theory
    15–16
  at Mamirauá 160–6
  movements 3–11
  and rational choice theory
    15–20
  on the Transamazon highway
    202–4
Programa Agroecológico da
  Transamazônica (PAET) 189
  support for 210n.41
Programa de Apoio ao
  Desenvolvimento do
  Extrativismo (PRODEX)
  120, 234
Programa de Crédito Especial de
  Reforma Agrária
  (PROCERA) 235, 241n.17,
  235
Programa de Polos Agropecuários e
  Agrominerais da Amazônia
  (POLAMAZONIA) 48
Protocolo Verde 235, 242n.18

rational choice theory 15, 41
resource governance functions 11,
  221
resource mobilisation theory
  15–20
Ricúpero, Rubens 61
rubber
  boom and bust 93–4, 125n.6
  estate system 95–6, 128n.29
  price of 116
  tax on (TORMB) 116, 130n.40

Index

rubber tappers 91
  council (CNS) 98
    political unity of 112–14
    stand-offs 96–7, 126n.11, 231, 233, 241n.12
    struggles 76, 96–102
  rural unions 97–8, 178–9, 190–2, 197–9

Secretaria da Amazônia Legal 61, 85n.46
Secretaria de Asuntos Estratégicos (SAE) 59, 63–5
Secretaria Especial do Meio Ambiente (SEMA) 54
Seixas Lourenço, José 85n.46
Serviço de Informação e Vigilância da Amazônia (SIVAM) 64, 86n.53
shifting cultivation 174, 205n.8
Silva, Marina 120
Sistema de Proteção da Amazônia (SIPAM) 64, 85n.51
Sistema Nacional de Unidades de Conservação (SNUC) 227, 240n.7
Sistema Nacional do Meio Ambiente (SISNAMA) 59
social movements 2
  see also productive conservation, movements
socio-political multiplier effect 232
Superintendência do Desenvolvimento da Amazônia (SUDAM) 49, 79n.11

tragedy of the commons
  definition of 12–15
  and fishing 136–7
Transamazon highway 47, 49, 171
  agroforestry projects on 177 (Fig. 5.1)
  migration waves to 193–4
Transamazônica see Transamazon highway

United Nations Conference on the Environment and Development (UNCED) 57

várzeas
  in Amazonia 134–5
  cross-section of 142 (Fig. 4.2)

World Bank 57, 81n.24, 84n.37, 99, 111, 127n.15